Potters' fields

What happens to the corpses of those who die poor or unclaimed in NYC

"NO ONE WHO sleeps there had a dollar to their name in life...the bodies interred here are as utterly forgotten and wiped away as if they never existed." This is how the *New York Herald* described Hart Island in 1874, five years after the city began burying its poor on the island off the Bronx. A century and a half later the poor and unclaimed are still buried in pine coffins, usually marked only with numbers, not names. These are stacked three deep in a trench, three feet below the surface. Each trench holds 150 adult coffins. Roughly 1,200 people are buried there each year.

Jurisdictions across America are wrestling with what to do with their unclaimed dead. A state fund in West Virginia, which has been hit hard by opioid overdoses, ran out of money to bury the unclaimed dead last year. Some cities, including Los Angeles, cremate the unclaimed after a certain period, which is cheaper than burial. In North Carolina unclaimed bodies are cremated, then stored for three years before being scattered at sea. In Washington's King County, which includes Seattle and its suburbs, the poor and the unclaimed are cremated and stored until a biennial burial ceremony. Because of the high number of migrant deaths in Pima County in Tucson, Arizona, its medical examiner's office handles more unidentified remains relative to population than any office in America.

Those who die without the means to pay for a funeral, which costs nearly $9,000 on average, end up on Hart Island. Nearly two-thirds had next of kin who opted for a public burial. In all about 1m people lie there. The earliest victims of AIDS were buried there in 1985, far away from the other graves. Hart Island may be the largest cemetery for victims of the epidemic. During heavy rains bones are sometimes washed away and end up on nearby beaches.

The island, which has a stark beauty, is under the jurisdiction of the city's Department of Corrections. Four days a week eight inmates from Rikers, New York's biggest jail, travel to the island to dig graves and lower coffins into them. They are paid a $1 an hour.

Because of Hart Island's close connection with jail and prisoners, it is difficult for relatives (or anyone else) to visit. "It is clear to me we can do better, much better for the people buried on Hart Island," says Corey Johnson, the Speaker of the city council. "This needs to be changed immediately." He is backing a bill that would transfer operations to the Parks Department, create an office to help those who need help with a burial and make travel to the island easier. The city also needs to think about what to do when Hart Island is full. The Department of Corrections says there will only be space for eight or ten more years.

Cold, cold Hart

Potter's Field

The Chanate Historic Cemetery in Santa Rosa, California

A History of the Old Sonoma County Cemetery
Plus a Biographical Record of Burials, 1881-1944

Jeremy Dwight Nichols

HERITAGE BOOKS
2009

HERITAGE BOOKS

AN IMPRINT OF HERITAGE BOOKS, INC.

Books, CDs, and more—Worldwide

For our listing of thousands of titles see our website
at
www.HeritageBooks.com

Published 2009 by
HERITAGE BOOKS, INC.
Publishing Division
100 Railroad Ave. #104
Westminster, Maryland 21157

International Standard Book Numbers
Paperbound: 978-0-7884-5010-5
Clothbound: 978-0-7884-8202-1

Contents

Introduction

"I alwuz liked dead people, en done all I could for 'em."
Jim, in *Huckleberry Finn*, by Mark Twain

The story of the Chanate Historic Cemetery is the story of Sonoma County. It is the story of the ordinary people who contributed in their way to the place many today call home. The people of the gold rush are here as are the immigrants who came looking for a new life or the chance to strike it rich in the land of the Golden Mountain. The men who farmed the land and the sea, built the Golden Gate Bridge, and worked on the railroad or fell off of it are here too. The terrors of earthquake and fire are here as well as the heartbreak of the Great Depression. The stories of failure, be they of crops or investments gone wrong, are here.

The major sources of information for the records in this book are abbreviated, underlined, and listed at the end of the first paragraph for each person. The key to these abbreviations is in the "Sources of Information" section at the back of the book. The use of abbreviations and acronyms is not recommended by the writers of style guides but I have justified it based on the number of references needed. Census and newspaper records, when included, are listed separately for each person in the book. Census records are from *Heritage Quest* unless otherwise referenced. Other references are listed as I used them. When qualifiers such as "may" or "possibly" are used, it means that the facts were not clear from the available evidence. All newspaper articles and obituaries and all material in quotes are exactly as found. Accuracy and completeness, while always desired, is not guaranteed. Some of the referenced materials contain apparent contradictions. In some cases, I have been able to resolve these contradictions but the reader should confirm all references.

Some politically incorrect terms are used in this book. Words such as "inmate" and "idiot" have different connotations today than they did when the county cemetery was in use. Further, our sensibilities have changed and we no longer say someone is "feeble minded" or a "pauper." However, in the 1800s and early 1900s, people did use those terms and in order to paint a clear picture of what it was like back then, I must use them too.

This is a Sonoma County story of the eighteenth and early nineteenth centuries. The people buried in the Chanate Historic Cemetery and in other paupers' cemeteries were for the most part contributing members of society. Their only failure was in not having family, friends, or money to provide for themselves in death, or of being a member of the 'wrong' race. It is bad enough for them to be buried in disgrace. If we can do nothing more for them, we should at least not ignore them.

The cemetery described in this book was created by Sonoma County on the county's farm property north of Santa Rosa. Between 1877 and 1944 it was used for the burial of at least 1,561 persons based upon the numbered grave markers. The names of 1,316 of these burials are known and another 28 are partially known but the remainder is completely unknown. Following the cemetery history is a biographical directory, alphabetical by last name, of the 1,344 persons for whom at least some information has been found. Another 43 names are included in the directory to correct errors.

For most of its life, the cemetery did not have a formal name, being referred to as the "county cemetery," "poor farm cemetery," or in similar terms. In 2006, the cemetery was named "Chanate Historic Cemetery" by the Sonoma County Board of Supervisors.

One of the responsibilities of municipal government has been to arrange burial for those who could not afford it. Such persons were known as "paupers" or "indigents" and included both residents and non-residents or "transients." The tradition of burial at public expense for the poor goes back as far as human history records it.

One of the best-known examples is found in Chapter 27 of the Book of Matthew in the New Testament of the Christian Bible. From it we get the term "potter's field," meaning a cemetery for those without means of paying for their own grave.

Then Judas, which had betrayed him, when he saw that he was condemned, repented himself, and brought again the thirty pieces of silver to the chief priests and elders,

Saying, I have sinned in that I have betrayed the innocent blood. And they said, What is that to us? see thou to that.

And he cast down the pieces of silver in the temple, and departed, and went and hanged himself.

And the chief priests took the silver pieces, and said, It is not lawful for to put them into the treasury, because it is the price of blood.

And they took counsel, and bought with them the potter's field, to bury strangers in.

The Parking Lot

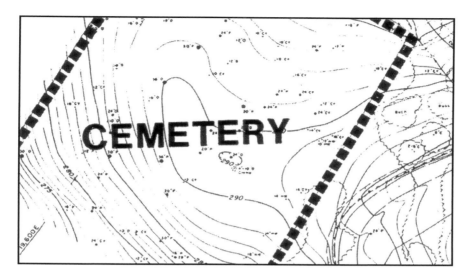

The staff of the Sonoma County Architect's Office wasn't even looking for a cemetery. They were inventorying trees for a parking lot project. Being sent to "count the trees" was an old Russian curse; people exiled to the Czar's Siberia were said to have nothing to do but count trees. The architect's staff had plenty to do, in part due to those darn tree huggers. They'd convinced the state legislature in Sacramento to require all large trees cut during government projects to be replaced. The Family Health Center, part of the county hospital complex, had expanded by putting a new building in the old parking lot. A replacement was needed and the details were to be worked out by the architect's office.

So there they were in the summer of 1987, wading through the poison oak, noting the size and type of the trees on their map, when one of them tripped on a . . . metal can? Well, it looked like an old rusty soup can but it was too heavy to be just a can. They picked the thing up and found it was full of cement. Even stranger, the cement had a number pressed into it. What was it?

They looked around, found more cans. Some of the cans were sitting in "puddles" of cement that had been poured onto the ground. Others were loose, like the first one, as if they'd come apart from their bases. It was strange. Were these markers of some kind? They couldn't be grave markers, could they? What kind of grave would have a can of cement instead of a tombstone? It was weird and almost spooky. They wrote the numbers on their map along with the trees, went back to the office and told what they'd seen. Grave markers. Yeah, sure.

The old heads talked it over. Better be safe, check it out. Anyone know of a cemetery out there? "Yes," someone said, "long ago. It's been abandoned for years, was used for Chinese or something."

What now? Ask the County Counsel . . . "Cemeteries are protected." Forever? "'Fraid so. You'd have to move each and every grave." But we don't even know how many there are! "Well, there's your first job, then. Figure out what the thing is and, in the meantime, put a hold on that parking lot . . ."

The Sonoma County Cemetery

The earliest burials in Sonoma County by Europeans were at the Russian colony of Ross (1812), Mission San Francisco Solano at Sonoma (1823), and in the St. Francis Solano Cemetery in Sonoma (1835). Once California was acquired by the United States and became the 31st state, the duty of burying indigents (those who had no money for their own burial) fell upon local governments. Large urban areas often had city facilities for their indigents but in rural counties such as Sonoma it fell on the shoulders of the Board of Supervisors. The earliest indigents were buried "where they fell," with whoever was willing to dig a grave being paid a dollar or two by the county. As cemeteries were started in various parts of the county, indigents were buried in the closest one, with a fee being paid the operator by the county.

Early indigent burials in Santa Rosa took place in the Santa Rosa Cemetery, now Santa Rosa Rural Cemetery, which was established in 1854. The exact date when indigent burials began is unknown but probably was soon after the founding of the cemetery. No written reference to this arrangement between the cemetery and the county has ever been found. The cemetery probably provided burial space at no charge as a public service. Over the next twenty years, as the Santa Rosa area grew, the number of burials in the "county section" increased to about 200, taking up more and more of the valuable land in the cemetery. Their public service must have appeared to the cemetery management to have become a nuisance and a liability.

The conflict was resolved, quite unintentionally, when the county supervisors bought a 100-acre farm just north of Santa Rosa. The county fathers had four things in mind when they contracted to buy Lewis A. Murdoch's farm in January 1874. First, the farm could be used as an almshouse, a home for poor people who needed only a meal and a place to stay. Second, the crops grown on the farm could be used to feed the 'inmates' or residents of the almshouse, the patients in the hospital, and even the prisoners in the county jail. Cash crops, especially wine grapes and hay, could be grown to generate income, offsetting the expense of caring for the poor. Third, the supervisors were looking ahead to the day when the county hospital, then on Humboldt Street in the "northern suburbs" of Santa Rosa, could be moved out of town. Fourth, the land could be used for an indigent cemetery.

The supervisors' contract with Lewis Murdoch required him to guarantee the county's use of the water springs on the Murdoch-owned land known as the "B. F. Goodin place"; Murdoch was to guarantee the right of way, today's Lewis Road, along the line dividing his property from Richard Fulkerson's; Murdoch was to provide access to a building site by 1 April 1874; full possession to be given to the county on November 1, 1874. Mr. Murdoch was to be paid $500 upon his filing a performance bond; $2000 without interest to be paid November 1, 1874; the balance of $2500 to be paid November 1, 1875 with interest from November 1, 1874 at one per cent per month. The total purchase price was $5000. Most of this land still belongs to Sonoma County today and is the land along Chanate Road where the Sutter Medical Center, Public Health offices, Coroner, Bird Rescue, etc., are located.
[Minutes of the Sonoma County Board of Supervisors, v.5, p.307, 1-09-1874.]

On May 7, 1874, shortly after Murdoch's contract was signed, Mr. Holmes and Mr. Thompson, representing the Santa Rosa Cemetery Association, attended a meeting of the Sonoma County Supervisors. They were probably determined to make the county pay for their graves in Rural Cemetery or go elsewhere. Holmes and Thompson, who obviously knew about the recently purchased county farm, presented a $200 invoice for the county lots in their cemetery. This must have really riled the supervisors, for they rose up and, on motion of Supervisor Beacom, rejected the invoice. They then went on to order ". . . that from and after this date, all paupers dying in this county, shall be buried in the south-east corner of the land known as the 'county farm.'" [Minutes of the Sonoma County Board of Supervisors, v.6, p.377, 5-07-1874.]

This first county cemetery, now on Hidden Valley Drive, was used for only a few years between 1874 and perhaps 1877. Probably no more than two or three dozen burials were made; no list of names or map has survived. This property is still owned by Sonoma County and looks like a vacant lot with nothing to indicate that the land was ever a cemetery. As regards Native Americans, no evidence has ever been found that there was an Indian Burial Ground in this area.

The next change happened in March of 1877 when the City of Santa Rosa's Common Council voted

"An Ordinance, to establish sanitary regulations for the health of the city and to stop the spread of infectious diseases . . . [section 11] A pest house and small pox hospital is hereby ordered to be erected and constructed at some suitable place upon the land of the county farm for the reception and care of any and all patients in the city infected with the small pox, and all persons now infected or who may become so hereafter, may be removed to such house and hospital for care and treatment." [Minutes of the Common Council, Book A, page 222, 3-09-1877; *Santa Rosa Times*, 3-15-1877]

The word "pest" is short for "pestilence;" a pest house was an isolation hospital for persons with contagious and usually fatal diseases such as typhoid, malaria, measles, and cholera. Pest houses were often placed near cemeteries so the deceased could be buried as quickly as possible. This must have done wonders for the patients' self-esteem.

The Santa Rosa pest house was built on the west side of the county farm. A new cemetery was placed next to the pest house, as far from the inhabited buildings of the county farm as possible. This work was probably done in 1877.

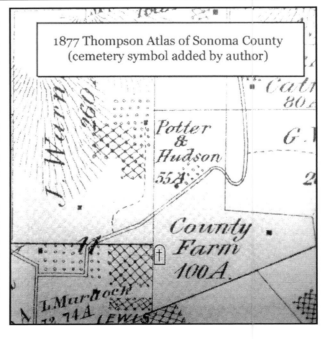

1877 Thompson Atlas of Sonoma County
(cemetery symbol added by author)

Confirmation that the new cemetery was in use soon after the pest house was built comes from an 1878 complaint to the supervisors by Mr. James Warner, whose property abutted the west side of the county farm. The *Sonoma Democrat* explained the problem.

"Mr. Howe [who had the contract to bury indigents] appeared before the Board to make a statement in relation to the indictment of the indigent poor that was brought up by James Warner yesterday. He stated that Mr. Warner was about to build a house on his farm just opposite where the poor are buried, and was desirous of having the graveyard removed and took this means to affect [*sic*] his purpose; that it was true that a corpse was buried in the water, but the grave was bailed out as much as could be, but the water ran in as fast as it was thrown out, and was storming hard at the time; the funeral had been postponed one day in consequence of the storm, and was buried temporarily as a matter of necessity, with the intention of burying the corpse deeper when the weather would permit. The storm continued the next day, harder than before, and three days afterward being a fair day, the corpse was exhumed and reburied full six feet under the ground. Mr. Howe was anxious that the Board should examine the matter for themselves, and not take the word of either Mr. Warner or himself in the matter. Although the expense to the county is only $5.75, the interments are as good as any that are conducted in any county in California." [*Sonoma Democrat*, 3-09-1878.]

Why didn't Mr. Warner also complain about the pest house? One would think a cemetery would have made a nicer, quieter neighbor than a house full of dying smallpox victims. This puzzle was solved on July 11, 1878 by the *Healdsburg Enterprise*, which reported a Grand Jury visit to the county farm. The jurymen noted that a pest house, <u>built, but never occupied</u>, was on the grounds of the farm. [Author's emphasis]

Finally, in its issue of December 13, 1884, the *Sonoma Democrat* confirmed the location when it said, "The pest house and grave yard are located some distance from the road at the <u>western end of the farm</u>." [Author's emphasis]

Burials in the county cemetery were put out to bid every year. One or another of the local mortuaries won the bid and, for a few dollars per burial, contracted to provide a casket made of "first-class redwood lumber," clothing for the deceased, transport to the cemetery in a "proper dead wagon," digging of the grave and the burial, and a wooden grave marker or headboard, "with two coats of white paint and the initials and hospital number of the deceased in black paint." Local ministers took turns providing the burial service.

Reproduction wooden headboard

L.S. 3031

Lester Swamp (1892-1928)

During the 1930s, Sonoma County, lacking a separate facility for tuberculosis (TB) patients, sent them to the Silverado Sanitarium in Calistoga, Napa County. If they died, as most did, they were brought back to Sonoma County for burial and, if indigent, they were buried in the county cemetery.

In 1939, the Oak Knoll Sanatorium was completed on the grounds of the county farm and opened for indigent tuberculosis patients. As it turned out, the sanatorium was next to the cemetery and in plain sight. The view of hundreds of white headboards shining in the morning sun must have upset the tuberculosis sufferers, who knew the cemetery was almost certainly their next stop. They complained of the "depressing" sight and the county agreed to remove the headboards.

To mark the graves, cans from the county hospital's kitchen were filled with cement, numbered, and buried flush with the ground. This marked the graves in a subtle manner and satisfied the patients. The newest graves at the east side of the cemetery received the lowest numbers and the oldest graves on the far western side got the highest numbers. The lowest number was probably "1", although "20" is the lowest number found to date, and the highest number was "1561" in the far southwest corner of the cemetery.

A "soupcan" grave marker

During the replacement process, a list was kept of the initials and hospital numbers, and the corresponding cement marker number. This list was compared to the hospital records and a master document was created, a *"Catalogue of Grave Markers,"* which contained names, dates of death, and marker numbers. Unfortunately, the hospital records went back only about ten years, limiting the list to the most recent 453 people, with a few exceptions. Because of this, only these people, less than one-third of the total, have known graves. The rest of the original list has not been located and probably was discarded.

The cemetery eventually was expanded to cover an acre and a half and was used until World War II, when it became full. In anticipation of this, the county in March 1944 bought from Frank and Ada Welti a three acre parcel, part of "H. H. Moke's subdivision of J. P. Stanley's addition to Rural Cemetery," which is today still the "county cemetery." [608 Official Records 3, and 22 Maps 15, Records of Sonoma County.] Although nothing confirms it, I believe the old cemetery was abandoned as soon as the new one went into use. When the County Architect's staff found the old cemetery in 1987, it had been almost completely forgotten.

Unfortunately, when the new cemetery went into use, the record keeping was not good. A complaint registered to the supervisors at that time noted that "several dozen" burials had occurred in the new cemetery without any recordation of the graves. Even today, the earliest burials shown on the map of the "new" county cemetery are in the 1960s. In the later 1940s, death certificates continued to list people as being buried in the "county cemetery" without noting whether it was the old one or the new one. Because of this, I have decided that burials in the old cemetery must have stopped soon after the new one was purchased. A break in the records suggests that burials in the new cemetery began after May 1944. Felice Cocci, who died May 20, 1944, thus has the dubious honor of being the last person buried in the Chanate Historic Cemetery.

The Old Cemetery is Found

Eureka!

In 1987, the county hospital had been on the farm property for one hundred years and was called Community Hospital. When a parking lot project led to the rediscovery of the old cemetery, news spread quickly around the county campus. One of the hospital staff remembered an old list of names and dug it out of the files. It was the "*Catalogue of Grave Markers*," listing 453 names, with date of birth and death and another number, which turned out to be the number on the concrete "soup can" marker.

Was that all? Were there more than 453 persons in the cemetery? A volunteer was set to work searching the county's death records. Records filed in and after 1905 listed the place of burial, so the volunteer was told to look for any record with "county cemetery" or something similar. What a job that must have been, poring through the old volumes, one by one. The list grew and grew, eventually totaling 1,139 names of people who had died between 1905 and 1964. The list included people who had been buried in the Chanate Road cemetery as well as the new one next to Santa Rosa Rural Cemetery.

The "Lost Cemetery," as the press dubbed it, made news all over the nation and many letters were written to the supervisors, especially to Helen Rudee, whose third district included the cemetery. "Don't put the cemetery on the back burner," urged one writer. Plans were made to restore the cemetery but funding was not available. In the end, the brush was cleared by a county inmate crew, a sign was erected to mark the cemetery, and some records were copied into a notebook and placed in the county library. A smaller parking lot was completed and for the second time the cemetery was abandoned.

Sonoma County Cemetery Proposed 1988 Improvements

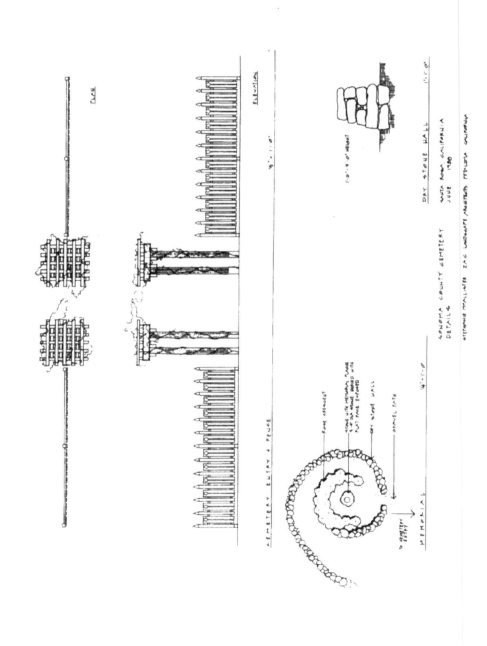

(From the files of the Sonoma County Architect)

Waiting

"Patience is for the dead."
Commander Dolum (Reptilian Xindi)
Star Trek Enterprise, 2004

Following the county's work in 1988, the old cemetery slept for another 13 years until I discovered it in early 2001 during the research for my book, *Cemeteries of Sonoma County, California, A History and Guide* (Bowie, Md: Heritage Books, 2002). Other than the sign naming it "Old County Cemetery," there was no sign the 1987 work had ever been done. I waded through the weeds, avoided the poison oak as best I could, found a few of the "soup can" grave markers but nothing else.

In 2003, following completion of my cemetery book, I looked for another project. The old county cemetery was the largest overgrown cemetery in the county, both in area and in number of burials. I decided to clean up the cemetery and document the burials.

Since the cemetery was public property, I first turned to the office of Tim Smith, who was at that time the Sonoma County Supervisor for the third district, in which the cemetery lay. Who administratively "owned" the old cemetery? To whom should I go with my clean-up request? In August 2003, a meeting was arranged by General Services Manager Dave Kronberg (since retired). Attending the meeting were Mike Wagner of the Real Estate office, County Architect Rob Kambak, Allan Darrimon from Regional Parks, Dave Kronberg and myself.

It would have been easy for the meeting attendees to deny me access to the old cemetery on grounds of "safety" or "privacy." To their credit, they were all in favor of my proposal. At least part of this dated back to the failed 1987 restoration project. Dave Kronberg had been involved in 1987; he undoubtedly was keenly disappointed that they were unable to proceed at that time.

The problem still was one of funding. Cleaning up an acre and a half of "cemetery turned forest" would take a lot of time. Erecting monuments and grave markers would take a lot of money. The county was short on both. What could we do? Finally, Dave Kronberg asked, "What can we do with volunteers and donations?" That was the first step forward.

One of my concerns for the old cemetery was that it had no legally recognized boundaries. The cemetery was part of the original 100-acre "county farm" property that Sonoma County had purchased in 1874. The cemetery had been fenced, probably several times over the years, but the boundaries in 2003 were as vague as the old fence. The cemetery abutted county land on three sides but across the fourth, western boundary was private property. No one could be blamed for accidentally driving a bulldozer across the unmarked boundary into the cemetery.

To the rescue came my surveyor friend Bob Curtis of *Curtis and Associates* in Healdsburg, California. Bob offered to survey the old cemetery at no charge and to record a map. This would place the cemetery in the legal record in the event of future development on adjacent properties. The action would also keep the county in compliance with state law. [State of California, Health And Safety Code, Section 8125-8137.]

Modern Parcel Map of the County Farm and Hospital Area

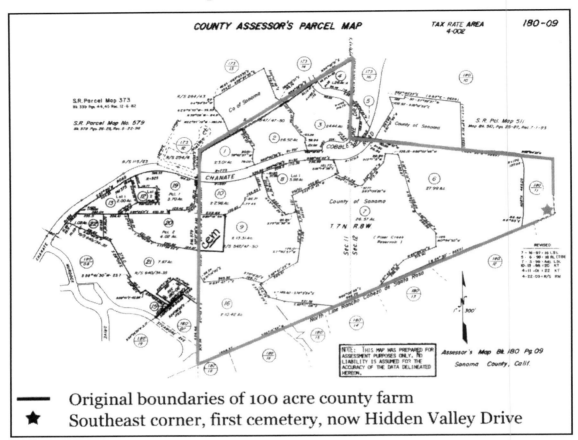

—— Original boundaries of 100 acre county farm
★ Southeast corner, first cemetery, now Hidden Valley Drive

[Records of Sonoma County Assessor's Office]

Bob's first challenge was to find any previous record showing the cemetery. Historically, the old burial ground was one of those places "everyone" knew and hence no one felt the need to make a written record. The official county maps showed the larger parcel but not the cemetery. Finally, Bob found a 1938 map made by the then-County Surveyor, M. M. Wallace, which showed the cemetery to scale. On the ground, we had a few old surveyors' marks and the remains of the fence.

On April 17, 2004, Bob Curtis and his son Brian surveyed the cemetery and I was an interested observer. We started from a surveyor's "monument" or locating pin in the middle of Chanate Road and measured from there to the cemetery, which was marked by previous surveys of the adjacent property and by the old fence posts. We found the 1938 Wallace map and our modern measurements to agree quite well. Given the apparent age of the fencing materials, they may have dated from the same period as the Wallace map.

Once the boundaries were confirmed and some new corner markers placed, the Curtis team drew a new map and submitted it to the county. On August 17, 2004, the Sonoma County Board of Supervisors authorized the recordation of the survey and map with the County Recorder.

Sonoma County Farm and Hospital, M. M. Wallace, 1938

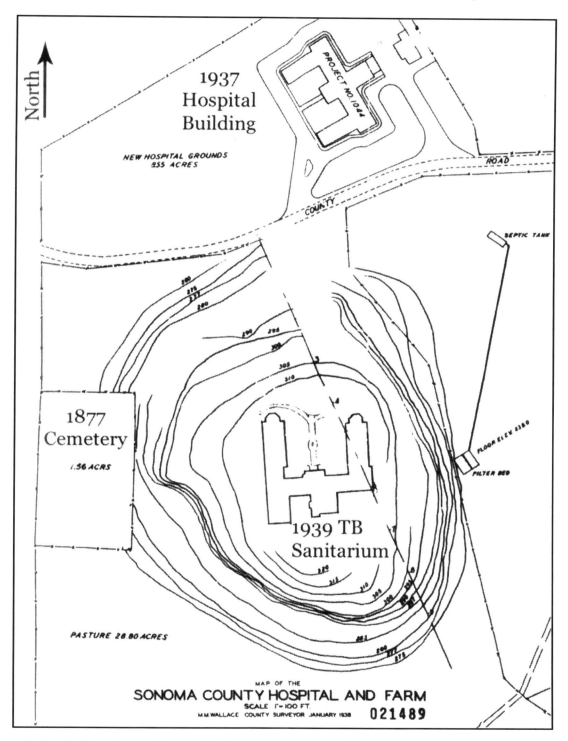

[M.M. Wallace, Jan. 1938, Records of Sonoma County. Labels added for clarity by the author.]

Survey Map of the Chanate Historic Cemetery by Curtis and Associates

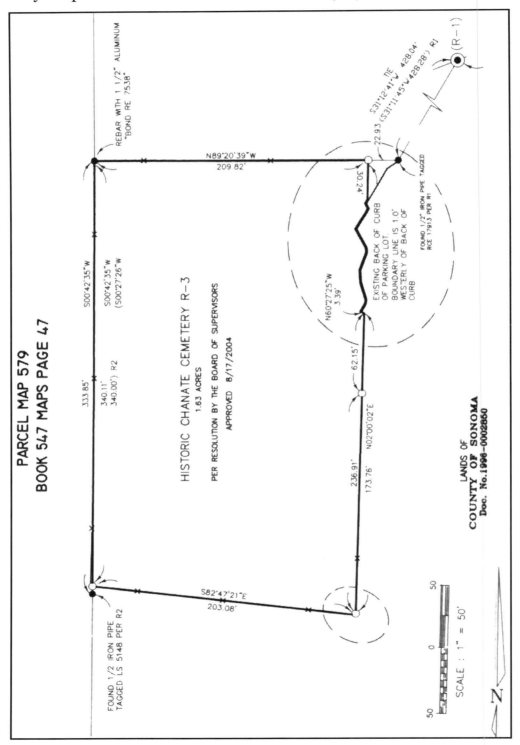

[Records of Sonoma County, 676 Maps 37]

Restoring the Old Cemetery

The restoration of the cemetery began on September 17, 2003 with the United Way's annual "Day of Caring." Since 1990, United Way has championed an annual day in which citizens go out and help those in need. The City of Santa Rosa and the County of Sonoma are both involved in this effort and offered to share some of their people to begin the cleanup.

When fifteen people showed up on that first day in 2003, the cemetery was a solid mass of vegetation. Visibility through the branches was no more than a few feet. It looked more like "the woods" than a cemetery. By the end of the day, the "woods" had been pushed back twenty feet or more and the first row of grave markers had been found. These first markers were numbered from 100 to 112 and were all in a line with more to come, beyond the small section we cleared. This was the first clue that the graves in the cemetery were organized, rather than randomly placed.

Each September since then, the United Way volunteers have returned to clear a little more of the cemetery. Also working at Chanate have been the Spring Clean group and the young people of DeMolay.

A regular search for grave markers at Chanate began in September 2005 and went on for almost two years. To my friend John Dennison must go much of the credit for pushing me to meet him at the cemetery every week. Other volunteers joined me from time to time but all except John were soon defeated by the ubiquitous poison oak.

Beginning in September 2005, John Dennison and I met every Wednesday for twenty-one months. John brought his metal detector and did most of the "finding" while I recorded the "soup can" number on a map and placed a small flag so the grave could be found again. Most of the markers were under several inches of leaf litter and dirt. The metal detector was able to find many of the markers but others had so rusted away that the electronic sensor was baffled. With experience, we found we could predict where the next marker would be found. We often had success by simply moving over three or four feet and digging.

As time passed and more markers were found and mapped, it became clear that the cemetery was full of graves. From border to border, the acre and a half was packed with unfortunate souls. The lowest numbered marker found was "20" while the highest number, in the far southwestern corner of the property was "1561." Over 1,300 markers were found and flagged; the other markers were missing but spaces on the ground and on the map showed that the graves were still there.

A puzzling piece found during the Day of Caring in September 2005 was part of the top of a soup can marker. The piece was broken and only part of the number was legible. It was "something-21." The first number was curved, so it could have been "321," "621," "821," or "921." I agonized over this fragment for weeks but in the end had to wait until the other three markers were found, over a year later. When the other markers finally were located, the damaged one was proven to be "821." The broken piece, unfortunately, has never been found.

[821]

[321]   [621]   [921]

Two monuments to the dead have been installed at the entrance to the Chanate Historic Cemetery. One was purchased by the Sonoma County Historical Society with funds contributed by members of the public and the other was provided by the members of the Redwood Empire Chinese Association.

The historical society's monument refers to "over 1300" burials because the exact total was not known and even today is still uncertain.

Also located at the entrance to the Chanate Historic Cemetery are a new sign to replace the "Old County Cemetery" sign, an informational kiosk and a bench. These were designed by the Sonoma County Architect's Office and purchased with county funds.

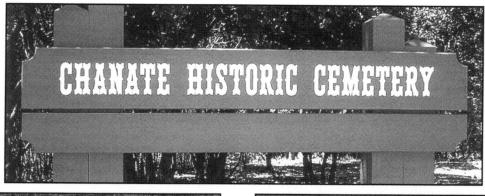

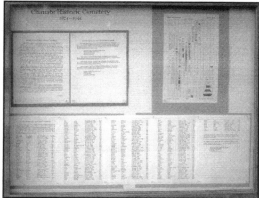

During the annual "Spring Clean" volunteer day in 2008, a path was built for a self-guided tour of the cemetery. Graves of people with interesting stories were marked with signs and a leaflet was made available at the entrance to tell the stories.

Finally, a series of 24 x 36 inch cast bronze plaques have been designed to honor all of the people in the cemetery whose names are known. As of this writing, one plaque has been purchased, money is in hand to buy the second, and fund raising is under way for the final two. These plaques will be placed in the entrance area of the cemetery.

Plaque number one of four

The Burial Records

"Eleanor Rigby died in the church and was buried along with her name . . ."
Eleanor Rigby, The Beatles, 1966

A compilation such as this one is dependent upon the accuracy of the source material. Critical to any list of burials is the documentation on which a person's inclusion or exclusion from the list is based. Whenever possible, I have used original documents such as death certificates, many of which list the place of burial. To the simple facts of name and date of death, I have added such biographical information as was available with a reasonable amount of research. Although this descriptive material makes it easier to distinguish between persons who have the same name, it is also more likely to contain errors.

Original documents such as death certificates contain both primary and secondary information. The accuracy of the information in the death certificate is usually subject to some doubt, since the deceased by definition was not there to fill out the form. Many of the death records on which this book is based were made from information given by persons as they checked into the county almshouse (poor farm) or the county hospital. This information should be accurate, excepting those cases where the person was seriously ill or injured and unable to communicate.

Beyond name and date of death, however, death certificates can also contain a wealth of personal information that may or may not be accurate depending on the source. Similarly, Census records were based upon the information given to the enumerator by whoever answered the door. Errors have been known to be made. For example, in the 1910 Census of the Sonoma County Poor Farm, the enumerator did not even interview the inmates, but rather worked from records in the office (and said so on the Census form).

Although the Chanate Cemetery probably began as early as 1877, no burial records earlier than 1881 have been located. Death records as such did not exist, and what little survives today has been gleaned from doctors' journals and morticians' records. This book lists the 1,344 persons whose burial in the old county cemetery on Chanate Road has been determined with certainty.

The largest source of information for the present compilation is a list compiled in January 1988 by an unknown county volunteer who went through the death records one by one, finding all persons for whom the place of burial was "county cemetery" or some similar term. A stenographer's notebook was used to record 1,139 names and dates of death. The notebook survives in the files of the Sonoma County recorder's office with a copy in the Sonoma County Library. The volunteer did an outstanding job with only a few errors.

An earlier, smaller list was compiled sometime after 1939, when the wooden headboards were replaced with numbered concrete "soup can" markers. This list was created by cross-referencing the initials and hospital number on each headboard to the hospital records. Unfortunately, the hospital records covered only the most recent ten years, i.e., the 1930s, so that the resulting *"Catalogue of Grave Markers"* contained only 453 names. Some of these names duplicate the 1988 list and some are unique.

A third source was a list found in the files of the Sonoma County Genealogical Society. Never before published, this list of names was extracted from a record book of burial permits probably discarded by the county when the 1910 courthouse was demolished in 1966. The book, which covered the time period 1914-1917, was apparently rescued from a dumpster, the names and dates extracted, and the resulting list organized by cemetery. Unlike other published burial lists, this one included burials in the county cemetery. There are 101 records of county cemetery burials with dates between October 1914 and June 1917.

Found late was a set of Sonoma County records entitled "Burials of Indigents." Covering deaths between 1937 and 1967, this document was purportedly authored by the Sonoma County Coroner's Office. The only known copy of this document is a 1973 microfilm in the Family History Library of the Church of Jesus Christ of Latter-day Saints (LDS or "Mormons") in Salt Lake City, Utah. Extensive inquiries in Sonoma County have failed to find the source of the document. A total of 135 Chanate burials are in this record.

Additional sources that occasionally mention county cemetery burials include the Sonoma County Coroner's office, the early, pre-1905, county death record books, the county physician's reports, the minutes of the Sonoma County Board of Supervisors, and various local newspapers. Combining all of these sources, I created the master list of 1,344 names on which this book is based.

This list is clearly incomplete. The "soup cans" mark the locations of a maximum of 1,561 graves. Most of these markers have been located on the ground and spaces between the graves suggest they were all present at one time. This means there are over 200 totally unknown burials in the cemetery. Although some additions to the list may be made from time to time, the bulk of the missing burials will remain forever unknown. Most of these missing burials are early deaths, pre-1905, in which there was no record or only a partial record; the rest are probably people whose death records list only "Santa Rosa" as the place of burial.

The records in this book are listed alphabetically by last name. The spelling chosen is either the one in the Sonoma County death record, for deaths up to 1905, or the California Death Index (CADI), for deaths in 1905 and later. This was done to make this book conform as much as possible with the legal record. For persons not found in either record, a reasonable spelling based upon available records is used.

Alternate spellings are appended to each record as an "aka" (also known as). In a few cases where the spelling in CADI is clearly incorrect, I have used another spelling, with an explanatory note. Significant spelling variations are handled in the text with a cross-reference, e.g., "* GUAY see QUAY."

The minimum record contains the name of the deceased and the date of death. Additional information was added if it was available. Death records are the most common source of information; these often contradict Census records and the reader is given the responsibility of resolving these conflicts. The source of the information (underlined) is always the last item in the first paragraph of any individual's record. Additional information includes the number of the "soup can" grave marker in [brackets], the person's date and place of birth, and other personal details. A **bold** grave number means the grave marker has been located. References, abbreviations, etc., are at the end of the text. Place of birth follows the two-letter U.S. Postal Service convention for U.S. states; foreign countries are spelled out in full.

A uniform code for death certificates and other vital records has existed in California since 1905. Officials of the state's 58 counties are required to send a copy of all death certificates to Sacramento, where they are filed and made into a statewide list, the California Death Index (CADI). Through 1939, CADI contains only the name, initial of spouse's given name, age, date and county of death, and a state index number. In 1940, the index was expanded to add the decedent's birth date and birthplace and the names of the parents, but the spouse's initial was dropped. This index is available at libraries and on the Internet. There are separate indices for before and after 1940 as well as a separate index for "fetal deaths" (stillborn infants).

U.S. Census records were used to flesh out a person's life. If a Census record does not clearly belong to the person in question, it is listed as a "possible" Census record. Some of the persons in this list were inmates (residents) of the almshouse at the Sonoma County Farm or patients of the Sonoma County Hospital immediately before their deaths and were enumerated at those institutions.

A person's "hospital number" was issued upon entry into the Sonoma County Hospital as a patient. The numbers appear to be serial by date of admission, but bear no relationship to date of death. Registration numbers seem to have been assigned for Poor Farm (almshouse) inmates also, but few records mention them, and there is no way to differentiate a "hospital number" from a "poor farm number."

A few persons have been inferred into the county cemetery. For example, applicants for care in the county hospital or the county almshouse were required to turn over to the county what little money they possessed. If the person later left, they could take the money with them. If they died while in the care of the county, their money went into the public purse. These funds were kept and accounted for by the county physician. Following the death of such a person, the county physician included a note with the amount in his regular report to the Board of Supervisors. The existence of such a note implies the decedent was receiving care as an indigent and from this I have inferred burial of the decedent by the county. Because this is the weakest of all methods of determining indigent burial, I have resorted to it for only four early cases in 1881 and 1889), where there is no contradictory information.

In some death records, place of burial is impossible to ascertain. Prior to 1905, death records were not legally required in California. Most early death records were created after the fact from doctors' journals or mortuary records. Many do not state the cemetery in which the deceased was buried. Although death certificates beginning in 1905 should list the cemetery in which the deceased was buried, they sometimes give only the city. Similarly, death certificates for persons who died outside of, but were buried in, Sonoma County typically do not give the cemetery to which the body was "removed."

In the 1930s, tuberculosis patients were transferred to the Silverado Sanitarium at Calistoga in Napa County. Such patients, dying outside of Sonoma County, were brought back for burial; some even got a Sonoma County death certificate in addition to one in Napa County. There are thirteen such Napa County deaths between 1932 and 1937 in the Chanate burial records. This practice stopped in 1937 after the new county hospital was built. The tuberculosis patients were brought back from Calistoga and housed in the old (1887) hospital until the Oak Knoll Sanatorium was built in 1939. In addition to being able to keep its tuberculosis patients "home," there were financial advantages for Sonoma County beyond the obvious savings from not having to pay an outside institution. Sonoma County was missing out on available state aid for counties with indigent tuberculosis patients: the Silverado Sanitarium in Calistoga did not qualify with the state.

The clerks who filled out the death certificates were not always consistent in the name they wrote down for the place of burial. Many Sonoma County death records list only "Santa Rosa" as the place of burial. This could be one of four cemeteries: Calvary, County (Chanate), Odd Fellows/Memorial Park, Rural.

This confirms that "Santa Rosa" burials, which one thinks primarily as occurring in Odd Fellows, Rural, or Calvary, could in fact include the county cemetery. Therefore, at least some people buried in Chanate will have death certificates listing their place of burial as "Santa Rosa." This also partly explains why Chanate has 1,561 marked graves while there are only 1,344 names in this list. I have not included people buried in "Santa Rosa" unless there was another source that confirmed they were buried at Chanate.

Newspaper references are sometimes valuable in determining whether a person was buried in the county cemetery. The phrase "buried in a local cemetery" is often used to hide in plain sight the fact that the deceased is receiving a pauper's burial. Similarly, "in a local hospital" usually refers to the Sonoma County Hospital. Such usage seems to have been adopted early in the 1900s – earlier obituaries were more likely to name names. Persons who were reported to have "no known living relatives" were more likely to be buried in the county cemetery, especially if they had no money.

It is standard procedure even today to note racial information on death certificates. Readers of old newspapers know that, until relatively recently, this information was also given in the press. In the 1800s, the racism was blatant, as in the headline, "A Chinaman Whipped" (Jim Mahoney, 1886). As the 1900s began, the racial identification was still there: "Negro Drops Dead," (Edward Jones, 1901). This survived until at least the 1960s.

A few persons were, according to their death records, buried at Chanate, but evidence also exists to show they were buried elsewhere. For example, Andrew Soule's death certificate states he was buried at Chanate, but the records of the Santa Rosa Rural Cemetery also list him, and he even has a tombstone there. There are also some entries for persons who were shown as buried at Chanate due to an error in a source. These burials are listed in the present work along with an explanatory note. All such records are preceded by an asterisk (*) and do not count towards the 1,344 persons in this book. Over 200 burials at Chanate are now unknown. Some were unknown when they died while others may have been known at the time, but their records have vanished.

Some of the people buried by the county were "unknown" in that they were new to the county – fell off of a train or washed up on the beach, for example – or could not be identified for some other reason. Those unfortunates were listed in the death records under various labels such as "John Doe" or "Unknown Male." Following the lead of the California Death Index, I have listed the 28 such persons in the Chanate Historic Cemetery as "ZZ Unknown" and put them at the end of the list.

The Chinese

See the stranger, fear the stranger;
Hate the stranger, kill the stranger.

The Chinese first came to Sonoma County in the 1860s to work in logging, farming, and especially on the building of the railroad. When the Chinese railroad workers were displaced by Peter Donahue's Irish laborers, many of them settled in Santa Rosa, where they created a Chinatown that lasted for more than eighty years. [LeBaron, *Santa Rosa, A Nineteenth Century Town,* 43.]

Unlike other Sonoma County residents, most of the Chinese were not settlers but rather sojourners. Almost exclusively male, they had come to America as contract laborers, leaving their families behind in China. Instead of assimilating, they retained their Chinese way of life and sent their earnings back to China in support of their families. Their hope was to strike it rich in the land of the "Golden Mountain" and return home to China as wealthy men.

Prejudice against the Chinese was widespread, even as many white families employed them in their homes as domestics and on their farms as inexpensive laborers. Formation of the Anti-Chinese League in 1886 led to a campaign to rid Sonoma County of all Chinese. It was very nearly successful. The Chinese were harassed for their "pigtail" hair, their clothing, and their food. Since they spent little with local merchants and sent much of their meager pay to their families in China, they were accused of not supporting the local economy.

One of the ways in which society demonstrated its ill will was by denying the "pagan" Chinese the ability to bury their dead in the local cemeteries. At that time, most Chinese were in America to earn a living for their families. A very few returned home rich men. If they died here, their wish was to send their bodies back to China for burial. Failing that, burial in a Chinese cemetery in San Francisco was desirable.

As a last resort, Sonoma County officials allowed Chinese to be buried with the paupers in the county cemetery. Although 89 Chinese burials are documented in the Chanate Historic Cemetery, the actual total is probably about one hundred, based on the percentage of all identified graves. Discriminated against during their lifetimes, in death the Chinese became equals. Their graves were not restricted to a separate part of the county cemetery but were placed side by side with the non-Chinese.

In spite of the anti-Chinese campaign, many Sonoma County residents retained their Chinese employees and simply kept them out of sight. Prejudice against the Chinese dropped with their numbers but the cemetery policy stayed in force until World War Two, when China became our ally in the Pacific war. Even Tom Wing Wong, a respected, well-to-do Santa Rosa merchant and labor contractor, was denied burial any place other than the county cemetery.

The first documented Chinese burial in Santa Rosa Rural Cemetery was not until 1937. The grave belongs to Young Moon, who was an uncle of Song Wong, daughter of Tom Wing Wong. Young Moon was for many years a cook but later became janitor at the Elks Club. Moon was a favorite of the Elks and when he died, the funeral was held under their auspices. His is the only Chinese tombstone in Rural Cemetery.

"Young Moon, Died Feb. 16, 1937"

Military Veterans

" . . . to care for him who shall have borne the battle . . . "
Lincoln's Second Inaugural Address, March 4, 1865

On March 15, 1889, the California State Legislature passed *An Act to provide for the burial of ex-Union soldiers, sailors, and marines in this State who may hereafter die without leaving sufficient means to defray funeral expenses.* This new law, which forbade the 58 California counties from burying indigent veterans in pauper cemeteries, was passed at the behest of the G.A.R. (Grand Army of the Republic), a Civil War veterans group, politically active and very powerful in the 1880s and 1890s. At the G.A.R.'s peak in the 1890s, 10% of all Union Civil War veterans were members.

The law stated, in part, that "it shall be the duty of the Board of Supervisors of each county in this State to designate a proper person in the county, whose duty it shall be to cause to be decently interred the body of any honorably discharged soldier, sailor, or marine who served in the army or navy of the United States during the late war, or in the war with Mexico, who may hereafter die without having sufficient means to defray funeral expenses. Such burial shall not be made in any cemetery or burial ground or any portion of such cemetery or burial ground used exclusively for the burial of the pauper dead."

The "proper person" designated by the Board of Supervisors was one Joel D. Barnett, himself a veteran of the Civil War. He was appointed in 1889 and served until January 1893, when he resigned and was replaced by Milo S. Davis, a veteran and a local undertaker. Today, the function is filled by the Veterans Services Officer, who is part of the Sonoma County Human Services Department. [Minutes of the Sonoma County Board of Supervisors, Book 10, p.15 (1-09-1893).]

The law is still in effect today as part of the Military and Veterans Code.

MILITARY AND VETERANS CODE
SECTION 940-950

943. Such burial shall not be made in any cemetery or burial ground, or any portion thereof, used exclusively for the burial of the pauper dead . . .

The rub came in the timely identification of the veteran, especially the indigent veteran. If a person had lived in Sonoma County for many years and was known to all as a veteran, there was no problem. Transients or new residents were another matter. Although many a veteran carried his discharge papers "next to his heart," others possessed none. Additionally, the law initially covered only Union veterans of the Civil War, not Confederates. Later, the law was expanded to cover Confederate Civil War veterans as well as veterans of later wars.

Even with this law and its successors, still in effect today, some military veterans were buried in the county's pauper cemetery. This was not deliberate but rather a problem with identification. The decedents were probably strangers and not known to be veterans, or proof of their service was not available. The following persons, known or strongly suspected to have served in the armed forces of the United States, are buried in the Chanate Historic Cemetery. There are probably more.

CRONIN, Frank, World War 1 (a transient, originally from Alameda County, California).

DAVIS, Benjamin, Civil War (from Connecticut; newspaper obituaries explicitly noted his military service as a "Union soldier").

JONES, Edward, Civil War (newly arrived in Santa Rosa, proof of service was not immediately available).

SWAMP, Lester, World War 1 (originally from Wisconsin, he came to the Guerneville area looking for work after he was released from the Army at The Presidio).

Trivia

Numbers

- Lowest numbered grave marker: "20"
- Highest numbered grave marker: "1561"
- Number of people buried in the cemetery who have been identified: 1,344
- Number of people buried in the cemetery who are known by name: 1,316
- Number of graves identified as to <u>both</u> name and location: 453

Oldest person (tie)

- Ah PING, age 100 (1817 −1917)
- Thomas TOMBOTAS, age 100 (1828−1928)

First known Chinese burial

- Seven CHUNG (July 7, 1887)

Earliest born person

- Elijah PRESBY (1810−1887)

Husband and wife

- Katherine <u>and</u> Martin ESKERICA (1938)
- Tom Wing WONG (1918) <u>and</u> Tong Chow WING (1893), Lo Kim WING (1898), Toy Lon WING (date of death unknown)
- William <u>and</u> Johanna STROHMEIER/STROMIER (1912, 1919)

Mother and baby

- Sylvia BROWN <u>and</u> "Baby Boy" (1921)
- Rachel [Raphel] SAIS <u>and</u> Angela SAIS (1910)

Siblings

- BARONE (BARONI) babies (1935, 1936)
- Mary Lee <u>and</u> Ralph HILLIGAS (1938, 1939)
- Helen <u>and</u> James LEMMON (1938, 1939)
- Archibald <u>and</u> Thomas MARBLE (1939, 1940)
- RHINE twins (1931)
- Martin <u>and</u> Morris SHEPARD (1905)

Homicide (killers and their victims)

- James CAPENINI (1939) − victim
- Hom HONG (1917) − victim
- Mrs. Delta MORRISON (1938) − victim
- Benjamin RENALDS (1921) − killer (murder/suicide)
- Baby THOMAS (1909) − victim

Burials in the Chanate Historic Cemetery, 1881–1944

"He was a quiet and inoffensive prisoner.
He shall be decently interred in the cleanest sack we can find."
The Count of Monte Cristo, Alexandre Dumas

> Source codes are at the end of the text. Names marked with * are not buried in Chanate, but are included in order to correct an error in the historical record.

ABEL, Charles, June 14, 1905, laborer, died at the county hospital; 1900 Census (Russian River Township) T623-114-228, b.December 1834 Germany, a.65, single, emigrated 1880, naturalized citizen, day laborer. CADI, CEN, DC, MIC

ABETI, Guiseppe, October 20, 1938 [**181**] b.1879, a.79, county hospital [patient] #3462 and died there. BOI, CADI, CAT, DC

ABITIA, Joe, September 27, 1936 [**217**] b.1899, a.37. CADI, CAT, DC

ABITIA, Susie, June 1, 1934 [**516**] b.1921, a.13 (CADI gives a.10), Mexican, a resident of Healdsburg. CADI, CAT, MIC

Newspaper records
"Funeral Rites for Girl," *Sotoyome Scimitar,* 6-07-1934.
"Funeral Rites For Healdsburg Girl," *Healdsburg Enterprise,* 6-07-1934.

ACKEN, Charles S., November 10, 1938 [**179**] b.1863, a.75, a resident of Tuolumne County, which paid $25 to Sonoma County for the expenses of burial; possible 1930 Census (Township 4, Tuolumne County) T626-224-4A, "ACKEN, Charles S.," a.66, b.NJ-NJ-NJ, single, tanner on farm. BOI, CADI, CAT, CEN, DC

ADAMS, Hugh, May 6, 1938 [**129**] b.1-21-1862 NY, a.76, "ranch worker," 36 years in California, 6 years in Sonoma County, "lived in Decker street;" 1930 Census (Vernon Township, Sutter County) T626-224-10B, "ADAMS, Hugh A.," a.68, b.NY-Scotland-Irish Free State, single, fruit farm laborer. BOI, CADI, CAT, CEN, DC, NEW

Newspaper records
"Hugh Adams Dies," *The Press Democrat,* 5-08-1938.

ADAMS, John, September 3, 1941, b.2-18-1938 CA. CADI, DC

ADAMS, Wesley N., September 6, 1939, a.73, at death a resident of the county hospital; 1930 Census (Healdsburg) T626-222-6A, "ADAMS, Wesley N.," a.64, b.OH-OH-OH, widowed, sheep ranch laborer. No Healdsburg obituary. BOI, CADI, CEN, DC

ADDUCCA, Paola, May 30, 1888, b.1857 Italy, resident of Marin County, left $1.00 to the county. DEA, PHY

ALADIO, Baby Girl, December 2, 1916, stillborn; burial permit "Inf dau of m/m Francisco Lodio 12-22-1916." Comment: The infant is listed in Fetal CADI as "ALADIO, ZZ." BP, CADI, DC

ALAMO, Robert, April 29, 1935 [**380**] b.1908, a.27, aka "ALANO, Robert." CADI, CAT

ALAMODA, John, June 10, 1893, b.1855 Portugal, hospital #594, left $2.00 to the county. DEA, PHY

ALDRICH, Edgar, February 14, 1929 [**701**] b.1850, a.78. CADI, CAT

ALEXANDER, Rufus, April 9, 1909, b.NY, a.77, widower, 23 years 8 months in California, hospital #5389; possible 1860 Census (Olema, Bolinas Township, Marin County) M653-60-727, a.24, laborer. CADI, DC, NEW, REG

Newspaper records
"Dies in Santa Rosa," *The Press Democrat*, 4-11-1909.
"A Pioneer Passed Away," *Petaluma Argus*, 4-12-1909.

ALFARE, Max, July 22, 1919, a.55. CADI, DC

ALLEN, E. Frank, July 5, 1913, a.82. CADI, DC

ALLEN, Harry, September 12, 1940, born "about 1882," age "about 58," an itinerant prune picker, died en route to the county hospital due to multiple fractures and shock following an auto accident on the Redwood Highway (now US-101) at Mark West, buried 9-19-1940 in the "Co. Cemetery." CADI, DC, MIC, NEW

Newspaper records
"Aged Man Hit By Car, Killed," *The Press Democrat*, 9-12-1940.

ALMON, Pasquali, June 7, 1893, b.Italy, a.60. CC, DEA, REG

ALPEN, Peter, April 13, 1943, b.7-15-1865, a resident of the county hospital, mother VACK, died in Santa Rosa. BOI, CADI, DC

AMAN, Caspar, March 23, 1895, b.Austria, a.55, d.Fulton, suicide. COR, DEA, REG

AMEDEO, Lewis, October 14, 1915, age "about 29," day laborer, died at the county hospital, #7479. Comment: Mr. Amedeo died as a result of burns and other injuries received in the Cloverdale Hotel fire. The fire started in a restaurant at the front of the hotel, both of which were managed by Joe Swindell. Mr. Swindell had lit his gasoline stove for the start of the business day and then gone to check his fuel supply. He returned to discover the stove had exploded. The fire spread from the kitchen through the old wooden hotel and eventually consumed the entire block of buildings. BP, CADI, CC, NEW, REG

Newspaper records
"Cloverdale's Big Fire," *The Press Democrat*, 10-15-1915.
"Fire Takes Life And Property," *Cloverdale Reveille*, 10-16-1915.
"Three Lose Lives in Burning Hotel," *San Francisco Chronicle*, 10-15-1915.

ANDERSON, Alfred, April 3, 1910, a.68. <u>CADI, DC</u>

ANDERSON, Edith J., September 14, 1931 [**533**] b.1867, a.63; 1930 Census (Sonoma County Farm and Hospital) T626-222-222A, a.62, b.Sweden, patient, married 23 years, emigrated 1885, naturalized citizen, wife of John ANDERSON, boat builder of Bodega Bay (1920 Census T625-150-81). <u>CADI, CAT, CEN, DC</u>

ANDERSON, Gustafson, April 7, 1930 [679] b.1861, a.55. <u>CADI, CAT, DC</u>

ANDERSON, Henry, July 6, 1938 [**126**] b.1857, a.81, died in the county hospital. <u>BOI, CADI, CAT, DC</u>

<u>Newspaper records</u>
"Petaluman Dies," *The Press Democrat*, 7-07-1938.

ANDERSON, John, January 25, 1917, b.2-28-1841 Sweden, a.75 years 10 months 28 days, single, farm laborer, parents Anders BENSON (b.Sweden) and Anna ANDERSON (b.Sweden), 8 years in California, 2 years 4 months 17 days at the place of death, hospital #7143, buried in the Sonoma County Farm Cemetery. Comment: Did the deceased take his mother's last name or is he "John, son of Anders?" <u>BP, CADI, MIC, REG</u>

ANDERSON, John A., July 8, 1910, a.67; 1910 Census (Sonoma County Farm and Hospital) T624-109-29B, a.60, b.Sweden, single, emigrated 1864. <u>CADI, CEN, DC</u>

ANDREW, John, May 6, 1886, b.1831 Norway, left $12.50 to the county. <u>PHY</u>

APPLE, Henry, April 30, 1911, a.58. <u>CADI, DC</u>

AQUISTAPACE, Dominico, January 3, 1937 [**193**] b.1857, a.80, aka "ACQUISTAPACE, Domenico." Comment: DC error, has 1936 as year of death. <u>CADI, CAT, DC, NEW</u>

<u>Newspaper records</u>
"Kenwood Rancher, Long Ill, Passes," *The Press Democrat*, 1-05-1937.

ARBUCKLE, Robert, March 26, 1920, b.1849 NY, age "about 71," single, laborer, parents Daniel ARBUCKLE (b.NY) and Eliza MEINS (b.Scotland), 50 years in California, suffered a pulmonary embolism at Freestone [his residence?], hospital #696, buried at the county farm. <u>CADI, DC, MIC</u>

ARRIGHI, Charles, June 18, 1939 [**121**] b.1864, a.75, aka "ARIGHT, Charles S." <u>CADI, CAT, DC</u>

ASHTON, Frank M., December 26, 1915, b.CA, a.50, Indian, single, day laborer, life in California, died in Mendocino Township, "Porter Creek 9 miles from Healdsburg," buried 12-28-1915 in the Sonoma County Cemetery. <u>BP, CADI, DC, REG</u>

ASMUSSEN, Andrew, December 7, 1935 [**376**] b.7-23-1875 Germany, a.59, a resident of Boyes Springs, parents Andrew ASMUSSEN and Annie MILLER; 1920 Census (Orange County) T625-123-148, a.44, b.Germany, single, laborer, emigrated 1911, naturalized citizen. CADI, CAT, CC, CEN, DC, MIC

ASMUSSEN, Henry, December 18, 1925, a.81, aka "ASSMUASSAM, Henry;" 1920 Census (Analy Township) T625-150-51, a.76, b.Denmark, widowed, emigrated 1900, naturalized citizen, farm laborer. CADI, CAT, CEN

ATWELL, Cassus, March 8, 1912, a.65. CADI, DC

AVERY, James, October 10, 1924, age "about 90," single, 7 months 16 days at the place of death, died in the county hospital, buried in the county cemetery. CADI, DC, MIC

AVILLA, James M. Lain, October 15, 1937 [**581**] a.1 hour, aka "AVELLA, Infant." CADI, CAT, DC

BACCI, Antonio, April 3, 1938 [**148**] b.1883, a.54, died in the county hospital, aka "BACCI, Tony." BOI, CADI, CAT, DC

BACCI, Santi, May 7, 1935 [446] b.7-29-1849 Italy, a.85, widowed, farm laborer, parents Antonio BACCI (b.Italy) and Mary PADESTA (b.Italy), 67 years in U.S., 62 years in California, 7 years a resident of the county farm; 1930 Census (Sonoma County Farm and Hospital) T626-222-222A, a.80, b.Italy, emigrated 1875, inmate [an "inmate" was a resident of the Sonoma County Farm or Almshouse, as opposed to a hospital "patient" or a jail "prisoner"]. Comment: Mr. BACCI fell out of bed at the county farm and fractured his femur; while hospitalized, he suffered a cerebral hemorrhage and died. CADI, CAT, CEN, MIC

BAILEY, Clarence W., May 17, 1908, a.63, divorced [ex-wife not named], carpenter, father b.KY, 10 years in California, 3 months at the place of death, died in the county hospital, #5273, buried 5-25-1908 in the Sonoma County Farm Cemetery; possible 1900 Census (661 Grove Street, Oakland, Alameda County) T623-82-304, "BAILEY, Clarence W.," b.August 1846 OH-VA-KY, a.53, married (8 years), engineer "Goo Co" (?), wife Alice (b.December 1859 CA-WI-MO, a.40, no children). Comment: An Alice BAILEY is in the 1910 Census for Alameda County but the details are wrong; she apparently is not Clarence's widow. Perhaps the widow Alice BAILEY remarried before 1910 and so has a different last name. CADI, CEN, DC, MIC

BAILEY, James William, August 12, 1896, hospital #1047, left $4.75 to the county; 1880 Census (Bodega Township) T9-84-255, b.1814 ME-Ireland-Ireland, a.66, widower, fisherman. CEN, PHY

BAINBRIDGE, Ben, November 3, 1924, b.1849 England, a.75, married, farmer, 12 years 10 months 3 days at the place of death, buried in the county cemetery; 1920 Census (Sonoma County Farm and Hospital) T625-151-12B, a.79, b.England, widowed, emigrated 1853, naturalized citizen, inmate. CADI, CEN, DC, 1914 GR, MIC

BAKER, John A., August 22, 1916, b.9-14-1850 PA, a.65 years 11 months 8 days, widowed, laborer, parents John BAKER (b.Switzerland) and Mary SMITH (b.Switzerland), 20 years in California, died in the county hospital, #7698, buried 8-25-1916 in the Sonoma County Farm Cemetery. BP, CADI, DC

BAKER, Levy, March 23, 1935 [443] b.1850, a.84, died in Napa County (tuberculosis patient?); 1930 Census (Sonoma County Farm and Hospital) T626-222-222A, a.79, b.PA-PA-PA, inmate. Comment: In the mid-1930s Sonoma County sent its tuberculosis patients to the Silverado Sanitarium in Calistoga. Those patients who died of their affliction (most did) were returned to Sonoma County for burial. Some even had their deaths recorded in Sonoma County, although Mr. Baker was not one of those. CADI, CAT, CEN, MIC

BALDASARIA, Giorgi, December 22, 1910, a.27; 1910 Census (Spain Street, Town of Sonoma) T624-109-169, "BADASSARI, George," a.26, b.Italy, married (1st time, 3 years), emigrated 1910, alien, laborer (odd jobs). Comment: The wife and children (if any) are not listed in the Census. Might he have left them in Italy or in some other part of the U.S.A.? CADI, CEN, DC

BALDWIN, John, March 5, 1920, b.1858 Ireland, age "about 62," single, parents William BALDWIN (b.Ireland) and Elizabeth HEATON (b.Ireland), 41 years in the U.S., 40 years in California, 2 months 11 days at the county hospital, hospital #59, buried 3-08-1920 in the county farm cemetery. CADI, DC, MIC

BAMFILL, Maude, Mrs., February 11, 1912, a.67; 1910 Census (Washington Township, Yolo County) T624-110-189, "BANFILL, Maud," a.55, b.Scotland, widow, 7 children born, 4 alive, housekeeper, emigrated 1860. CADI, CEN, DC

BANKS, Joseph, September 23, 1913, age "about 55," labor, marital status unknown, parents unknown, died in Stewart's Point of "acute alcoholism," buried September [date obliterated] 1913 in the Sonoma County Farm Cemetery. Not found in the 1910 Census of California. CADI, CEN, DC, MIC

BAPTISTA, Margolfo, April 23, 1894, b.1849 Italy, a.45, hospital #1169, left $3.95 to the county. DEA, PHY

BARALOGY, Steven, January 19, 1929 [735] b.1862 Switzerland, age "about 67," widowed, laborer, father Domenick BARALOGY (b.Switzerland), 27 years in the U.S.A. and in California, 2 years at the place of death, died in the county hospital, #7277, buried 1-21-1929 in the Sonoma County Farm Cemetery, aka "BARALONY, Steven." Comment: Not found in the 1920 Census of California. CADI, CAT, CEN, MIC

BARBY, Frank, November 26, 1931 [531] b.6-25-1867 Canada, a.64, single, itinerant, father Henry BARBY (b.Canada), mother unknown (b.Canada), died at the county hospital (suicide), aka "DARBY, Frank." CADI, CAT, DC, MIC

BARDSLEY, Emmett Noel, February 5, 1916, b.5-30-1915 CA, a.8 months 6 days, son of Fred and Delia W. BARDSLEY (both b.CA), a resident of Santa Rosa Township, buried 2-05-1916, in the Sonoma County Farm Cemetery. BP, CADI, DC, MIC, REG

BARONE, Baby Boy, March 13, 1935 [460] stillborn, parents Saul BARONE (b.Azores) and Laura FREITAS (b.Portugal), aka "BARBONI or BARONI, Infant." CADI, CAT, DC, MIC

BARONI, Baby Boy, July 13, 1936, son of Laura BARONI. Comment: Probably another stillborn child of Saul and Laura BARONE. CADI, DC

BARRON, William, September 13, 1887, b.1822 Ireland, single, died at the county hospital, left $2.50 to the county; 1880 Census (Sonoma County Farm) T9-84-100C, a.58, b.Ireland, single, "inmate, pauper." CEN, DEA, PHY

BARRY, Daniel, January 19, 1930 [**682**] b.1856, a.73, aka "BARRY, David." Comment: Not found in the 1920 Census of California. CADI, CAT, DC

BARRY, Ray R., May 30, 1935 [**379**] b.1-04-1892 Sanger (Fresno County, California), a.43, age 43 years 4 months 26 days, a resident of Cazadero, rancher, spouse Nellie BARRY, parents Blueford BARRY (b.MO) and Lida FIDLAR (b.OH), life in California, died at the Yost Sanitarium (Route 5, Santa Rosa), aka "BARRY, Roy." CADI, CAT, CEN, DC, MIC, NEW

Comment: The correct first name would seem to be "Roy," not "Ray." The error might have been made by whoever filled out the death certificate and then picked up by Sacramento when the record was filed.

Census records
1900 (Lolo Precinct, Shoshone County, ID) T623-234-51, "BARRY, Roy," a.8, b.January 1892 CA-OH-IA, parents "Bluff and Eliza BARRY."
1910 (1919 D Street, Sacramento County) T624-93-200, "BARRY, Roy Richard," a.18, single, b.CA-OH-IA, teamster in cement works, living with parents "Bluford N. BARRY" (a.62, b.OH-OH-NY, 2nd marriage) and "Eliza A. BARRY" (a.52, b.IA-IL-OH, 1st marriage). The parents had been married 30 years, 10 children born, 7 alive.
1920 (Yuba City) T625-153-265, "BARRY, Roy," a.27, b.CA-CA-CA, married, truck driver, wife "Millie" (a.17, b.CA-CA-CA).

Newspaper records
"Cazadero Rancher Claimed by Death," *The Press Democrat*, 5-31-1935.
"Funeral Rites Held," *The Press Democrat*, 6-02-1935.

BARSOCHINI, Antonio, October 27, 1912, b.Italy, age "about 65," resident at 509 Adams, Santa Rosa, single, laborer "around hotel," suicide by gunshot, aka "BAROSHINITAKES or BAROSBINITAKSO, Antonio;" 1910 Census (Mendocino Township) "BARSOCHINI, Antone," T624-109-246, a.50, b.Italy, single, laborer, "odd jobs." CADI, DC, MIC

BASILIO, Marnelli, November 1, 1906, a.63. Not in the 1900 Census of California. Comment: To this author, "Basilio" does not sound like a surname; were the last and first names accidentally reversed? CADI, DC

BASSI, Peter, July 5, 1935 [**237**] a.70. CADI, CAT, DC

BATES, John Joseph, December 25, 1941, b.1870 CA, a.71, mother BATES, father BATES. CADI, DC

BAUER, Charles, January 7, 1915, a.70; possible 1910 Census (Bloomfield, Analy Township) T624-109-2, "BAUER, Charles," a.69, b.Germany, single, emigrated 1865, naturalized citizen, laborer (odd jobs). BP, CADI, CEN, DC

BAUERS, Charles, February 18, 1923, a.79. Not found in 1920 Census of Sonoma County. CADI, DC

BAUMBERG, William, July 27, 1905, b.1831 New Orleans, a.74, single, sailor, resident at the county farm, died at the county hospital, aka "BARRMBERG or BARRONBERG, William." CADI, DC, MIC

* BAVETTO see RAVETTO (1930).

BAXTER, Joseph, February 1, 1943, b.10-14-1876 CA; 1930 Census (Sonoma County Farm and Hospital) T626-222-222A, age 57, b.CA-New Brunswick-Northern Ireland, single, inmate. CADI, CEN, DC

BAZONI, Louis, March 27, 1889 (40 Deaths 5) b.Italy, a.54, single, died in Santa Rosa, left $0.90 to the county (County Physician's 1889 Annual Report, p.8). DEA, PHY, REG

BEACH, Riley, February 15, 1936 [249] b.1867, a.68. CADI, CAT, CEN, DC

Census records
1870   (Chico Township, Butte County) M593-70-58, a.3, b.CA, with parents Thomas (a.32, b.NC) and Martha (a.26, b.CA).
1880   Not found.
1900   Not found.
1910   (Josephine County, Oregon) T624-1281-91, a.40, single, b.CA-U.S.-U.S., farmer.
1920   (Analy Township) T625-150-49, a.52, divorced, b.CA-NC-IA, laborer (fruit farm).
1930   (Bodega Township) T626-221-245, a.62, widowed, b.CA-U.S.-U.S., fruit farm laborer.

BEAL, Charles, December 30, 1937 [134] b.12-02-1865 ME, a.72, laborer, widower, resident at 3 South Main St., 11 months 23 days in Santa Rosa, 27 years in California, parents Thomas BEAL and Betsy NORMAN (both b.ME), fractured hip, then got pneumonia, died in the Sonoma County Hospital; BOI has "Son 641 Ag" but this terminology is without explanation; 1920 Census (Anderson Township, Mendocino County) T625-121-7, "BEAL, Charles F.," a.55, b.ME-ME-ME, married, farmer, wife Jane F. BEAL, a.65, b.ME-ME-VT. Comment: For the wife, CADI has "BEAL, Jane F., d.7-13-1920 Sonoma County, a.66, spouse C.T." The meaning of the comment in BOI is unclear; was he an agricultural worker? BOI, CADI, CAT, CEN

BEALL, Daisy L., February 25, 1929 [622] a.47, died in San Francisco, aka "BELL, Daisy;" 1920 Census (Sonoma Township) T625-150-268, "BEALL, Daisy L.," a.45, b.CA-VA-OR, no occupation, living with her cousin, James L. LaFITTE, a widowed farmer (a.50, b.LA-Cuba-LA). CADI, CAT, CC, CEN, MIC

Comment: The Sonoma County physician occasionally sent indigent patients to San Francisco for advanced care. Those who died were brought back to Sonoma County for burial. Daisy Beall was apparently such a person. Unfortunately, CAT listed her only as "Bell, Daisy, no date, 622." The misspelled last name, missing date of death, and out-of-county death made finding records of her a challenge.

BECK, Andrew, March 1, 1908, a.70; 1900 Census (Bodega Township) T623-114-47, a.72, b.November 1827 France, emigrated 1838, naturalized citizen, day laborer. Comment: Date of death also 2-10-1908. CADI, CEN, DC

BELLINGER, John, January 4, 1926, a.74. CADI, DC

BENEDETTO, Frank, May 26, 1917, b.4-10-1880 Italy, a.37 years 1 month 16 days, married, spouse unknown, occupation cook, parents Frank BENEDETTO (b.Italy) and Alemeno ROSSI (b.Italy), 24 days at the place of death, 20 years in California, died in the county hospital, buried 6-09-1917 in the Sonoma County Farm Cemetery. CADI, CC, REG

BENNETT, Jack, March 4, 1935 [**440**] b.1875, a.59. CADI, CAT, DC

BERGLOFF, Alexander, January 10, 1941, b.1877, a.64, aka "BERGLOFF, Alex." CADI, DC

BERGMANN, Otto, August 4, 1915, a.43, aka "BERGMAN, Otto." BP, CADI, DC

BERNANDO, Ben, May 28, 1898, b.CA, a.60, Indian, d.Knapp Ranch, widower, buried at the county farm. DEA, COR

BERNSTEIN, Fredrick, May 11, 1910, a.75, aka "BERSTEIN, Fredrick." CADI, DC

BERTA, Peter, June 4, 1903, b.Switzerland, a.35, single, cook, "indigent," died at the county hospital. REG

BERTI, Lorenzo, August 9, 1936 [**222**] b.1875, a.61. CADI, CAT, DC

BERTON, Thomas, December 9, 1899, a.74, married, died in the county hospital, buried at the county farm. DEA, REG

BERTOZZI, Angelita, May 20, 1931 [**535**] b.1894, a.36, spouse "B. BERTOZZI," aka "BERIOZZI, Angelena." CADI, CAT, CC, DC

BERTRAM, Albert, October 7, 1899, b.Germany, a.47, died in the county hospital, "buried at the county farm." DEA, REG

BESSE, Maurice, January 27, 1899, b.Switzerland, a.33, "indigent, county farm." DEA, REG

BIAVASCHI, Baby Boy, May 13, 1928 [366] stillborn (premature) at the county hospital, #2059, parents Antone BIAVASCHI (b.MT) and Ellen CUICELLO (b.Sebastopol). CADI, CAT, MIC

BIERER, John, February 27, 1912, a.38. CADI, DC

BIGLOW, Jerry, November 28, 1933 [**420**] b.1883, a.50. CADI, CAT, DC

BILLY, Joseph, May 11, 1942, b.3-18-1881 CA, a resident of the county hospital. BOI, CADI, DC

BINEGER, William F., April 25, 1916, b.1-26-1849 Harrison County, WV, a.67, single, laborer, father George BINEGER, mother Elizabeth CONSTABLE (b.PA), 1 year 3 months 30 days at the place of death, 35 years in California, died in the county hospital, #7229, buried 4-26-1916 in the Sonoma County Farm Cemetery. <u>BP, CADI, CC, DC, REG</u>

BIRD, William, October 8, 1912, a.60. <u>CADI, DC</u>

BISCHOFF, James <u>or</u> John, July 25, 1941, b.1-23-1878 NY, a.63, a resident of Penngrove, hospital #8089. Comment: CADI has two entries, James and John, for the same person. Sonoma County records including BOI give the man's name as "BISCHOFF, James." <u>BOI, CADI, CC, DC</u>

BISHOP, Mattie, October 20, 1907, b.England, a.72, female, widowed, 18 years in California, 3 years 6 months in the county hospital. <u>CADI, DC, MIC</u>

BLAGG, Donald, August 15, 1941, b.4-12-1941 AZ, a.4 months, mother McCAULEY, father BLAGG. <u>CADI, DC</u>

BLOCK, Elizabeth, November 15, 1893, b.Denmark, a.35, died at the county hospital #1085 (childbirth), buried at the county farm. <u>DEA, REG</u>

BLOOMSTROM, Charles, January 17, 1934 [**426**] b.9-22-1872 Finland, a.61, laborer, in California since 1882, father Isac [*sic*], mother Katrina, aka "BLOOMSTRAM, Charles." <u>CADI, CAT, DC, MIC, NEW</u>

<u>Newspaper records</u>
"El Verano Man, 61, Dies in Hospital," *The Press Democrat*, 1-18-1934.

BLUM, Charles, May 15, 1903, b.CA, a.40, single, laborer, "indigent." <u>REG</u>

BOAKES, Jacob N., May 7, 1917, b.4-26-1850 NY, a.67, widowed, occupation baker, a resident of Petaluma, parents Nenery BOAKES (b.Waterberry [*sic*], CT) and Miss HORTON (b.NY), 15 days at the place of death, 7 years in California, died in the county hospital, #7983, buried 5-11-1917 in the Sonoma County Farm Cemetery; possible 1880 Census (Essex County, New Jersey) T9-781-222, "BOAKES, Jacob H.," a.33, b.NY-CT-NY, baker, wife Emma, five children. <u>CADI, CC, NEW, REG</u>

<u>Newspaper records</u>
"John Boakes Passed Away," *Petaluma Argus*, 5-08-1917.

BOHL, Fred, July 14, 1932 [**416**] b.8 Mar 1845 Prussia, a.87, single, a resident of Petaluma, 32 years in California, 65 years in the U.S., died in the county hospital; 1920 Census (Petaluma Township) T625-151-18, "BOHL, Frederick," a.73, b.Prussia, widowed, emigrated 1868, naturalized 1876, poultry farm laborer. No obituary. <u>CADI, CAT, DC, MIC</u>

BON, Wong Hang (Mong), June 7, 1893, b.China, a.56, married, died in Santa Rosa, buried at the county farm, aka "BON, Hong W." Comment: The name "BON, Wong Hang (Mong)" is given here exactly as it appears in county records; no explanation of the parenthetical "Mong" was found. CC, DEA, REG

BONTELLE, Helen, February 27, 1934 [**394**] b.1849, a.84. CADI, CAT, DC

BOONE, Kenneth, September 9, 1919, b.3-03-1919, a.6 months, Indian, died at the county hospital. CADI, DC, MIC

BORGAS, Joloses, August 30, 1925, a.55. CADI, DC

BORST, Arthur, October 13, 1936 [**209**] b.1861 NY, a.76-9-16, divorced (ex-spouse now Mrs. F. M. BERG of 1601 Manbert St., San Leandro), resident and died "near Glen Ellen," parents Jerry BORST and Adeline DUEL (both b.NY), 12 years in Santa Rosa, 35 years in California. CADI, CAT, DC, MIC

BOWEN, Albert, November 18, 1940, b.2-26-1865 CA, mother BUSMORE. CADI, DC

BOWER, Mary Frances, March 18, 1902, b.MA, a.53, married, "died in Santa Rosa . . . indigent . . . new resident." REG

BOYES, John, June 21, 1912, a.75. CADI, DC

BOZICH, John, October 9, 1936 [**210**] b.1-20-1892, a.44, died at the west end of Third Street in Santa Rosa, transient, laborer. CADI, CAT, DC, MIC

BRADLEY, James, January 30, 1937 [**187**] b.1867 NY, a.70. BRADLEY had lived on Second Street for two years, coming from Napa County, where he had lived for 47 years. Comment: No Napa County records of BRADLEY were found in the U.S. Census. CADI, CAT, DC, NEW

Newspaper records
[No title] *The Press Democrat*, 1-31-1937.
[No title] *The Press Democrat*, 2-04-1937.

BRADLEY, Wayne, December 31, 1938 [**585**] b.6-20-1938 Santa Rosa, a.6 months 11 days, resident on Route 1, Glen Ellen, died at the county hospital, parents Carl BRADLEY (b.Weatherford, TX), and Merle PIKE (b.Poolville, TX). BOI, CADI, CAT, DC, MIC

BRADT, George Washington, September 24, 1916, b.7-01-1868 MI, a.48 years 2 months 24 days, widowed, woodsman, father Robert BRADT (b.NY), mother Maria TAYLOR (b.Canada), 2 months 24 days at the place of death, died in the county hospital, #7707, buried 10-21-1916 in the Sonoma County Farm Cemetery. BP, CADI, DC, REG

BRADY, Lee, February 14, 1938 [**141**] b.1888, a.49, spouse W. BRADY, a resident of a "hobo camp." Comment: A coroner's inquest was held. BOI, CADI, CAT, DC, NEW

Newspaper records
"Brady Rites Held," *The Press Democrat*, 2-27-1938.

BRADY, Sarah A., July 21, 1931 [**664**] b.1876, a.54; 1930 Census (Sonoma County Farm and Hospital) T626-222-222A, a.53, b.IN, married 23 years, patient. CADI, CAT, CEN, DC

BRADY, Thomas, January 7, 1908, b.Ireland, a.70, single, laborer, parents unknown but b.Ireland, 43 years in California, 1½ months local, died at the county hospital, #5226, buried 1-02-1908 in the "Sonoma Co. Farm Cem." Comment: Not found in the 1900 Census for California. CADI, CEN, DC, MIC

* BRANDERBURG see HOLLINGSWORTH (1936).

BRAY, Baby Boy, September 16, 1908, father F. J. BRAY (b.CA), mother Crystal E. ALDRIDGE (b.MN), premature birth (about 5 months). CADI, DC, MIC

BRAZIL, Thomas, June 27, 1914, a.61. Comment: DC has 6-24-1914 for the date of death. CADI, DC

BREWSTER, Charles, March 27, 1891 (40 Deaths 6) [**976**] b.NY, a.72 or 73, white, male, single, died in the county hospital, #665. Comment: No obituary, not in GR or Census, yet someone bought him an expensive tombstone. CAT, DEA, GR, PV, REG

BRIMHALL, William H., July 16, 1933 [**521**] b.1855, a.78. CADI, CAT

BROCK, Leullian H., April 15, 1907, a.67. CADI, DC

BRODERSEN, Peter, October 13, 1934 [**433**] b.1891, a.43, aka "BRODERSON, Peter." CADI, CAT

BROKA, Larry, November 25, 1933 [**419**] b.6-13-1870 Austria, a.63, single, laborer, a resident of Petaluma, father John BROKA, mother Sophia PIROKA (both b.Austria), 30 years in California, 7 days at the hospital and died there, buried in the county cemetery, aka "BROKO, Tony," or "BROKA, Lany." Comment: CADI has the first name "Lany," a misreading of the death certificate's handwritten "Larry." CADI, CAT, DC, MIC, NEW

Newspaper records
"Local Man Dies At Santa Rosa," *Petaluma Argus-Courier*, 11-27-1933.

BROOKS, Andrew, May 9, 1918, b.3-07-1849 Holland, a.69 years 2 months 2 days, widower, farmer, father Alfred BROOKS (b.Holland), mother unknown, residence Santa Rosa, 25 years in California, 2 months 5 days in the county hospital, #23, buried in the county farm cemetery. CADI, DC, REG

BROOKS, Frank, July 22, 1940, b.10-18-1870 OK, a.69 years 9 months 4 days, single, gardener, not a veteran, resident on Orchard Street, Santa Rosa, father Adolph J. BROOKS (b.TX), mother Martha ROUNDTREE (b.PA), 25 years in California, 9 years local, 9 days in the hospital, died in the county hospital, buried 7-23-1940 in the "Co. Cemetery." Comment: Not found in Census records. BOI, CADI, DC, MIC

BROWN, Alice, May 14, 1943, b.11-05-1877, a resident of the county hospital, mother ROLAND, father EDMELO. BOI, CADI, DC

BROWN, Baby Boy, August 11, 1921, son of Miss Sylvia BROWN, father unknown, stillborn, Indian, at the county hospital. Comment: Not found in CADI. See "BROWN, Sylvia." CADI, DC, MIC

BROWN, Nellie B., July 4, 1926, a.45. CADI, DC

BROWN, Richard, November 22, 1939, a.74. CADI, DC

BROWN, Sylvia, August 11, 1921, b.2-14-1907 Humboldt County, a.15 years 5 months 27 days, died in childbirth at the Sonoma County Hospital, parents Nelson BROWN and Pearl DUNCAN (both b.CA). Comment: See "BROWN, Baby Boy." CADI, DC, MIC

BROWN, Walter, September 3, 1932 [**409**] b.1859, a.73. CADI, CAT, DC

BROWNE, Frederick S., June 23, 1916, b.2-10-1854 Providence, RI, a.61 years 4 months 13 days, single, laborer, father James P. BROWNE (b.Southfield, MA), mother Elizabeth HOWARD (b.VA), 31 years in California, died in the county hospital, #7665, buried 6-26-1916 in the Sonoma County Farm Cemetery. BP, CADI, DC, REG

BRUINES, Martin, July 12, 1941, b.10-22-1882, mother TINEN, father BRUINES. CADI, DC

BRUSH, James, April 23, 1900, died at the county hospital, buried at the county farm. DEA, REG

BUCHI, Henry, May 1, 1920, a.82. CADI, DC

BUCHLER, George F., December 6, 1923, b.5-19-1848, a.75, 55 years in California, died at the county hospital, buried on 12-07-1923. CADI, DC

BUCKLEY, Lawrence, March 15, 1936 [**252**] b.1866, a.70. CADI, CAT, DC

BUE, Young, April 18, 1906 [a victim of the 1906 earthquake] b.China, a.19, male, "yellow," single, merchant, died of "injuries sustained by earthquake," buried in the "S. R. County Farm Cem.," aka "DOEBUE, John" or "John Doe #1." CADI, CC, DC, MIC

Comment: Following the earthquake, Bue was initially unidentified, so his death record read "John Doe #1." When his name was determined, harried officials simply wrote "Young Bue" over "John Doe #1." A later misreading of this record then produced "John Doebue."

BUFORD, LeRoy, May 22, 1937 [**289**] b.1869, a.68, aka "BUFFORD, LeRoy." CADI, CAT, DC, NEW

Newspaper records
"Bufford Rites Held," *The Press Democrat*, 5-25-1937.

BUNTING, Geo. A., May 22, 1933 [**575**] b.1865, a.67. CADI, CAT

BURIANI, Joseph, December 3, 1891, b.Italy, a.37, married, ex-Occidental, d.Santa Rosa, buried at the county farm. MIC, REG

BURIESI, Frank, March 1, 1938 [**131**] b.1875 Italy, a.63, a resident of Cloverdale, died of "toadstool poisoning," aka "BRISSI, Frank;" 1930 Census (Ukiah Twp., Mendocino County) T626-177-276, a.55, single, b.Italy, farm laborer; aka "BRACCI, Frank." <u>CADI, CAT, CEN, DC, MIC, NEW</u>

<u>Newspaper records</u>
"Brissi, County Farmer, is Dead of Mushrooms," *Santa Rosa Republican*, 3-02-1938.
"Fungus Poison is Fatal to Rancher," *Petaluma Argus-Courier*, 3-02-1938
"Brissi Funeral Held," *The Press Democrat*, 3-05-1938.

BURKE, John, April 7, 1931 [**547**] b.1881, a.49. <u>CADI, CAT, DC</u>

BURKES, Harriet, July 21, 1939 [**196**] b.1913, a.25, a transient, spouse "O. BURKES." <u>BOI, CADI, CAT, DC</u>

BURNIGHT, Baby Boy, July 8, 1913, a.60 minutes, son of Ethel A. BURNIGHT. <u>CADI, DC</u>

BURNS, John, December 22, 1922 [**875**] b.1854, a.68; 1920 Census (Sonoma County Farm and Hospital) T625-151-12A, "BURNES, John," a.57, b.CA-Ireland-Ireland, divorced, inmate. <u>CADI, CAT, CEN</u>

BURNS, Thomas, September 29, 1910, a.66. <u>CADI, DC</u>

BURNS, William, May 1, 1915, a.80. <u>CADI, BP, DC</u>

BUSS, Louis, August 5, 1906, b.Canada, a.45, parents unknown, single, laborer, 5 years in California, 1 month at the county hospital; 1900 Census (Mendocino Township) T623-114-109, "Lewis BUSS" b.January 1839 Canada, a.61, single, emigrated 1886, naturalized citizen, wood chopper. Comment: Note the age difference between the Census and the death record. No *Press Democrat* obituary was found. <u>CADI, CEN, DC, MIC</u>

BUTCHER, Harry, September 9, 1936 [**216**] b.1868, a.68. <u>CADI, CAT, DC</u>

BUTLER, Almon, February 1, 1926, a.60. <u>CADI, DC</u>

BUTON, Otto, September 30, 1932 [**408**] b.1876, a.56, aka "BOUTON <u>or</u> BUTOW, Otto." <u>CADI, CAT, DC</u>

BUTTLER, Frederick A., December 7, 1907, a.59; 1900 Census (Santa Rosa Township) T623-114-250, "BUTLER, Fred," a.52, b.May 1848 Ireland, emigrated 1882, farm laborer. <u>CADI, CEN, DC</u>

BUTTS, John L., June 24, 1925, a.71. <u>CADI, DC</u>

BUZZINI, John, March 31, 1939 [**112**] b.4-04-1866 Switzerland, a.72 years 11 months 27 days, single, occupation "ranch hand," parents unknown, died at home on Fulton Road, 31 years in California, 2½ years local, buried 4-05-1939 in the county cemetery. <u>CADI, CAT, MIC, DC, NEW</u>

Comment: Mr. Buzzini is one of only a few persons

13

buried in Chanate for whom living relatives have been found.

Newspaper records
"John Buzzini Dies," *The Press Democrat*, 4-02-1939.

CADDEN, Katherine, October 25, 1909, a.60. CADI, DC

CADERAU, John, April 28, 1910, a.68; 1910 Census (Sonoma County Farm and Hospital) T624-109-29B, "CADERAN, John," a.68, single, b.France, emigrated 1882. CADI, CEN, DC

CALINI, Joseph, January 30, 1911, b.Italy, a.53, "common laborer," a resident of Santa Rosa, father Victor CALINI, mother Santini MOYER (both b.Italy), 26 years in California, 1 day at hospital, buried in the county farm cemetery. CADI, DC, MIC

CALLAHAN, John, November 10, 1908, b.CA, age 38, hospital #5395. CADI, DC

CALYSAIL, Valte, March 23, 1914, a.44, aka "CALISAIE, Vaelte." CADI, DC

CAMENATA, Bartiste, February 27, 1925, b.1852 Italy, a.73, single, died in the county hospital after 14 years 5 months 25 days, aka "CAMERATA, Bartiste." CADI, DC, MIC

CAMPBELL, Charles, September 15, 1939, b.7-14-1883 PA, a.56, rancher, married, wife Eleanor CAMPBELL, father John CAMPBELL (b.PA), 7 years on the ranch and in California, died at home on Faught Road north of Santa Rosa, buried in the county cemetery, aka "CAMBELL, Charles."
Comment: The name on the death certificate clearly spells the name "CAMBELL" in three different places although it is "CAMPBELL" in CADI and the newspaper. The death certificate has an "Investigation pending" note on it but there is no additional information. CADI, DC, MIC, NEW

Newspaper records
"Death Claims C. L. Campbell," *The Press Democrat*, 9-16-1939.
"Campbell Services Set," *The Press Democrat*, 9-17-1939.

CAMPBELL, John, February 1881. Comment: The 1881-82 Sonoma County Financial Report noted a credit of $2.11 from the "Estate of Jno. Campbell, deceased." Campbell, like all persons requesting shelter at the county almshouse, was required to turn over all assets to the county upon admission. These assets, usually small amounts of cash, could be drawn upon by the inmate for personal expenses or withdrawn if the inmate was discharged. Should the inmate die, the county was the legal "heir" and kept any funds in the inmate's account. Evidence of such funds being retained by the county is therefore proof the person was an inmate of the county almshouse and died there or at the county hospital. The logical conclusion is that the person was buried in the county cemetery. FIN

CANESI, John, August 7, 1910, a.60. CADI, DC

CAPENINI, James, October 11, 1939, b.8-27-1881, a.58, single, laborer, a resident of Cotati, father Secondi CAPENINI (b.Italy), inquest held, verdict homicide. Comment: CADI has County 47 (Siskiyou) for place of death. This is an error; the death record clearly states Capenini died at the Sonoma County Hospital. The error probably occurred when a clerk in Sacramento misread '47' (Siskiyou) for '49' (Sonoma). The death record does not list the place of birth; Italy is the most probable. CADI, DC, MIC, NEW

Newspaper records
"Aged Inmate Slugs Helpless Paralytic to Death With Board," *The Press Democrat*, 10-12-1939.
"Where Violent Death Struck," *The Press Democrat*, 10-13-1939.
"Aged Inmate Slugs Helpless Paralytic to Death With Board," *The Press Democrat*, 10-12-1939
"Aged Killer Due to Face Court Today," *The Press Democrat*, 10-13-1939.
"Coroner's Jury Blames Robinson in 'Farm' Murder," *The Press Democrat*, 10-14-1939.
"DeMeo to Defend Nelson Robinson, Poor Farm Slayer," *The Press Democrat*, 10-14-1939.
"Poor Farm Death Hearing Is Slated This Afternoon," *The Press Democrat*, 10-18-1939.
"Preliminary for Slayer Postponed," *The Press Democrat*, 10-19-1939.
"Poor Farm Slayer Due for Hospital Commitment Today," *The Press Democrat*, 11-28-1939.
"Poor Farm Slayer Taken to Asylum As Trial Evaded," *The Press Democrat*, 11-29-1939.

CARDINAL, N., April 3, 1910, a.57. Comment: Not found in 1900, 1910 Census in California. CADI, DC

CARDORA, Jesu, March 24, 1921, a.60; 1920 Census (Sonoma County Farm and Hospital) T625-151-12A, "CARODORA, Jean" (male) a.61, b.Mexico, inmate. CADI, CEN, DC

CARDOVA, Floyd James, February 14, 1914, a.5 months, birth date not given (September 1913?), male, Indian, father Mac CORDOVA (b.CA), mother Lizzie TRIPPO (b.CA), died in the county hospital, #6946, buried 2-14-1914 in the Sonoma County Farm Cemetery, aka "CORDOVA, Floyd James." Comment: The "CARDOVA" spelling is from CADI but the death record clearly spells it "CORDOVA." The family was not found in the 1910 Census for Sonoma County under either spelling. CADI, CEN, DC, MIC

CARLSON, Frank M., February 20, 1916, b.9-12-1878 Singkopoking, Sweden, a.38, single, rancher, father Carlson A. ERICKSON, mother Anna LARSON (both b. Singkopoking, Sweden), 3 months 24 days in the county hospital, buried in the Sonoma County Farm Cemetery. BP, CADI, DC, MIC, REG

Comment: The death record has his age at death 36 years 5 months 8 days. This does not compute. If the dates of birth and death are correct, the age at death must be 37 years 5 months 8 days. (Age 38 is from CADI; they must have rounded up the number.)

CARLSON, John, September 9, 1926, a.86. CADI, DC

CARLSON, Kittie, June 13, 1922, a.69, spouse B. CARLSON. Not found in the 1920 Census. CADI, DC

CARPENTER, William, June 18, 1937 [**294**] b.4-09-1873 MI, a.64, parents George CARPENTER (b.MI) and Emma GREENFIELD (b.MI), in California 33 years, WPA employee, fell and broke his back. He was survived by a son living in Mendocino County. CADI, CAT, DC, MIC, NEW

Newspaper records
"WPA Worker Dead," *The Press Democrat*, 6-19-1937.

CARR, William, June 19, 1923, a.77. CADI, DC

CARROLL, Baby Girl, May 6, 1935 [**457**] stillborn at the county hospital, father John H. CARROLL (b.AL), mother Rena SANDERS (b.CA), resident on Route 2, Santa Rosa. CADI, CAT, DC, MIC

CARTER, Frank, August 30, 1923, a.75. CADI, CEN, DC

Census records
1910 (Sonoma County Farm and Hospital) T624-109-29A, a.54, b.England, single, emigrated 1857, inmate.
1920 (Sonoma County Farm and Hospital) T625-151-12A, a.72, b.England, widowed, emigrated 1849, naturalized citizen, inmate.

CARUBBI, John, February 24, 1943, b.1-05-1875 Italy, father CARUBBI, mother SANTA, wife Annie, 31 years in California, a resident of Geyserville, buried in the county cemetery. CADI, DC

CASEY, Mary, April 26, 1935 [445] b.1900, a.34, spouse "CASEY, T. H." Comment: DC has "Marv," a transcription error. CADI, CAT, CC, DC

CASEY, Patrick, February 5, 1934 [**233**] b.1885, a.48. CADI, CAT, DC

CASSIO, Lenora Rose, June 15, 1934 [**459**] a.1 day, 6 hours, female, Indian, born in Santa Rosa, father Richard MEDINA, mother Wiwona CASSIO (b.CA), died in the county hospital, buried 6-19-1934 in the Sonoma County Cemetery. Comment: The death record has information from which one could infer an age of either 6 hours or 1 day 6 hours; CADI chose to use 1 day 6 hours. CADI, CAT, DC, MIC

CASTANADA, Joseph, April 17, 1929, b.10-11-1849 CA, a.79, widowed, laborer, buried 4-23-1929 in the Sonoma County Farm Cemetery. CADI, DC, MIC

CASTELLO, Ed, March 17, 1888, b.1847 Ireland, died in the county hospital, left $2.25 to the county. DEA, PHY

CASTERA, Casimir J., December 28, 1905, b.France, a.35, single, resident of the Town of Sonoma, hospital #2069, buried in the "Santa Rosa Farm Cem." Comment: The term "Santa Rosa Farm Cem." is unusual since the land containing the cemetery was not annexed into Santa Rosa until the middle of the twentieth century. It indicates that others whose place of burial was given only as "Santa Rosa" may also have been buried in Chanate. CADI, MIC

CASTI, Nicholas, September 11, 1923, a.83, 43 years in California and U.S.; 1920 Census (Sonoma County Farm and Hospital) T625-151-12B, a.81, b.Turkey, widowed, emigrated 1875, inmate. CADI, CEN, DC

CATON, Anna, July 10, 1916, a.65, widowed, 11 years 2 months 23 days at the place of death, 45 years in California, died in the county hospital, #1906, buried 7-13-1916 in the Sonoma County Farm Cemetery; 1910 Census (Sonoma County Farm and Hospital) T624-109-29A, a.70, b.Portugal, widow, emigrated 1865. BP, CADI, CEN, DC, REG

CAUZZA, John, October 27, 1914, a.80. BP, CADI, DC

CAVEDON, Virgil, May 9, 1941, b.6-09-1872, mother RURO. Comment: Date of death also given as 10-31-1941. CADI, DC

CHALSI, Besel, February 28, 1933 [**569**] b.6-14-1872 Switzerland, a.60 years 8 months 14 days, male, single, laborer, a resident of Bloomfield, father John CHALSI (b.Switzerland), mother Antonia BADETTA (b.Switzerland), 43 years in California and the U.S.A., 10 days in the hospital, buried 3-03-1933 in "Santa Rosa."

Comment: Here is an example of incomplete information occuring in a few Sonoma County death records. A "Santa Rosa" burial could be in any one of four cemeteries: Calvary, Chanate, Odd Fellows, or Rural (which includes Fulkerson, Moke, Stanley, and "Old Rural"). Because of this, Mr. Chalsi does not appear in the 1988 DC list. Fortunately, he was in the earlier *Catalogue of Grave Markers* (CAT), so he can be included here. CADI, CAT, MIC

CHAMPION, Victor, August 2, 1912, a.60. CADI, DC

CHANDITO, Pent, April 23, 1915, a.59. CADI, BP, DC

CHASE, Wilmot, October 16, 1918, b.1830 IA, a.87, widowed, laborer, father Allen CHASE (b.IA), mother Aralia HAYES (b.NY), 15 years 4 months 10 days in California, 9 months 21 days in the hospital, #849, buried in the county farm cemetery. CADI, DC, REG

CHEW, Young Gee, September 13, 1923, age 75, widowed. CADI, DC

CHILLI, Antonio, July 21, 1909, a.32, aka "CHILILLI, Antonio." CADI, DC

CHIN, Gee, July 21, 1899, b.China, a.40; buried in the county cemetery, aka "GEE, Chin." DEA, OLE, REG

CHITWOOD, Joseph, March 16, 1886, b.1853 TN, died at the county hospital, left $2.55 to the county; 1880 Census (Shasta County) T9-82-26, a.60, single, b.TN-VA-KY, miner. CEN, DEA, PHY

CHONG, Quong, August 5, 1938 [**123**] b.1868 China, a.70, resident of Sebastopol, died in the county hospital. BOI, CADI, CAT, DC, MIC

CHONG, Young, February 27, 1933 [**568**] b.1856, a.77, aka "CHANG, Young;" 1930 Census (Sonoma County Farm and Hospital) T626-222-222A, a.78, single, emigrated 1877, patient. CADI, CAT, DC

CHOW, Hong, July 4, 1916, b.China, age "about 62," male, widowed, laborer, died in the county hospital, buried 7-05-1916 in the Sonoma County Farm Cemetery. BP, CADI, DC, REG

CHOW, Yun, October 2, 1909, a.65. CADI, DC

CHOY, Ah Chun, June 4, 1901, b.China, a.42, d.Sebastopol, buried in the county cemetery. DEA, OLE

CHRELLI, Joseph, February 16, 1912, a.79. CADI, DC

CHRISTENSEN, Martin, September 13, 1936 [213] b.1883, a.52. CADI, CAT, DC

CHRISTIE, Horatio, August 7, 1913, a.80. CADI, DC

CHRISTINO, Serafino, July 24, 1912, a.62. CADI, DC

CHUNG, Charlie, November 1, 1930 [667] b.1858, a.72. CADI, CAT, DC

CHUNG, Seven, July 7, 1887, b.China, a.39, male, married, died at the county farm, aka "SEVEN, Chung." DEA, REG

CISNEAROS, Leandro, May 11, 1937 [288] b.1887, a.50, died near Santa Rosa, informant Sonoma County Sheriff's Office. CADI, CAT, DC, MIC

CLARK, Edward, October 26, 1906, a.73. CADI, DC

CLARK, Fred, December 12, 1925, a.60. CADI, DC

CLARK, Juan Waldo, August 27, 1941, b.1883. CADI, DC

CLAUKE, Oskar, April 14, 1940, b.1870. CADI, DC

CLAUSE, Peter, June 17, 1905, b.1828 Germany, a.77, laborer, died at the county hospital. CADI, DC, MIC

CLEMENS, John, August 17, 1907, b.LA, a.76, male, Negro, laborer, father b.PA, 10 years in California, 8 months at the county hospital, #4071, buried in the Sonoma County Farm Cemetery. CADI, DC, MIC

CLINE, Frank, July 12, 1914, b.10-15-1880 Philadelphia, a.33, occupation stone cutter, father John CLINE (b.Germany), mother Mary WAGNER (b.PA), died at the county hospital, #7063, buried in the Sonoma County Farm Cemetery, aka "ELINE, Frank." CADI, DC, MIC

COAKLEY, John, February 20, 1919, b.1850 MA, a.69, married, wife Ellen, laborer, father Cornelius COAKLEY (b.Ireland), mother Ellen DAVIS (b.Scotland), 62 years in California, 6 years at the place of death, buried 2-24-1919 in the county farm cemetery; 1910 Census (Sonoma County Farm and Hospital) T624-109-29A, a.59, b.U.S., widowed. CADI, CEN, DC, 1914 GR

COCCI, Felice, May 20, 1944, b.5-18-1886 Italy, a.58, male, single, died in the county hospital, buried in the county cemetery, aka "CROCCI, Helene." Comment: Thought to be the last person buried in the old county cemetery. The new property next to Rural Cemetery was purchased just before his death. BOI, CADI, DC

CODIGA, Joseph, April 25, 1908, a.75. CADI, DC

COLE, Edwin T., August 16, 1913, a.73; 1910 Census (Sonoma County Farm and Hospital) T624-109-29A, a.73, b.U.S., single, inmate. CADI, CEN, DC

COLLI, Frank M., January 17, 1916, b.Italy, a.72, divorced, father Padro COLLI (b.Italy), mother Mary MECORDIA (b.Italy), 45 years in California, died in the county hospital, #6932, buried 1-29-1916 in the Sonoma County Farm Cemetery. BP, CADI, DC, REG

COLLINGS, Alexander F., October 4, 1932 [**529**] b.1850, a.81, spouse "COLLINGS, A.;" 1920 Census (Santa Rosa) T625-151-243, a.69, b.IL-KY-KY, wife Louise A., son Elven. CADI, CAT, CEN

COLLINS, Samuel, June 20, 1924, a.67. CADI, DC

COLSTON, Enoch, December 1, 1929 [**685**] b.1880, aka "COLSTON, F." CADI, CAT

COMETTA, Dalmiro, June 12, 1935 [**234**] b.1872, a.63, died in Napa County. Comment: COMETTA was probably a tuberculosis patient sent to the Silverado Sanitarium in Calistoga. Patients with tuberculosis were sent out of county during the latter part of the 1930s until the Oak Knoll Sanatorium was completed in 1939. When the patient died (and most did) he or she was brought back to Sonoma County for burial. Some, like COMETTA, had their deaths registered in Sonoma County as well as in Napa County. CADI, CAT

CONKEL, Roy, September 29, 1942, b.6-15-1866 OH, mother WALLER. CADI, DC

CONNERS, Michael, June 9, 1929 [**695**] b.2-25-1875 ME, a.54, single, laborer, hospital #2266, aka "CONNORS, Michael." CADI, CAT, CC, DC, MIC

CONSOLASIO, Joseph, May 2, 1928 [**714**] b.1871, a.57. CADI, CAT

CONWAY, Patrick, January 20, 1911, b.Ireland, a.73, parents b.Ireland, divorced, farm laborer, 8 years in the hospital, 63 years in California, hospital #35, buried in the Sonoma County Farm Cemetery, aka "COURVAY or CONRVAY, Patrick;" 1910 Census (Sonoma County Farm and Hospital) T624-109-29A, a.71, divorced, b.Ireland-Ireland-Ireland, emigrated 1848. Comment: How CADI managed to read the name on the death certificate as "CONRVAY" is unknown but so it is in the record. CADI, CEN, DC, MIC

COOPER, Charles A., July 25, 1912, a.58. CADI, DC

COOPER, John, October 8, 1909, a.49. CADI, DC

COOPER, Mary, April 7, 1916, a.79, d.San Francisco. Comment: Mary COOPER was probably one of those people who, as [an indigent] patient of the Sonoma County Hospital, was sent to San Francisco for care not available in Sonoma County. Even though her death occurred in San Francisco, she was the responsibility of Sonoma County so she was buried here. CADI, BP

CORCORAN, Patrick, April 5, 1914, a.74; 1910 Census (Sonoma County Farm and Hospital) T624-109-29A, a.71, b.Ireland, single, emigrated 1869. CADI, CEN, DC

CORDA, Pasquale, March 17, 1939 [**111**] b.1872, a.67, spouse "M. PASQUALE," died in the county hospital. Born in Switzerland and a former resident of Petaluma and Sonoma, Mr. CORDA was survived by a sister, Evaline CATTANEO in Switzerland. BOI, CADI, CAT, DC, NEW

Newspaper records
"Pasquale Corda Dies," *The Press Democrat*, 3-18-1939.

CORDOVA, William, July 26, 1911, a.1. <u>CADI, DC</u>

* CORDOVA <u>see</u> CARDOVA (1914).

CORNELSAN, Peter, December 12, 1937, a.78, aka "CORNELSON, Peter;" BOI has his residence in a community called 'Grand View.' Comment: Grand View was located northwest of Sebastopol in the Cherry Ridge area. <u>BOI, CADI, DC</u>

CORRADINO, Francisca, December 28, 1907, a.63. <u>CADI, DC</u>

CORS, Louisa, July 24, 1932 [**417**] b.1861, a.70, aka "CORS, Louise;" 1930 Census (Sonoma County Farm and Hospital) T626-222-222A, a.68, b.Switzerland, home language French, widow, patient. <u>CADI, CAT, CEN</u>

CORVETTO, August, October 28, 1931 [**554**] b.1847, a.84; 1930 Census (Sonoma County Farm and Hospital) T626-222-222A, a.82, b.Italy, single, emigrated 1869, inmate. <u>CADI, CAT, CEN</u>

COSTANTINO, Lago D., November 22, 1939, a.51, born in Italy, a resident of Sebastopol for 15 years, aka "CONSTANTINO <u>or</u> CONSTANTINI, Logo <u>or</u> Lago." <u>CADI, DC, NEW</u>

<u>Newspaper records</u>
"Lago Constantini," *The Press Democrat,* 11-23-1939.

COSTELLO, Martin, April 4, 1909, b.England, age 59, single, hospital #5558. <u>CADI, DC</u>

COTA, Sabina, September 14, 1937 [**309**] b.12-31-1869, a.67, male, parents Joseph COTA and Bessie BASHUE, a resident of Healdsburg, spouse "R. COTA," aka "CATO, Sabino." Born in Baja California and survived by his wife. No Healdsburg obituary. <u>CADI, CAT, DC, MIC, NEW</u>

<u>Newspaper records</u>
"Local Resident Dies," *The Press Democrat,* 9-15-1937.

COX, Isaac, July 16, 1898, b.MA, a.73, died in the county hospital. <u>CEN, CHSQ, DEA, GR, NEW, REG</u>

Comment: Isaac Cox was a three-term member of the Oregon State Legislature (representing Josephine County) and the author of two books. He is listed in *The Political Graveyard* <<u>http://politicalgraveyard.com/</u>>.

<u>Census and voter registration records</u>
1860   (Siskiyou County) M653-69-154, a.30, b.MD, farmer.
1870   (Josephine County, OR) M593-1286-445, a.41, b.MD, farmer.
1880   (Siskiyou County) T9-083-266B, a.52, b.MD-MD-MD, single, miner.
1890   (Siskiyou County) Great Register, a.54, b.MD, registered 6-09-1879.

<u>Newspaper records</u>
"Local Briefs," *Santa Rosa Daily Republican,* 7-16-1898.

COYLE, John, April 7, 1937 [**285**] b.1850, a.76. <u>CADI, CAT, DC, NEW</u>

<u>Newspaper records</u>
"John Coyle Dies," *The Press Democrat*, 4-08-1937.

CRAIG, Belva, January 21, 1936 [**245**] b.1890, a.46, spouse CRAIG, J.D., aka "GRAIG, Belva;" 1920 Census (Payne County, OK) T625-1483-3, Belva (wife of Jefferson) CRAIG, a.30, b.KS-KS-KS. Mrs. CRAIG, a native of Kansas, was the wife of Jefferson D. CRAIG and had four children, George, Melvin, Darrell and Margaret CRAIG. <u>CADI, CAT, CEN, DC, NEW</u>

Comment: During the 1987 study of the old county cemetery by Sonoma County authorities, a daughter of Belva Craig telephoned county officials from Bakersfield, having heard about the project. The descendant said her mother had been buried in plot number 47, near the eastern fence. Indeed, there is a marker numbered 47 in this location but the county records show Mrs. Craig's grave to have been buried with marker number 245. In this latter location are buried others who died in January 1936, so the current location seems most appropriate for Belva Craig's grave.

<u>Newspaper records</u>
"Windsor Wife Dies Suddenly," *The Press Democrat*, 1-23-1936.

CRAIG, John L., July 23, 1932 [**412**] b.1850, a.82. <u>CADI, CAT</u>

CRAIG, William S. "Old Pike," July 27, 1903, b.MO, a.72, woodcutter, buried in the county farm cemetery; 1900 Census (Sonoma County Farm and Hospital) T623-114-257B, b.May 1830 MO-VA-GA, a.70, single, pensioner. <u>CEN, DEA, NEW</u>

<u>Newspaper records</u>
"'Old Pike' is Dead," *The Press Democrat*, 7-29-1903.

CRAIN, William Kennan, December 3, 1941, b.8-07-1870 KY, a.71, father CRAIN. <u>CADI, DC</u>

CRANE, Tactinas, November 4, 1911, a.49. <u>CADI, DC</u>

CRAW, William, February 5, 1936 [**247**] b.1853, a.82, aka "GRAW, William." <u>CADI, CAT, DC</u>

CRENSHAW, Ida May, October 28, 1938 [**176**] b.1898, a.40, spouse "L. CRENSHAW." <u>CADI, CAT, DC</u>

CRESWELL, Luther, December 26, 1938 [**122**] b.1866, a.72, a resident of Healdsburg, aka "CRISWELL <u>or</u> GRISWELL, Luther." Comment: Chanate has three markers numbered "122." CRESWELL could be buried in any one of them. The other two "122" graves are unidentified. <u>BOI, CADI, CAT, DC, NEW</u>

<u>Newspaper records</u>
"Luther Creswell, Ranch Hand, Dies," *The Press Democrat*, 12-27-1938.

CRONIN, Barry, October 7, 1911, a.66. CADI, DC

CRONIN, Frank, June 2, 1938 [**158**] b.1893 San Francisco, a.45, iron worker, "transient, investigation pending," died in the county hospital, buried 6-08-1938 in the county cemetery; BOI notes as his residence "County Jail (Hobo)." Comment: CRONIN may have been a veteran of World War One. BOI, CADI, CAT, DC, MIC, MIL, NEW, POL

CROSBY, Ole, July 28, 1937 [**297**] b.1873, a.64. CADI, CAT, DC

CROSS, Isaac, November 11, 1931 [**556**] b.1865, a.66; 1930 Census (Sonoma County Farm and Hospital) T626-222-222A, a.64, b.IN-VA-U.S., single, inmate. CADI, CAT, CEN

CRUSE, Bena, February 25, 1908, a.13, female, Indian, single, parents unknown, life in California, 1 year 8 days at the county hospital, #5022, died of tuberculosis, buried in the Sonoma County Farm Cemetery. CADI, DC, MIC

CRUSE, Joseph, July 23, 1936 [**225**] b.1880, a.56. CADI, CAT, DC

CRUSEN, William E., January 8, 1907, a.77. CADI, DC

CRUZ, Pedro, August 17, 1942, b.Philippines, a.85, resident on West 8th Street [in Santa Rosa?]. BOI, CADI, DC

CRUZE, Joseph, March 26, 1940, b.1889 CA, aka "CRUZ, Joseph." CADI, DC

CULLERTON, John, April 2, 1935 [383] b.1868, a.67; aka "COLLERTON, John." CADI, CAT, DC

CURTIS, George, January 19, 1941, b.1874 Sonoma County, a.66, parents unknown, marital status unknown, post office address General Delivery, Healdsburg, residence address county farm, 2 years 8 months 14 days in the hospital and died there, buried 1-24-1941 in the county cemetery. BOI, CADI, CEN, DC, MIC

Census records
1920 (Sonoma County Farm and Hospital) T625-151-12B, "CURTISS [*sic*], George C.," a.45, b.CA-CT-OH, divorced.
1930 (Sonoma County Farm and Hospital) T626-222-222A, a.56, divorced, b.CA-Canada-OH, inmate.

CUSTA, Dina, September 9, 1934 [401] a.12 hours. CADI, CAT

DALE, Charles, January 23, 1941, born "about 1880," a.61, died at his residence on West Third Street in rural Santa Rosa, father DALE, informant "papers in possession," buried 1-27-1941 in the county cemetery. CADI, DC, MIC

* DARBY see BARBY (1931).

DARLING, Willis, February 3, 1940, b.2-03-1886 Michigan. CADI, DC

DAUGHERTY, Michael, December 4, 1913, a.67. CADI, DC

DAUTZLISEN, William, January 9, 1915, a.63. BP, CADI, DC

DAVIDSON, John Jack, August 26, 1917, b.11-01-1835 Scotland, a.82, single, laborer, father Jack DAVIDSON (b.Scotland), mother's name unknown (b.Scotland), 10 years 9 months at the place of death, buried 8-31-1917 in the Sonoma County Farm Cemetery. CADI, DC

DAVIS, Benjamin, November 14, 1892 (40 Deaths 26) b. CT, a.53, widower, Company F, 7th Connecticut Infantry, Civil War, died at the county hospital, #922, "interred at county farm;" Great Register of Voters, b.CT, carpenter, blue eyes, brown hair, light complexion. No Healdsburg or Petaluma obituary. Comment: As a veteran, DAVIS should not have been buried in a pauper's grave. DEA, GR (1884-1892), NEW, REG

Newspaper records
[No title] *Santa Rosa Daily Republican*, 11-15-1892.
"A Deceased Veteran," *Sonoma Democrat*, 11-19-1892.

DAVIS, Helma, May 13, 1939 [**115**] b.1863 Finland, a.75, spouse Joseph DAVIS, a resident of Santa Rosa for 33 years, died at her home in North Orchard street. CADI, CAT, DC, MIC, NEW

Newspaper records
"Mrs. Helma Davis," *The Press Democrat*, 5-16-1939.

DAVIS, Joe, May 31, 1941, b.10-02-1878, living in the Empire Hotel, father DAVIS, mother MYKIE, a.62. BOI, CADI, DC

DAVIS, John, June 20, 1913 [**120**] b.1847 England, a.66, hospital #1874. CADI, CAT, MIC

DAY, Isaac, January 30, 1937 [**188**] b.1864 NY, a.72, moved to California in 1899, a resident of Agua Caliente since 1931. Mr. DAY was survived by a sister in New York. CADI, CAT, DC, NEW

Newspaper records
[No title] *The Press Democrat*, 1-31-1937.
[No title] *The Press Democrat*, 2-02-1937.

DAY, William, June 30, 1936 [**265**] b.1850, a.86. CADI, CAT, DC

DECKER, August, January 24, 1920, a.78; 1920 Census (Sonoma County Farm and Hospital) T625-151-12A, a.78, widowed, b.Germany, emigrated 1873. CADI, CEN, DC

DELAGE, Max, April 26, 1910, a.55. CADI, DC

DELANEY, John, January 17, 1926, a.55. CADI, DC

DELANY, Joseph, November 29, 1919, a.66. CADI, DC

DELONG, Frank, November 15, 1887, b.1852 NY, left $5.50 to the county. DEA, PHY

DELONG, John, August 1, 1929 [**693**] b.1852. CADI, CAT

DEMING, William, January 29, 1907, a.87. CADI, DC

DENKER, Carl, May 6, 1938 [**130**] b.2-22-1848 Germany, a resident of the county farm, retired restaurant operator, aka "DENKER, Carlo," 6 years in Santa Rosa, 53 years in California, 54 years in U.S. <u>BOI, CADI, CAT, DC, MIC, NEW</u>

Newspaper records
"Death Claims Carl Denker," *The Press Democrat*, 5-07-1938.

DERRICK, Ludwig, July 11, 1909, a.79. <u>CADI, DC</u>
DESMOND, Harry, February 13, 1935, a.55. <u>CADI, DC</u>

DETRICK, Alice, September 20, 1931 [**359**] b.1930, a.1, aka "DEITRICK, Alice." Comment: Alice was almost two years old, hence the difference between her official death certificate age and the newspaper. <u>CADI, CAT, DC, NEW</u>

Newspaper records
"Convulsions Fatal to 2 Year Old Girl," *The Press Democrat*, 9-23-1931.

DETTIS, Michael, February 22, 1910, a.80. <u>CADI, DC</u>
DEUBERRY, Edward, July 8, 1906, a.61. <u>CADI, DC</u>

DEVINCENZI, Augustino, January 28, 1937 [**186**] b.1893 Italy, a.43, resident on Route 3, Santa Rosa, died at a Napa County sanitarium, probably of tuberculosis (not in Sonoma County records). <u>CADI, CAT, NEW</u>

Newspaper records
"Dies At Napa," *The Press Democrat*, 1-30-1937.

DEVINE, Jerry, September 16, 1933 [**503**] b.1859, a.74. Comment: CAT has [**508**] for Mr. DEVINE, which duplicates that of William SHAW, probably due to mis-reading "508" for "503." Based on the sequence of dates of death, [**503**] is correct for Mr. DEVINE. <u>CADI, CAT</u>

DIAS, Antonio, January 18, 1934 [**427**] b.9-16-1867 Portugal, a.66, male, farmer, father Jookan DIAS, mother Anna Marie JULS, aka "DIAS, Antonia." Comment: the handwritten names on the death certificate were hard to read. <u>CADI, CAT, DC, MIC, NEW</u>

Newspaper records
"Antonio Dias Dead," *The Press Democrat*, 1-19-1934.

DICKEY, George Washington, November 8, 1942, b.2-02-1869 CA, a.73, father DICKEY. <u>CADI, DC</u>
DINUCCI, Bartolamso, February 14, 1913, a.58. <u>CADI, DC</u>

DISHWINDOR, Joseph D., August 15, 1911, b.Switzerland, a.46, single, "common laborer," father b.Switzerland, mother b.France, 2 years 4 months in California (Sonoma County?), hospital #6184, buried in the county farm cemetery, aka "DESCHWANDY or DESCHWANDEN, Joseph." Comment: This person cannot be found in CADI, probably due to a misspelling of the last name. CADI, CC, CEN, DC, MIC

Census records
1900 (Ten Mile River Township, Mendocino County) T623-93-170, "DESCHWANDY, Joseph," a.35, male, white, b.Switzerland, emigrated 1884, 16 years in USA, papers applied for, dairyman.
1910 (Santa Rosa Township) T624-109-11, "DESCHWANDEN, Joseph," a.45, b.Switzerland, single, farm laborer, emigrated 1894, naturalized citizen.

DIXON, Joseph, January 29, 1915, a.85. BP, CADI, DC, 1914 GR

DOE, Jr., Edgar, October 17, 1932 [**528**] b.14 Mar 1927, a.5. No obituary. CADI, CAT, DC

DOEHLER, Gustave, December 2, 1942, b.2-19-1858. CADI, DC

DOMENCCI, Carlo, March 19, 1935 [**442**] b.1860, a.75, aka "DOMENICCI or DONFANGO, Carlo." CADI, CAT, DC

DOMINGUEZ, Lilly E., January 2, 1937 [**197**] b.5-10-1912, a.24, Indian, parents Frank PETE and Mary MAMAL, aka "DOMINGUES, Lilly," spouse Frank E. DOMINGUEZ (died May 1936). CADI, CAT, DC, MIC, NEW

Newspaper records
"Lilly Dominguez, 24, Succumbs Here," *The Press Democrat*, 1-03-1937.
"Services Held for Lilly Dominguez," *The Press Democrat*, 1-06-1937.

DONAHUE, John, June 17, 1938 [**161**] b.June 1874 Ireland, a.64, 4 years in Santa Rosa, 8 years in California; BOI has him residing in Occidental. BOI, CADI, CAT, DC, MIC

DONG, Wong Jung, May 29, 1915, a.47. BP, CADI, DC

DONNATO, Nicola, April 1, 1898, b.Italy, a.30, male, single, drowned; inquest "DAMATI, Nicola," occupation block maker, buried in the county farm cemetery. COR, DEA, REG

DONOVAN, Daniel, November 25, 1934 [391] b.1884, a.50, aka "DONOVAN, Dan." CADI, CAT, DC

DONOVAN, Daniel, September 1, 1936 [**218**] b.1871, a.66. CADI, CAT, DC

DOO, Lee, August 26, 1915, a.60, burial permit August 27, 1915. BP, CADI, DC

DORAN, William, February 4, 1910, a.53. CADI, DC

DORSEY, Frank, May 6, 1936, a.50. CADI, DC

DOUGLAS, Joseph, March 11, 1908, a.80. CADI, DC

DOWNEY, Morris, April 25, 1914, a.77. CADI, DC

DRAGHI, Luigi, November 22, 1887, b.1842 Italy, left $5.00 to the county. <u>DEA,</u>
<u>PHY</u>

DRAY, Alfred, March 21, 1937 [**281**] b.1862, a.74. Comment: The first name "Alex"
in the *Argus-Courier* obituary appears to be an error. The large number of
siblings in the Census records suggests collateral relatives of Alfred DRAY
may be found in Iowa, Missouri, and/or Oklahoma. <u>CADI, CAT, CEN, DC,</u>
<u>NEW</u>

Census records
1880 (Page County, Iowa) T9-358-348, "DRAY, Alfred H.," living with parents
"DRAY, A. H. and Susan," the eldest of ten siblings, blacksmith.
1900 (Jasper County, Missouri) T623-867-204, "DRAY, Alfred H.," blacksmith.
1910 (Stockton, San Joaquin County) T624-103-47, " DRAY, Alfred H.," a.47,
b.England, emigrated 1875, naturalized, blacksmith in carriage factory, wife
Elizabeth, son Wendell, daughter Katherine.
1920 (Manteca, San Joaquin County) T625-143-33, "DRAY, Alfred H.," a.56,
b.England, married, blacksmith.

Newspaper records
"Alex Dray is Called by Death," *Petaluma Argus-Courier*, 3-23-1937.
"Petaluman Expires," *The Press Democrat*, 3-23-1937.

DRIMMER, David, May 29, 1937 [**291**] born "about 1909" in New York, a.28, buried
6-12-1937 in the county cemetery. Comment: DRIMMER was the only
automotive fatality in Sonoma County resulting from the festivities
celebrating the opening of the Golden Gate Bridge, held over the Memorial
Day weekend of 1937. He accepted a ride to Sonoma County from WALLACE,
who was intoxicated. WALLACE hit another car in Cotati, DRIMMER went
through the windshield, and was killed. <u>CADI, CAT, CRT, DC, NEW</u>

Newspaper records
"Autoist Killed in Cotati Crash," *The Press Democrat*, 5-30-1937.
"Holiday Crowd Sets New County Record," *The Press Democrat*, 6-01-1937.
"Autoist Killed in Cotati Crash," *The Press Democrat*, 5-30-1937.
"Fatal Accident At Cotati As Car Is Sideswiped In Mad Saturday Night Dash," *Petaluma*
Argus-Courier, 5-31-1937.
"Auto Victim Identified By Prints," *Petaluma Argus-Courier*, 6-03-1937.
"Inquest in auto death set Friday," *The Press Democrat*, 6-08-1937.
"Trial is set for motorist in death case," *The Press Democrat*, 7-10-1937.
"Negligent homicide case is set Monday," *The Press Democrat*, 9-14-1937.
"Prosecution in crash case is nearing close," *Santa Rosa Daily Republican*, 9-21-1937.
"Autoist in fatal crash was drunk, witness claims," *The Press Democrat*, 9-21-1937.
"Physician says Wallace drunk night of crash," *Santa Rosa Daily Republican*, 9-22-1937.
"Wallace trial nearing close, open argument," *Santa Rosa Daily Republican*, 9-23-1937.
"Wallace fate will be given to jury today," *The Press Democrat*, 9-23-1937.
"Wallace Fate Near Jury's Hand," *Petaluma Argus-Courier*, 9-23-1937.
"Wallace is held guilty in auto death case here," *Santa Rosa Daily Republican*, 9-24-1937.

"Wallace guilty of negligent homicide," *The Press Democrat*, 9-24-1937.
"Earl Wallace Found Guilty Of Negligent Homicide In Hitch-Hiker's Death," *Petaluma Argus-Courier*, 9-24-1937.
"Wallace asks probation in auto killing," *The Press Democrat*, 9-28-1937.
"Wallace Given Year In Jail, And $500 Fine," *The Press Democrat*, 10-31-1937.

DROPER, Joseph L., December 15, 1933 [**578**] b.1851, a.82, aka "DRAPER or DROFER or DROKER, Joseph L." CADI, CAT, DC

DRYER, Louis, March 20, 1923, a.83. CADI, DC

DUBOIS, Abel, June 1, 1924, b.3-08-1848 Canada, a.76, single, died in the county hospital. BOI, CADI, DC

DUBOIS, Alfred, June 24, 1893, b.1869 France, hospital #984, left $4.35 to the county. DEA, PHY

DUBOIS, Leon, January 27, 1944, b.3-01-1868 France, 41 years in California, 6 years 9 months in hospital. CADI, DC

DUCK, Ah, January 8, 1928, b.1868, a.60, male, cook, died in Santa Rosa. Comment: Some records have the name as "DORK" but the spelling in CADI and DC is clearly "DUCK." CADI, DC, MIC

DUGAN, Nelson L., June 9, 1936 [**262**] b.1867, a.68. CADI, CAT, DC

DUN, Ham, November 23, 1925, a.61. CADI, DC

DUNBAR, (Reverend) Halahan Killigrew, November 2, 1904, b.9-26-1819 Dublin, Ireland, single, Anglican minister. Comment: Although possessed of considerable artistic talent, DUNBAR was unable to work as an artist for the usual reason, lack of a patron. DUNBAR studied at Trinity College in Dublin, received a Bachelor of Arts degree in 1844 and became a curate in the Church of Ireland. (In the churches of the Anglican communion, a curate is an assistant or deputy of a rector or vicar.) In the late 1860s, Rev. DUNBAR was curate at Belleek <http://www.belleek.ie/> home of the famous pottery firm, where he modeled a piece of statuary known as the "Group of Greyhounds." CEN, GR, IND, NEW, RUR

In 1869, Dunbar left the church and escorted his sister, Frances Holmes Dunbar, to Australia, where she was to be married. In Australia, Dunbar met a Canadian named Gilbert Jenkins; later, the men together emigrated to the United States where they were in business in San Francisco. In 1877, Dunbar and Jenkins moved to Sonoma County and bought a small ranch on Mark West Creek. Jenkins later married and had a family but Dunbar was a lifelong bachelor.

Dunbar was unable to succeed in his new home and fell upon the charity of the county. He died at the county hospital and was buried by the county. Jenkins, hearing of Dunbar's death and pauper burial, wished to have him removed to the Jenkins plot in the Stanley Cemetery (now part of the Santa Rosa Rural Cemetery) but there is no evidence this was ever accomplished.

Gilbert Jenkins's sister, Catherine Jenkins, lived in Santa Rosa and collected letters from family members and from Dunbar. Styling herself "C. Carlyon Jenkyns," she wrote from the letters a book entitled *Hard Life In The Colonies* (London:

T. Fisher Unwin, 1892). Although some of the descriptive writing appears to be imaginative, the Sonoma County section seems accurate. In any case, this is the only surviving "my life in California" written by a person buried in the Chanate Historic Cemetery.

Newspaper records
"Once Noted Man Dies In Poverty," *The Press Democrat*, 11-17-1904.

DUNBAR, Lucian A., September 5, 1932 [**410**] b.1851, a.80; 1930 Census (Sonoma County Farm and Hospital) T626-222-222A, a.78, b.MA-MA-NH, single, inmate. CADI, CAT, CEN

DUNLAP, James, September 9, 1939, a.80. CADI, DC

DUNLAP, Joseph, May 14, 1910, a.58. CADI, DC

DUNNING, Silas S., March 21, 1921, a.57; 1920 Census (Sonoma County Farm and Hospital) T625-151-12B, a.58, divorced, b.NY-NY-NY, inmate. CADI, CEN, DC

DURAND, Jaques, May 17, 1912, a.91; 1910 Census (Sonoma County Farm and Hospital) T624-109-29A, a.86, widowed, b.France, emigrated 1868; aka "DURAND, Jacque." CADI, CEN, DC

* DUULON, Maud, February 27, 1909. The name is actually "DUNTON, Maud." She was buried in the cemetery at the Sonoma State Home at Eldridge (now the Sonoma Developmental Center), not in Chanate (DC error). CADI, DC, MIC

DYE, Albert O., October 4, 1934 [**432**] b.1861, a.73. CADI, CAT, DC

EARLEY, Raymond Carl, March 15, 1940, b.7-16-1889 Iowa, mother McDOWELL, died in the "Mendocino Woodland Camp" (BOI), probably a CCC or WPA late depression-era operation. BOI, CADI, DC

EBBS, George W., January 6, 1934 [**400**] b.10-29-1875 Kansas, a.58, widowed, rancher, a resident of Sebastopol, father Henry EBBS (b.MO), mother Mary BURGES (b.KS), aka "WEBBS, George" (DC error). CADI, CAT, CEN, DC, MIC, NEW

Census records
1920 (Sacramento) T625-126-69, a.43, b.KS-MO-MO, carpenter in railroad shop, wife Bessie, a.38, b.SD-U.S.-U.S.

Newspaper records
"Funeral Held For Sebastopol Farmer," *The Press Democrat*, 1-09-1934

ECK, John, December 8, 1935 [**451**] b.10-30-1856 Germany, a.79, parents William ECK and Annie ORTHER, farm laborer, a resident of Bloomfield. CADI, CAT, DC, MIC

ECKERT, August, February 1, 1941, b.1861. CADI, DC

EHLERS, Henry, February 1, 1917, b.6-19-1857 Germany, a.59 years 7 months 14 days, single, butcher, father Hans EHLERS (b.Germany), mother Annie MASS (b.Germany), 30 years in California, died in the county hospital, #7755, buried 2-03-1917 in the Sonoma County Farm Cemetery. BP, CADI, MIC, REG

EHLICH, Henry, February 18, 1937 [**275**] b.NY, a.60, employed and resident at the ranch of Mrs. Kurt LYONS on the Star Route out of Petaluma, entered the "Santa Rosa" hospital in September 1936 and died there. Comment: A "star route" <http://www.postalmuseum.si.edu/starroute/sr_02.html> was a rural mail route carried by contractors. CADI, CAT, DC, NEW

Newspaper records
"Henry Ehlich Dies at Santa Rosa," *Petaluma Argus-Courier*, 2-19-1937.
"No Known Relatives," *The Press Democrat*, 2-19-1937.

ELISECHE, Ambrosio, August 4, 1907, b.Spain, a.33, male, single, laborer, father Simon ELISECHE (b.Spain), mother b.Spain, 3 years in California, died at the county hospital, #5105, buried in the Sonoma County Farm Cemetery. CADI, MIC

ELLIOTT, William, December 29, 1930, a.74. CADI, CEN, DC

Census records
1920 (Sonoma County Farm and Hospital) T625-151-12B, a.79 [*sic*], b.NY-U.S.-U.S., widowed, inmate.
1930 (Sonoma County Farm and Hospital) T626-222-222A, a.73, single, b.NY-Canada-MA, inmate.

EMERY, Francis, May 3, 1936 [**256**] b.1859, a.76 [CAT error, gives dates 1859-1931]. CADI, CAT, DC

ENNIS, Patrick, October 15, 1905, b.1847 Ireland, a.58, single, occupation "railroader," died at the county hospital (Dr. S. S. BOGLE). CADI, DC, MIC

EOKILA, Mathieu, January 25, 1931, b.7-01-1870 Finland, a.60, single, laborer, father Mathieu EOKILA (b.Finland), mother Annie (b.Finland), 33 years in U.S., 20 years in California, 1 month 25 days at the county hospital, buried 1-26-1931 in the county cemetery, aka "EUKILA, Mathieu." CADI, DC, MIC

ERICKSON, John, April 11, 1931 [**537**] b.1873, a.57; 1930 Census (Sonoma County Farm and Hospital) T626-222-222A, a.56, single, b.Sweden, emigrated 1892, patient. CADI, CAT, DC

ERIKSON, Eric, November 21, 1915, b.5-06-1853 Sweden, a.62 years 6 months 15 days, single, carpenter, father Peter ERIKSON (b.Sweden), mother Anna LUNDSTROM (b.Sweden), 25 years in California, died in the county hospital, buried 2-28-1916 in the Sonoma County Farm Cemetery. BP, CADI, DC, REG

ERNST, William, March 15, 1887, b.1824 Germany, left $3.00 to the county; 1880 Census (Town of Sonoma) T9-84-8, a.53, b.1827 Prussia, single, farm laborer. CEN, DEA, PHY

ESKERICA, Katherine, June 24, 1938 [**163**] b.1882 Austria, a.56, a resident of Geyserville, spouse Martin ESKERICA, aka "SKENNICA, Mrs. Katherine E." BOI, CADI, CAT, DC, NEW

ESKERICA, Martin, August 3, 1938 [**164**] b.1883 Italy, a.54, a resident of Geyserville, spouse was Katherine ESKERICA, served in the Serbian Army in WWI. BOI, CADI, CAT, DC, NEW

Newspaper records
"Mrs. Eskerica Dies," *The Press Democrat*, 6-26-1938.
"Martin Eskerica Dies," *The Press Democrat*, 8-04-1938.

EVANS, Baby Girl, October 13, 1924, stillborn, parents Everett EVANS and Alice Virginia NOBLE (both b.CA), a resident of Santa Rosa, died in the Mary Jesse Hospital (Santa Rosa). CADI, DC, MIC

FABRIA, Louis, August 24, 1929 [**690**] b.1876, a.53. CADI, CAT

FACCINI, Clement, June 18, 1936 [264] b.1858, a.77. CADI, CAT, DC

FAH, Charles, July 2, 1927, a.66. CADI, DC

FALCONER, Colin, December 26, 1888, b.1821 Scotland, left $18.00 to the county. DEA, PHY

FARMER, Jack, October 29, 1931 [**555**] b.1857, a.79. CADI, CAT, DC

FAURSCHOU, Nils, August 2, 1935 [**239**] b.1856, a.79. CADI, CAT, DC

FAUST, Rudolph, August 13, 1937 [**299**] b.1848 Switzerland, a.88, a resident of Sonoma County since 1898. FAUST, while washing, had a heart attack and fell into the wash basin, striking the hot water tap. He was scalded by the hot water although his death was attributed to the heart attack. CADI, CAT, CEN, DC, NEW

Census records
1910 (Silveyville, Vacaville Twp., Solano County) T624-108-78, FOUST, Rudolph, a.66, b.Switzerland, single, emigrated 1879, "papers applied for," fruit farm laborer.

Newspaper records
"Inmate Succumbs to Heart Attack in S. R. Hospital," *The Press Democrat*, 8-14-1937.

FEILING, Louis, December 17, 1935 [**452**] b.5-18-1867, a.68, parents Louis and Anna FEILING, divorced, a resident of Two Rock, laborer, in California 52 years. CADI, CAT, CC, DC, MIC

FELIC, Vitorell, November 25, 1902, b.CA, age 8 months, male, white, single, "indigent." REG

FELSINGER, John, September 19, 1925, a.74. CADI, DC

FERNENDEZ, Carlos, July 11, 1936 [**227**] b.1880. Comment: CADI has "FERNINDES, Carlos, a.55, d.7-11-1936 in county 28 (Napa)." He may have been a tuberculosis patient at the Silverado Sanitarium. CADI, CAT

FERRARA, Lugi, June 30, 1906, a.82, birth date not given, b.Italy, widower, farmer, parents unknown, 22 days in the hospital, died there, buried 7-02-1906 in the "S. Co. Farm Cem." Comment: This person could not be found in CADI. The handwritten name on the death record could also be "FENARA" or "FEMARA." DC, MIC

FERRARA, Richard Edward, June 26, 1934 [512] b.1863, a.70. Comment: CAT error, marker [512] duplicate, see McCLOSKEY [513]. CADI, CAT, DC

FERRERO, Ricardo, September 18, 1941, b.4-24-1875. CADI, DC

FERRETTI, Antonio, July 25, 1908, a.34. CADI, DC

FIELD, Baby Girl, February 5, 1934 [411] a.4 hours, father Lewis FIELD, mother Clara WALKER (b.PA). CADI, CAT, DC, MIC

FILLEY, Phillip, March 3, 1925, a.75. CADI, DC

FISHER, Fred, April 26, 1917, b.Switzerland, ranch laborer, a.60, thrown from a cart and died in the "Pine Mountain district" near the Napa County line, buried 4-30-1917 in the county cemetery. The newspaper obituary says he was the "keeper of the Ransom House [tavern? hotel?] sixteen miles above Santa Rosa." BP, CADI, DC, MIC, NEW, REG

Newspaper records
"Fred Fisher is Man Found Dead Yesterday," *The Press Democrat*, 4-28-1917.

FISHER, John Henry, June 11, 1916, b.12-16-1856 Holland, a.59 years 5 months 26 days, single, laborer, father Richard FISHER (b.Holland), mother Mary BASMAN (b.Holland), 21 days at the place of death, 29 years in California, died in the county hospital, #7663, buried 6-14-1916 in the Sonoma County Farm Cemetery. BP, CADI, DC, REG

FITZGERALD, James, May 19, 1905, b.Ireland, a.80, laborer, a resident of the county farm, buried in the "County Plot;" 1900 Census (Sonoma County Farm and Hospital) T623-114-257B, b.January 1834 Ireland, a.66, single, emigrated 1862, pensioner. Comment: There are unexplained birthdate differences (CADI = 1825, Census = 1834). It is possible that the man in the death record and the one in the Census are two different persons. CADI, CEN, DC, MIC

FITZIMMONS, Thomas, July 21, 1919, a.55, aka "FITZIMONS, Thomas." CADI, DC

FLAGE, Frederick, January 6, 1916, b.5-11-1858 in Sonoma County, a.57 years 7 months 27 days, single, farm laborer, father Henry FLAGE (b.Germany), mother Mary A. FELKER (b.IL), 46 years in California, died in the county hospital, #7516, buried 1-07-1916 in the Sonoma County Farm Cemetery. BP, CADI, DC, REG

FLAGG, Henry, July 8, 1887, b.1835 MA, left $5.15 to the county. DEA, PHY

FLAMING, John, February 16, 1940, b.5-9-1879, a.60. CADI, DC

FLAMMER, Charles, December 4, 1940, b.11-26-1873 MI, a.66, a resident of the county farm, mother DINKENTER. BOI, CADI, DC

FLANAGAN, James, June 8, 1925, a.75. CADI, DC

FLATLEY, Bernard, September 13, 1918, age "about 50," laborer, 18 days in the county hospital, buried 9-17-1918 in the Sonoma County Farm Cemetery. CADI, DC, REG

FLEMING, John, March 31, 1925, a.48. CADI, DC

FLINN, Michael, March 30, 1932 [**563**] b.1847, a.85. CADI, CAT

FLORES, Jesus, July 30, 1917, b.7-28-1917 in Sonoma County, a.2 days, father Jesus FLORES (b.Mexico), mother Rebecca VILLA (b.CA), died in Analy Township, buried 7-31-1917 in the Sonoma County Farm Cemetery. Comment: BP has date of death "June 30, 1917" in error. BP, CADI, DC, REG

FOGEL, Phillip, January 27, 1937 [189] b.1858, a.78, a native of Illinois and a 17-year resident of Petaluma, at the county farm since 1929; 1930 Census (Sonoma County Farm and Hospital) T626-222-222B, a.72, b.IL, single, inmate. CADI, CAT, CEN, DC, NEW

Newspaper records
"Petaluman Succumbs," *The Press Democrat*, 1-28-1937.
"Philip Fogel Is At Rest Near Santa Rosa," *Petaluma Argus-Courier*, 1-30-1937.
[No title] *The Press Democrat*, 1-31-1937.

FON, Wong, October 24, 1916, a.58, aka "FONG, Wong." BP, CADI, DC

FONG, Joe, March 8, 1926, a.60. CADI, DC

* FONG, Wong see WONG, Tong (1910).

* FOOTS see FOUTS (1912).

FORBES, Henry, October 20, 1907, b.Nova Scotia, a.52, married, parents b.Nova Scotia, 8 months in California, died at the county hospital, buried in the Sonoma County Farm Cemetery. CADI, DC, MIC

FORD, Angier B., March 3, 1935 [**439**] b.1-07-1849 Boston, MA, a.86 years 1 month 26 days, male, single, a resident of the county farm, father Thomas FORD (b.Duxbury, MA), mother Grace Fish BOYKTON (b.Duxbury, MA), 60 years in California, 7 years in Santa Rosa, died in the county hospital, buried 3-05-1935 in the Sonoma County Cemetery; 1930 Census (Sonoma County Farm and Hospital) T626-222-222B, a.81, b.MA-MA-MA, single, inmate; aka "FORD, A." Comment: CAT lists date of death as 1936 in error. CADI, CAT, CEN, DC, MIC

FORD, Guilford, July 19, 1941, b.10-06-1866 ID, mother RICHARDS. Comment: BOI indicates the expenses of burial were paid by Ukiah; was he a Mendocino County resident? BOI, CADI, DC

FORESCHI, Luigi, March 28, 1886, b.1852 Italy, left $1.00 to the county. DEA, PHY

FORTOLA, John, October 24, 1916, b.Italy, age "unknown, probably 65 years," parents b.Italy, 3+ years at the county farm, died at the county hospital, buried 10-26-1916 in the Sonoma County Farm Cemetery, aka "FORTOLA, K. John." BP, CADI, DC, REG

* FOSTER see KOSTER (1929).

FOSTER, George, October 21, 1919, a.75. <u>CADI, DC</u>

FOSTER, Walter, September 12, 1936 [**214**] b.1874, a.61. <u>CAT, DC</u>

FOSTOMANTUS, Francisco, December 4, 1907, a.76. <u>CADI, DC</u>

FOTHERGILL, John, September 3, 1939, b.3-11-1856 England, a.83, single, 50 years in U.S., 12 years resident at MAXWELL's Ranch, at death a resident of the county farm, aka "FATHERGILL, John." <u>BOI, CADI, DC, MIC</u>

FOU, Charlie, April 18, 1906, died at the Occidental Hotel of "injuries sustained by earthquake," b.China, age unknown, 22 years in California, male, "yellow," married, cook, buried in the county farm cemetery. <u>CADI, CC, DC, MIC</u>

FOUTCH, Molinda, July 23, 1925, a.67, spouse A. P. FOUTCH. <u>CADI, DC</u>

FOUTS, Frank, August 2, 1924, a.52. <u>CADI, DC</u>

FOUTS, Louis, March 6, 1912, a.38, single, parents unknown, fruit ranch laborer, a resident of the town of Sonoma, life in California, 2 months at the county hospital, buried in the Sonoma County Farm Cemetery, aka "FOOTS, Louis." <u>CADI, DC, MIC</u>

FOWLER, Fredrick, January 24, 1905, b.1886 NE, a.19, single, occupation "dairy-man," father b.IN. <u>CADI, DC, MIC</u>

FOX, James M., May 25, 1919, b.1847 Ireland, a.72, single, laborer, father John FOX (b.Ireland), mother Bess FAGAN (b.Ireland), 63 years in California, 6 days in the county hospital, buried 5-27-1919 in the county farm cemetery. <u>CADI, DC, REG</u>

FRANCISCO, George, October 30, 1926, a.73. <u>CADI, DC</u>

FRANKLIN, Edwin V., September 15, 1938 [**169**] b.1856, a.82. <u>CADI, CAT, DC</u>

* FRANKS, Charles <u>see</u> SWED, Frank (1938).

FRANTZEN, Oscar, July 10, 1938 [**125**] b.1879, a.59, a resident of Sebastopol; possible 1920 Census (Lawrence Township, Clearfield County, PA) T625-1553-46, "FRANTZEN, Oscar," b.Sweden, a.40, single, steel worker, naturalization papers applied for. Comment: this is the only Oscar FRANTZEN in the USA for the 1920 Census. The 1920 Census did not give the date of immigration for Oscar and he is not listed in the 1910 Census; the "Oscar FRANTZEN" in the 1900 Census of Biloxi, MS is too old. <u>BOI, CADI, CAT, CEN, DC</u>

FRASER, John, March 5, 1939 [**109**] b.1852 NY, a.86, a resident of Healdsburg. <u>BOI, CADI, CAT, DC, NEW</u>

<u>Newspaper records</u>
"John Fraser Dead," *The Press Democrat*, 3-07-1939.

FRAZIER, Richard, May 8, 1942, b.5-08-1942 CA, a.2 minutes, mother TOOLEY. <u>CADI, DC</u>

FRAZIER, Richard Edward, July 7, 1927, a.65. <u>CADI, DC</u>

FREITAS, Joseph, September 7, 1913, a.3 months. <u>CADI, DC</u>

FRIEDER, Nicholas, December 19, 1920, a.60. <u>CADI, DC</u>

FROMENT, George, March 8, 1937 [**279**] b.1880 France, a.56, farmer, resident on Rural Route #1, Santa Rosa, d.Napa County, brother of Adolph R. FROMENT of Santa Rosa, aka "FREMONT, George." Comment: FROMENT may have died of tuberculosis. In the 1930s, until January 1938, Sonoma sent its tuberculosis patients to the Silverado Sanitarium in Napa County. <u>CADI, CAT, NEW</u>

<u>Newspaper records</u>
"George Froment Dead," *The Press Democrat*, 3-09-1937.
"Graveside Service," *The Press Democrat*, 3-11-1937.

---

* FUGOLA, Lorenzo, September 29, 1907. DC error, not in Chanate, buried "Duncans" [Duncans Mills Cemetery] according to the Sonoma County death record. <u>DC, MIC</u>

FUHS, Nicholas, January 26, 1941, b.12-19-1863 IA, a.77 years 1 month 7 days, parents Michael and Margaret FUHS, 23 years in the community, died at his residence on West Third Street in rural Santa Rosa, informant Sonoma County Social Services, buried 1-28-1941 in the county cemetery. <u>CADI, DC, MIC</u>

FULLER, Charles, February 5, 1939 [**102**] b.1876, a.62. A ten-year resident of the Two Rock area, Mr. FULLER was born in Colorado. <u>CADI, CAT, DC, NEW</u>

<u>Newspaper records</u>
"Charles Fuller," *The Press Democrat*, 2-07-1939.

FUNG, Moy, November 17, 1917, a.70, aka "MEY, Fung." <u>CADI, DC</u>

FURGERSON, Levi, December 22, 1914, b.VA, a.84, single, laborer, parents b.VA, died at the county hospital, #6735, buried in the Sonoma County Farm Cemetery. <u>BP, CADI, DC, MIC</u>

GAGER, George, December 17, 1915, b.5-20-1826 MA, a.89 years 6 months 20 days, retired, 63 years in California, died at the county hospital, buried 12-19-1915 in the Sonoma County Farm Cemetery; 1910 Census (Santa Rosa Township) T624-109-37, a.83, b.CT-CT-CT, widowed, farm laborer. No obituary. <u>BP, CADI, CEN, DC, REG</u>

GALEGO, Thomas, March 29, 1887, b.1872 CA, a resident of Petaluma, left $2.00 to the county. No obituary. <u>DEA, PHY</u>

GALGANI, Joseph, September 12, 1936, a.58. <u>CADI, DC</u>

GALLI, Gaetano, December 25, 1928 [**733**] b.2-18-1873 Switzerland, a.55, single, farm laborer, father Domenico GALLI (b.Switzerland), mother b.Switzerland, 44 years in California and U.S., 3 years 9 months 14 days at the county hospital, hospital #2051, aka "GALLI, Gaethno," <u>or</u> "CALLI, Gaetano." <u>CADI, CAT, CC, DC, MIC</u>

GAMBO, John, December 17, 1936 [**199**] b.1861, a.75. <u>CADI, CAT, DC</u>

GANASCIA, Frank, December 8, 1938 [**177**] b.1877, a.61, a resident of Cloverdale. Comment: BOI noted the "man had $35 in Bank of America, Cloverdale." <u>BOI, CADI, CAT, DC</u>

* GANGLUAN <u>see</u> GAUGHRAN (1907).

GANZERT, William, July 21, 1941, b.2-07-1854 NY, aka "GENZERT, William." <u>CADI, DC</u>

GARCIA, Baby Girl, November 5, 1912, stillborn, father Antonio GARCIA (b.Spain), mother Anna CONEJO (b.Spain), residence Santa Rosa, buried in the county cemetery. Comment: DC has 11-06-1912. <u>CADI, DC, MIC</u>

GARCIA, Mary, May 2, 1926, stillborn, father Frank GARCIA (b.CA), mother Goldie GARDNER (b.MN), buried in the county cemetery. <u>CADI, DC, MIC</u>

GARDINI, Domenico, March 4, 1928, a.83. <u>CADI, DC</u>

GARDNER, Francis Delores, July 31, 1925, a.1. <u>CADI, DC</u>

GARE, Tomaso, January 22, 1907 (60 Deaths 67) b.Italy, a.45, male, single, laborer, 21 years in California, died in Santa Rosa, buried in the Sonoma County Farm Cemetery. Comment: This person cannot be found in CADI. <u>DC, MIC, REG</u>

* GARFIELD <u>see</u> RELYEA (1938).

GARNER, Lemuel, February 23, 1914, a.59, divorced, wood chopper, father Charles GARNER (b.PA), mother Sarah STEER <u>or</u> STEEN (b.PA), 6 years in California, died in the county hospital, #6968, buried 2-28-1914 at the "Sonoma County Farm," aka "GARNER, Samuel." <u>CADI, DC, MIC</u>

GARRITY, Thomas, December 5, 1924, a.68. <u>CADI, DC</u>

GAUGHRAN, Peter, April 8, 1907, b.Ireland, a.71, widower, laborer, died at the Sonoma County Hospital, #4075, buried in the "Farm Cemetery," aka "GANGLUAN, Peter." <u>CADI, DC, MIC</u>

GEE, Young, August 20, 1916, a.50, aka "GEE, Yong." <u>BP, CADI, DC</u>

GEIGER, Antonio, January 9, 1894, left $30.00 to the county; 1890 Census Substitute (p.97), b. 1830 Switzerland. <u>CS, PHY</u>

GEISLER, John, March 21, 1917, b.4-06-1855 PA, a.62, single, farmer, father Joseph GEISLER (b.Switzerland), mother Mary BRWE [*sic*] (b.Switzerland), died in the county hospital, #7228, buried 3-26-1917 in the Sonoma County Farm Cemetery. <u>BP, CADI, REG</u>

GELPI, Luigi, September 26, 1941, b.3-06-1878, a.63, mother VALI. <u>CADI, DC</u>

GELSI, Joseph, January 20, 1937 [**190**] b.1888 Italy, a.48, emigrated 1911, 7 years in Sonoma County, spouse Elba GELSI. <u>CADI, CAT, DC, NEW</u>

<u>Newspaper records</u>
"Joseph Gelsi, Here Seven Years, Dead," *The Press Democrat*, 1-21-1937.

GENGLAR, John, July 17, 1925, a.67, aka "GENGLER, John." <u>CADI, DC</u>

GENSCHMER, Max, May 17, 1939 [**116**] b.1852, a.87, a resident of the county farm, aka "GEMSCHMER, Max." BOI, CADI, CAT, DC

GENTHER, Rose Irene, August 19, 1936 [**501**] b.8-19-1936, stillborn. CADI, CAT, DC

GEORGE, Baby Girl, July 14, 1931 [**363**] stillborn in the county hospital, father Walter G. GEORGE (b.IN), mother Frances WILSON (b.NE), informant Walter GEORGE, Yuba City (Sutter County), buried 7-16-1931 in the county farm cemetery. CADI, CAT, DC, MIC

GEORGE, John, November 17, 1918, b.1885, a.43, single, father C. GEORGE (b.Italy), mother unknown, a resident of Redding, Shasta County, 1 day in the county hospital, buried 12-04-1918 in the county farm cemetery. CADI, DC, REG

GEORGE, Madeline Dorothy, May 12, 1936 [**496**] b.1936, a.1 day. CADI, CAT, DC

GERMAIN, Joseph, March 25, 1931 [**546**] b.1891, a.59. CADI, CAT, DC

GIBSON, James, June 18, 1934 [**514**] b.1879, a.54. CADI, CAT

GIBSON, John S., June 11, 1930 [**669**] b.1853, a.76; 1930 Census (Sonoma County Farm and Hospital) T626-222-222B, a.76, single, b.Canada, emigrated 1875, patient. CADI, CAT, CEN, DC

* GIBSON, Samuel J., July 4, 1927, b.TN, a.85, widowed, laborer, a resident of Cazadero, father John GIBSON (b.TN), mother Samara ROBINSON (b.KY) 25 years in California, 12 days in the hospital, #7149, buried 7-09-1927 in the "Sonoma Co. Farm Cemetery." CADI, DC, MIC, PRO

Comment: Although the death record plainly indicates a pauper's burial, other records contradict. Specifically, the Sonoma County probate records (file #9679) show the deceased left an estate of $644.06. Against this, the mortician D. H. Lafferty filed a $200 claim, including $25 for "preservation of remains complete" and $20 for a "single grave in Rural Cemetery."

Although the claim was filed on June 14, 1929, the expenses were dated July 21, 1927. The remainder after expenses was divided among two sons, David Gibson of Soldier Summit, Utah, and Silas W. Gibson of Gainesville, Texas.

Lucinda (Moore) and Samuel J. Gibson

(Photo credit: Dale Gibson Hoover, Ukiah, Cal.)

Since there is no claim for exhuming an already-buried body, this author is forced to conclude that while Mr. Gibson may have been slated for burial in the county cemetery and the death certificate filled out, the news of his positive financial condition must have arrived just in time, and the location quickly changed. Alternately, the burial location on the death certificate may simply have been in error.

GIFFORD, Edward, October 8, 1942, b.9-09-1869 IL, a.73, mother FLETCHER. CADI, DC

GILARDY, Joseph, January 30, 1941, b.11-12-1866 France, a.74 years 2 months 18 days, single, retired, parents unknown, not a veteran, a resident of the county farm, 46 years in the USA, 44 years in California, 10 years local, 7 years at the county farm (BOI says "Co. Hospital since 1934"), died in the county hospital, buried 1-28-1941 in the county cemetery, aka "GILLARDY or GALIRDY, Joseph." BOI, CADI, DC, MIC

GILLAM, John, August 15, 1917, b.1-06-1850 Liverpool, England, a.67, single, laborer, father John GILLAM (b.Ireland), mother Mary SMITH (b.Ireland), 40 years in California, died in the county hospital, buried 8-16-1917 in the Sonoma County Farm Cemetery. CADI, DC

GINGRICH, William, July 4, 1941, b.1-20-1868 MI, a.73, a resident of El Verano (near Sonoma), mother McDOWELL, father GINGIRCH (CADI typo?). BOI, CADI, DC

GIORGI, Nicola, September 18, 1928 [**723**] b.1883, a.45. CADI, CAT

GIOVANNINI, Aldopho, January 26, 1936 [**372**] b.1882, a.53. CADI, CAT, DC, NEW

Newspaper records
"Burial Rites Held For River Resident," *The Press Democrat*, 1-28-1936.

GIUSTI, Guiseppe (Joe), June 17, 1942, b.8-04-1881, a.60, a resident of the county hospital, mother POLIDORI, aka "GUISTI, Guiseppi." BOI, CADI, DC

GLASE, Charlie, December 6, 1939, a.85, a resident of the county farm, aka "GLACE, Chas.;" 1920 Census (Sonoma County Farm and Hospital) T625-151-12B, a.70, b.Germany, single, emigrated 1850, naturalized citizen, inmate. BOI, CADI, CEN, DC

GLEESON, David, August 12, 1937 [**300**] b.1877, a.60, died in Napa County, probably of tuberculosis. CADI, CAT

GOMEZ, Clara T., October 5, 1935 [**448**] b.1894, a.40, aka "GOMES, Clara." CADI, CAT, DC

GONG, Leoy, April 10, 1909, a.77, single, died at 640 2nd Street, Santa Rosa, aka "GONG, Leay." CADI, DC

GOODMAN, Aron [*sic*], January 4, 1917, b.1878, a.38, single, laborer, father Jacob GOODMAN (b.NY), died in the county hospital, buried 1-05-1917 at the Sonoma County Farm Cemetery. Comment: On November 18, 1916, Mr. GOODMAN was thrown from a Southern Pacific train at El Verano (near the town of Sonoma). His five-year battle with morphine addiction was listed as a contributing factor in his death. No *Press Democrat* obituary was found. BP, CADI, MIC, REG

GOODWIN, John, February 9, 1908, a.65. CADI, DC

GORDON, James Franklin, November 16, 1920, a.56; 1920 Census Mendocino Township, a.54, b.MO, divorced. <u>CADI, CEN, DC</u>

GORE, Charles R., July 18, 1914, a.82. <u>CADI, CEN, DC</u>

<u>Census records</u>
1900 (Sonoma County Farm and Hospital) T623-114-257B, b.October 1831 KY-TN-TN, a.68, single, pensioner.
1910 (Sonoma County Farm and Hospital) T624-109-29A, a.74, b.U.S.-U.S.-U.S., single, inmate.

GOREEN, Patrick, August 22, 1938 [**167**] b.1875, a.63, residence "unknown," aka "GORMEN, Patrick." <u>BOI, CADI, CAT, DC</u>

GOU, Chew, January 16, 1937 [**191**] b.1853, a.84. <u>CADI, CAT, DC, NEW</u>

<u>Newspaper records</u>
"Chew Gou Goes to Celestial Home of Departed Ancestors," *The Press Democrat*, 1-17-1937.

GRACO, Sadie Delores, September 21, 1925, stillborn, female, father Sam GRACO (b.Italy), mother Cora ALBERT (b.MO), buried in the county cemetery. <u>CADI, DC, MIC</u>

GRALEY, George, November 15, 1911, a.72. <u>CADI, DC</u>

GRANDULFI, Lugi, January 8, 1913, a.65, aka "GRANDULFI, Luigi." <u>CADI, DC</u>

GRANT, George, November 15, 1935 [**450**] b.1894, a.41. <u>CADI, CAT, DC</u>

GRATER, J. F., January 23, 1899, a.55, white, male, single, b.Switzerland, "indigent," buried at the county farm. <u>REG</u>

GRAY, Baby Boy, December 7, 1935 [**456**] stillborn, parents Elmer GRAY and Bessie WILCOX (b.MO). <u>CADI, CAT, DC, MIC</u>

GRAY, David, September 26, 1901, b.NY, a.62, died in the county hospital, buried at the county farm. <u>CEN, DEA, REG, NEW</u>

<u>Census records</u>
1880 (Monroe County, New York) T9-862-588, "GREY, David B.," a.41, b.NY-Scotland-Scotland, grain dealer, wife Ellen (a.35, b.NY-NY-NY).
1900 (Contra Costa County) T623-85-226, "GREY, D.B.," a.60, b.July 1839 NY-England-England, widowed, farm laborer.

<u>Newspaper records</u>
[No title] *Healdsburg Tribune*, 10-03-1901.

GREEN, George, November 22, 1907, a.75. <u>CADI, DC</u>

GREEN, James, February 11, 1935 [437] b.1872, a.62. <u>CADI, CAT, DC</u>

GREEN, Nelson F., April 13, 1906, b.6-21-1826 MS, a.79, single, laborer, father Richard M. GREEN (b.NC), mother Issabella [*sic*] FLEMING (b.MS), died at the Sonoma County Hospital, informant R. GREEN. <u>CADI, DC, MIC</u>

GREENMAN, William, August 19, 1938 [**166**] b.1861, a.77, died in the county hospital; 1920 Census (San Francisco) T625-137-109, San Francisco Hospital, patient. BOI, CADI, CAT, CEN, DC

GREGOR, Frank, December 31, 1911, a.81. CADI, DC

GREGORI, Camille, December 19, 1934 [**435**] b.8-01-1880 Italy, a.54 years 4 months 18 days, a resident of Healdsburg, male, married, laborer, father Antonia GREGORI (b.Italy), mother Rose GRIROLE (b.Italy), 28 years in California and the U.S., 18 years in Healdsburg, died in the county hospital, buried 12-21-1934 in the county cemetery. CADI, CAT, DC, MIC

GREGORY, Frank, August 15, 1906, a.68. CADI, DC

GREMLER, Richard, September 13, 1916, b.12-12-1880 Germany, a.35 years 9 months 1 day, single, machinist, 35 years in California, died in the county hospital, #7752, buried 9-14-1916 in the Sonoma County Farm Cemetery; 1910 Census (Tomales, Marin County) T624-88-301, a.56, single, b.Germany, emigrated 1853 (?), naturalized citizen, laborer (odd jobs). BP, CADI, CEN, DC, REG

GRIMSLEY, Baby Boy, June 19, 1938 [**582**] b.6-19-1938, a.6 hours 50 minutes, father Ernest GRIMSLEY (b.Red Oak, IA), mother Pearl GRIMSLEY (b.ID), transients. BOI, CADI, CAT, DC, MIC

GRISETTI, Frank, August 22, 1943, b.6-26-1875, mother LAZZARI, died in the county hospital. BOI, CADI, DC

GROETCSCH (probably CADI typo), Gustav, August 26, 1928, a.85, aka "GROETSCH, Gustav." CADI, DC

GROFTON, George, January 8, 1920, a.69. CADI, DC

GROSSO, Joseph, October 8, 1909, a.71. CADI, DC

GUAMAS, Antone, November 17, 1909, a.37. CADI, DC

GUAMEZ, Ben, September 21, 1937 [**307**] b.1880 Guam, a.57, "wanderer," father Ignacio GUAMEZ. Comment: His obituary says he had been a resident of Sonoma County for 27 years, which hardly makes him a "wanderer." CADI, CAT, DC, MIC, NEW

Newspaper records
"S. R. Man, Long Ill, Dies," *The Press Democrat*, 9-22-1937.

---

* GUAY see QUAY (1938).

GUE, Lue, April 30, 1905, b.China, a.59, male, single, buried in the county farm cemetery. DEA, REG

GUERA, Joseph, February 19, 1908, a.78. CADI, DC

GUESS, Wilson, April 19, 1909, b.NC, a.83, single. CADI, DC

GUIDI, Arturo, October 26, 1938 [**180**] b.1866, a.72, aka "GUIDI, Anturo." CADI, CAT, DC

GIULIANI, Philip, December 12, 1913, b.Italy, a.45, single, laborer, father Joseph GUILIANI [*sic*], mother Catherine ESCANNIL (b.Italy), 14 years in USA, died at the county hospital, buried in the Sonoma County Farm Cemetery, aka "GUILIANI, Philip." CADI, DC, MIC

GUILLERMIR, Marcel, March 5, 1942, b.8-25-1865, a.76, a resident of Cloverdale, mother GAUDEN, aka "GUILLEMERE, Marcel." BOI, CADI, DC

* GUINSENBERRY see QUISENBERRY (1933).

GUNIGNI, Gincinto, June 14, 1937 [**292**] b.1884, a.53, son of the late Mr. and Mrs. Bolo GUNIGNI of Healdsburg, died in Napa County "near Calistoga," aka "GUNIGAN, Gincinto." CADI confirms the Napa County death; GUNIGNI was probably a tuberculosis patient at the Silverado Sanitarium. No Healdsburg obituary. CADI, CAT, MIC, NEW

Newspaper records
"Former Rancher Dies," *The Press Democrat*, 6-15-1937.

GUSSMAN, Nancy Frances, January 30, 1934 [**395**] b.10-21-1847 MO, a.86, widowed, retired, a resident of Healdsburg, father Peter DAVIS (b.VA), mother Matilda BOWER (b.OH). CADI, CAT, DC, MIC

GUSTASSON, Jacob, July 21, 1941, b.12-10-1863, a.77, resident on Roberts Avenue in Santa Rosa, aka "GUSTAFFSON, Jacob." CADI, DC, NEW

Newspaper records
"Aged Santa Rosa Man Found Dead," *Santa Rosa Republican*, 7-21-1941.

GUTRIE, Walter, January 6, 1935, a.62. CADI, DC

GUY, Gordon H., October 31, 1937 [**318**] b.1891 VT, a.46. Comment: Gordon GUY was survived by his sons, Robert and GUY of Sonoma County and Gordon Jr. and William GUY of Fort Riley, Kansas. CADI, CAT, DC, NEW

Newspaper records
"Itinerant Succumbs," *The Press Democrat*, 11-02-1937.

HAARMANN, Joseph, December 1, 1939, a.60. CADI, DC

HACKNEY, Dave, October 16, 1941, b.1896, a.45. CADI, DC

HAFFE, Abe, November 25, 1936 [**200**] b.1852, a.84. CADI, CAT, DC

HALE, John Robert, February 10, 1922, a.71; 1920 Census (Stewarts Point) T625-150-246, "HALE, John B.," a.69, b.VA, maker of railroad ties. CADI, CEN, DC

HALEY, John, November 14, 1942, b.5-25-1864 OR, a.78, mother FORD. CADI, DC

HALL, Alta, January 4, 1941, b.7-27-1873 MO, a.67 years 5 months 16 days, female, widow, occupation "at home," a resident of Cloverdale, father Henry LUPER (b.unknown), mother BROWN (b.unknown), 10 years in California, 7 years local, autopsy (death due to a cancer-caused hemorrhage), buried 1-17-1941 in the "Co. Cemetery," aka "HALL, Aha." Note: The date of death in DC is 1-14-1941 due to a copying error by the 1988 volunteer. CADI, DC, MIC

HALL, Oran A., March 6, 1939 [**110**] b.1868, a.71, died in the county hospital. BOI, CADI, CAT, CC, NEW

Newspaper records
"O. A. Hall Dies," *The Press Democrat*, 3-07-1939.

HAMER, Sylvester T., September 9, 1905, b.2-09-1852 Lafayette, IN, a.53, formerly a resident of Upper Lake, Lake County, died at Dr. Burke's sanitarium, laborer, in California since 1854, father James A. HAMER (b.Dayton, OH), mother Louise M. STOOPS (b.Lafayette, IN), informant Belle HAMER (wife, a resident of Fulton). CADI, DC, MIC

HANSBURY, Patrick, July 4, 1915, a.76, aka "HANSBORG or HANSBARRY, Patrick." CADI, DC, 1914 GR

HANSEN, Fred, April 22, 1935 [**381**] b.1865, a.69. CADI, CAT

HANSEN, George, May 4, 1938 [**154**] b.10-08-1872 San Francisco, a.65, ranch hand, resident for 35 years on Route 3 (Bennett Valley), Santa Rosa. CADI, CAT, DC, MIC, NEW

Newspaper records
"Hansen Rites Today," *The Press Democrat*, 5-07-1938.

HANSEN, Maggie P., June 17, 1907, a.67. CADI, DC

HANSON, Olof, October 3, 1925, a.61. CADI, DC

HANSSON, Alfred, November 19, 1888, b.1837 Finland, left $4.55 to the county. DEA, PHY

HARDEY, Charles, December 17, 1933 [**404**] b.1875, a.58, aka "HARDY, Chas." CADI, CAT, DC

HARMISON, Douglas Donald, July 23, 1934 [**497**] b.7-19-1934 Santa Rosa (premature), a.4 days, father Leonard D. HARMISON (b.WY), mother Larue KIETH (b.IA), died in the county hospital, buried 7-26-1934 in the "Sonoma Co. Cem.," aka "HARRISON, Donald D." CADI, CAT, MIC

HARMS, Peter, March 28, 1935 [**386**] b.1840, a.94. CADI, CAT, DC

HARRINGTON, Charles, September 3, 1936 [**219**] b.1888, a.47. CADI, CAT, DC

HARRIS, Wylie, July 22, 1941, b.1-08-1930 TX, a.11, father John HARRIS (b.TX), mother Letha HAMMON (b.OK), residence Route 1, Sebastopol, died in the county hospital of second and third degree burns following an accident on the Ansel Banks Ranch near Occidental due to playing with gasoline, 3½ days in the hospital, 1 year in the community, buried 7-24-1941 in the "Co. Cemetery." CADI, DC, MIC, NEW

Newspaper records
"Death of Burned Boy an Accident," *Santa Rosa Republican*, 7-23-1941.

HARRISON, John J., January 23, 1893, b.MT, a.26, "died in Santa Rosa, intered [*sic*] at the county farm cem." <u>DEA, REG</u>

HARVEY, John Frances, November 22, 1916, b.9-15-1852 CT, a.64 years 2 months 7 days, single, laborer, father John HARVEY (b.Ireland), mother Julia DORSEY (b.Ireland), 1 year 8 months in California, died in the county hospital, buried 11-23-1916 in the county farm cemetery. <u>BP, CADI, DC, REG</u>

HARVEY, Rody, September 28, 1921, a.93. <u>CADI, DC</u>

HAST, Frank M., December 16, 1914, born "about 1844" IN, parents b.VA, a.70, widowed, farmer, 1 year 5 months at the hospital, #6778; possible 1900 Census (Lake County) T623-88-39, "HUST, Frank," b.November 1830 VA-Unk-Unk, a.69, father-in-law, widower, stock herder. <u>BP, CADI, CEN, DC, 1914 GR, MIC</u>

Comment: The name may be 'HUST.' The name was handwritten on the death record such that the second letter could be either "a" or "u." The writer made all other "a"s closed and all other "u"s very open; this letter is in-between and could go either way. The 1914 Great Register of Voters has 'HUST.' CADI uses the spelling 'HAST,' so that is used here.

HAUDFORD, John, May 9, 1909, b.England, a.89, single, hospital #1969. <u>CADI, DC</u>

HAWLEY, Delia Annie, July 4, 1916, b.3-21-1843 New Milford, CT, a.73 years 3 months 13 days, widowed, father Eli WORDEN (b.New Milford, CT), mother Lucy Adaline SHERMAN (b.New Milford, CT), 3 months 5 days at the place of death, 34 years in California, died in the county hospital, #7613, buried 7-13-1916 in the Sonoma County Farm Cemetery. <u>BP, CADI, CEN, DC, REG</u>

Census records
1900   (Alameda County) T623-82-174, b.June 1843 CT-CT-CT, a.56, married 27 years, 5 children born, 3 alive, spouse George T. HAWLEY.
1910   (Alameda County) T624-70-108, "HAWLEY, Adalia," a.67, b.CT-CT-NY, wife of "HAWLEY, George T."

HAYDN, Andrew, July 12, 1936 [**228**] b.11-28-1868 Hungary, a.67-7-24, widower, gardener, father Andrew HAYDN (b.Hungary), mother Mary SASHAY (b.Hungary), 30 years in California, 1 year 5 months 6 days at the place of death, buried 7-14-1936 in the Sonoma County Cemetery. Comment: Several possible 1900-1910-1920 U.S./California Census records exist for Andrew "HAYDN" or "HAYDEN" with birthplace Hungary or Czechoslovakia. <u>CADI, CAT, DC, MIC</u>

HAYES, John, October 15, 1918, b.1844 Ireland, a.74, single, farm laborer, father John HAYES (b.Ireland), mother Mary CONNORS (b.Ireland), a resident of Healdsburg, 27 years 4 months 2 days in California, 3 days in the hospital, #351, buried in the county farm cemetery. <u>CADI, DC, REG</u>

HAYES, Joseph, June 3, 1942, b.4-16-1884 CA, a.58, aka "HASE, John." Comment: CADI has two entries for this person, one for each spelling. <u>CADI, DC</u>

HAYES, William, March 4, 1929 [**700**] b.6-29-1853 England, a.75, single, 56 years in California, laborer, parents John HAYES and Anna BAKER. <u>CADI, CAT, MIC</u>

HAYNESS, John, November 29, 1907, b.Germany, a.51, single, laborer, parents b.Germany, 23 years in California, 1 year 2 months in the hospital, died at the county hospital, #5166, buried in the Sonoma County Farm Cemetery. <u>CADI, DC, MIC</u>

HAZZARD, John, September 13, 1888 (40 Deaths 50) b.SC, a.45, single, "a tramp who died on the street in SR, intered [*sic*] county farm." Comment: The death record indicates an inquest was held but the file is missing, not in COR. <u>COR, DEA, REG</u>

HEALY, James, October 30, 1937 [**314**] b.1860, a.76. <u>CADI, CAT</u>

HEATON, George, December 27, 1924, a.79. <u>CADI, DC</u>

HECKER, William Henry, January 30, 1915, b.8-29-1856 Germany, a.58, single, laborer, father Conrad HECKER (b.Germany), mother Barbara BICKER (b.Germany), 38 years at "place of death" [meaning Santa Rosa?], died at the county hospital, #712, buried in the Sonoma County Farm Cemetery. Comment: Not found in U.S. Census records in California. <u>BP, CADI, DC, MIC</u>

HECKLER, Henry, September 23, 1920, a.76. <u>CADI, CEN, DC</u>

<u>Census records</u>
1910   (Cloverdale Township) T624-109-143, "HEKELER, Henry," a.65, b.Germany, single, farmer.
1920   (Sonoma County Farm and Hospital) T625-151-13A, "HECKLER, Henry," a.75, b.Germany, single.

HEINECKE, August, July 27, 1910, a.65; 1910 Census (Sonoma County Farm and Hospital) T624-109-29A, "HEINRICKE, August," b.Germany, a.65, single, emigrated 1864, inmate. <u>CADI, CEN, DC</u>

HELSING, John, December 11, 1935 [**375**] b.9-13-1863, a.72, parents Nelson HELSING and Elizabeth ERICKSON, resident at the county farm 14 years, occupation "invalid;" 1930 Census (Sonoma County Farm and Hospital) T626-222-222B, a.67, b.Sweden, single, emigrated 1872, inmate. <u>CADI, CAT, CEN, DC, MIC</u>

HEMLER, George, February 17, 1893, a.44, single, hospital #923, left $4.10 to the county; 1880 Census (Orland, Colusa [now Glenn] County) T9-64-532, a.31, b.Germany, single, brewer. <u>CEN, DEA, PHY</u>

HENCHEN, Martin, May 19, 1912, a.60. <u>CADI, DC</u>

HENDERSON, Christ [*sic*], March 31, 1925, b.9-26-1852 Norway, a.72 years 6 months 5 days, single, laborer, father Hans HENDERSON (b.Norway), mother Malia OLSEN (b.Norway), 5 years in California, 15 days at the place of death, died in the county hospital of "senile gangrene," buried in the county cemetery, aka "HENDERSON, Chris." <u>CADI, DC, MIC</u>

HENDERSON, James H., December 19, 1922, a.76. <u>CADI, DC</u>

HENDREX, William T., November 8, 1936 [**203**] b.12-02-1860 Texas, a.69, single, laborer, parents unknown, a resident of rural Sebastopol, 46 years in California, 9 years at the place of death, died at the county hospital, buried 11-12-1936 in the Sonoma County Cemetery. No obituary found. <u>CADI, CAT, DC, MIC</u>

HENDRICH, Charles, July 15, 1902, b.Germany, a.85, died at the county hospital, "old inmate of county farm;" 1900 Census (Sonoma County Farm and Hospital) T623-114-257B, "HENDERICH, Charles," b.July 1828 Germany, a.71, 50 years in USA, alien, pensioner. <u>CEN, DEA, REG</u>

HENKLE, Charles, June 8, 1913, b.1848 Germany, a.65, divorced, hospital #6686. <u>CADI, DC, MIC</u>

HENRY, Clark C., January 10, 1926, a.73; 1920 Census (Mendocino Township) T625-150-184, a.67, widowed, b.NY-NY-VT, plumber at the Salvation Army Children's Home. <u>CADI, CEN, DC</u>

HERBIE, Michael, May 2, 1893, b.Germany, a.53, brewer, hospital #1000, left $12.05 to county, aka "HOERLY, Michael." <u>CC, DEA, PHY</u>

HERNANDEZ, James, December 23, 1939, b.CA, a.66, a resident of Upham Street in Petaluma. <u>BOI, CADI, DC, NEW</u>

<u>Newspaper records</u>
"Ranch Worker Dead," *The Press Democrat*, 12-26-1939.

HIGGENBOTTOM, Robert C., September 8, 1939, a.53. <u>CADI, DC</u>

HIGGINS, Allen B., February 9, 1906, b.Maine, a.76, single, carpenter, buried in the "County Farm Cem;" 1900 Census (Ocean Township) T623-114-138, a.67, b.June 1832 ME, single, occupation "forest laborer." <u>CADI, CEN, DC, MIC</u>

HILLIGAS, Mary Lee, July 1, 1938 [**583**] b.7-01-1938 in the county hospital and died there, a.6 hours, father Roy Lee HILLIGAS (b.Poe County, NE), mother Ruth SPORTSMAN (b.MO), residents of Graton, buried 7-05-1938 in the "Co. Cemetery." Comment: BOI lists this death as a coroner's case but the death certificate does not so indicate. <u>BOI, CADI, CAT, DC, MIC</u>

HILLIGAS, Ralph, August 7, 1939, born 8-05-1939 at home on Route 4, Sebastopol, a.2 days, father Roy Lee HILLIGAS (b.Poe County, NE), mother Ruth SPORTSMAN (b.MO), resident on Route 4, Sebastopol, died of jaundice (*icterus neonatorum* or Ritter's Disease) in the county hospital, buried 8-10-1939 in the "Co. Cemetery." <u>BOI, CADI, DC, MIC</u>

HINCKLEY, Elenor, November 6, 1916, b.5-02-1827 England, single, father Charles HINCKLEY, mother Mary BEGARY, both b.England, 33 years in California, 3 years at place of death, residence on Washington Street (Santa Rosa), buried 11-07-1916 at the "Sonoma Co. Farm." BP, CADI, CEN, DC, MIC

Census records

1900 (3rd St., Santa Rosa) T623-114-340, "HINCKLEY, Eleanore," b.May 1840 England, a.60, single, housekeeper, living with her sister, Emily BURNEY, emigrated 1883.

1910 (3rd St., Santa Rosa) T624-109-136, "HINCKLEY, Eleanor," b. [1838] England, a.72, single, emigrated 1883, living with family members.

HITCHCOCK, Jasper Newton, July 3, 1936 [**266**] b.8-27-1880 Mendocino County, a.55, father Isaac Newton HITCHCOCK (b.MO), mother Susan Isabelle HOPPER (b.MO). Note: A bronze grave marker for Mr. HITCHCOCK has been purchased with a contribution from the family. CADI, CAT, CEN, DC, FAM

(Photo: Patricia Hitchcock Hanson.)

Census records

1900 (Arena Township, Mendocino County) T623-93-13, with his parents.

1910 (Arena Township, Mendocino County) T624-88-41, with his parents.

1920 (Cuffey's Cove, Mendocino County) T625-121-67, "HITCHCOCK, Caspar N.," a.40, single, b.CA-MO-MO, brakeman on railroad.

1930 (El Verano, Sonoma Township) T626-222-249, "HITCHCOCK, Jasper," a.49, single, b.CA-MO-MO, woodsman in logging camp, living with his brother.

Comment: Jasper, the eleventh of twelve children, was nicknamed 'Jap,' long before World War II and the racist implications of the name. He was given his father Isaac Newton Hitchcock's middle name. Jasper lived with his parents until after he was 30 years old and never married. Most of his working years were spent as a teamster, logger, or brakeman on logging trains. In his WW I draft registration he is listed as being medium height, medium build with dark brown eyes and black hair. One of his employers was the Goodyear Redwood Company, where he worked as a conductor (head brakeman) on a logging railroad.

For more information, see *My Hitchcocks : William to Arthur Henry*, by Patricia Ann Hitchcock Hanson (Carson, Washington: P.A.H. Hanson, c2002).

JASPER NEWTON HITCHCOCK
1880 - 1936

HOBRICK, Peter, October 12, 1908, a.85. <u>CADI, DC</u>

HODDY, O. P., August 21, 1899, b.OH, a.62 years 11 months, printer, buried at the county farm; 1880 Census (Napa County) T9-69-414, a.41, b.OH-OH-OH, printer. <u>DEA, REG</u>

HOGAN, Fanny, September 18, 1923, b.2-18-1869 TX, a.54, widow, 2 years in California. <u>CADI, DC</u>

HOGENSON, James, February 28, 1917, b.1872, a.45, single, farmer, died in the county hospital, #7952, buried 3-22-1917 in the Sonoma County Farm Cemetery, aka "HOGENSON, C." <u>BP, CADI, REG</u>

HOGINSON, J., November 18, 1899, b.Italy, a.50, died in a rock quarry, buried at the county farm. <u>DEA, REG</u>

HOLGATE, Ernest, October 20, 1911, a.32. <u>CADI, DC</u>

HOLLINGSWORTH, Frank, January 15, 1936 [**244**] b.1863 OH, a.73, died at the Kunde Ranch, Kenwood, aka "BRANDERBURG, Delbert;" possible 1920 Census (Glendale, Los Angeles County) T625-102-164, "HOLLINGSWORTH, Frank," a.56, b.OH-OH-OH. Comment: Both names "Frank Hollingsworth" and "Delbert Branderburg" are listed in CADI with one State of California file number, 6963. The *Catalogue of Grave Markers* (CAT) lists only "Hollingsworth, F." The obituary gives his name as "Delbert Hollingsworth," an employee of the Kunde Ranch near Kenwood. <u>CADI, CAT, CEN, DC, MIC, NEW</u>

<u>Newspaper records</u>
"Ranch Worker Is Found Dead in Bed," *The Press Democrat*, 1-17-1936.

HOLMES, John H., July 20, 1935 [**238**] b.1864, a.71. <u>CADI, CAT, DC</u>

HOLST, Baby Boy, October 9, 1907, stillborn, parents Jacob E. HOLST (b.MN) and Dora DUCTHER [*sic*] (b.IA), a resident of Santa Rosa, hospital #5194, buried in the Sonoma County Farm Cemetery. <u>CADI, CEN, DC, MIC</u>

HOLTZ, Antone, August 16, 1938 [**165**] b.1867, a.78, a resident of Cloverdale. <u>BOI, CADI, CAT, DC</u>

HOLZ, Henry, November 6, 1915, b.Washington, D.C., a.66, single, laborer, father b.Ireland, died at the county hospital, #6258, buried 11-09-1915 in the Sonoma County Farm Cemetery. <u>BP, CADI, DC, REG</u>

HONG, Hom, March 11, 1917, born "about 1853" in China, age "about 64," farm laborer, died at "the Finley Ranch, on the Healdsburg Road, 5 miles northwest of Santa Rosa," homicide (gunshot), buried March 16, 1917 in the Sonoma County Farm Cemetery. <u>BP, CADI, CC, MIC, NEW, REG</u>
Comment: Hom Hong was killed by gunmen from San Francisco who believed him a member of a rival tong (Chinese family association). "Hom Hong, who was the boss of Finley's crew of workers, was a much respected member of the Bing Kong Tong Society. That year [1917] the Hop Sing and Suey Sing Tongs

---

ganged up against the more powerful Bing Kong Society." [Carmen Finley, *The Finleys of Early Sonoma County, California.* Bowie, Md: Heritage Books, 1997.]

HONG, Wong, September 20, 1897, b.China, a.51, died at Roberts Ranch, buried at the county farm, aka "AH, Hong." <u>COR, DEA, REG</u>

HOOD, James, March 27, 1923, a.61. <u>CADI, DC</u>

HOP, Wong, October 9, 1922, b.China, a.72, died at 635 2nd St., Santa Rosa, married, laborer, 18 years in Santa Rosa, 50 years in California, buried 10-11-1922 in the "County Farm Cem.," informant "Wong TAN," 642 2nd St., Santa Rosa, aka "WONG, Hop;" 1920 Census (Santa Rosa) T625-151-237, a.68 b.China. <u>CADI, CEN, DC, MIC</u>

Comment: Hop Wong is also listed in the Santa Rosa Rural Cemetery. Given the anti-Chinese bias that still existed, it seems unlikely he was buried there. For example, only four years earlier, Tom Wing Wong, a wealthy Santa Rosa merchant and "mayor" of Chinatown, had been denied burial any place other than the county cemetery.

<u>Newspaper records</u>
"Wong Hop, Chinese, Dies at Age of 72," *The Press Democrat*, 10-12-1922.

HOPKINS, James, December 16, 1927 [**709**] b.1845, a.82; 1920 Census (Sonoma County Farm and Hospital) T625-151-12B, a.75, b.RI-RI-RI, single, inmate. <u>CADI, CAT, CEN</u>

HOPPER, Harlow, December 20, 1928 [**734**] b.12-24-1849 NC, a.78, single, laborer, father Zacariah HOPPER (b.NC), mother Jane ENGLISH (b.TN), 7 years at the hospital, 71 years in California, died at the county hospital, #983. <u>CADI, CAT, MIC</u>

HORNER, John, October 6, 1911, a.59. <u>CADI, DC</u>

HOUSE, George Lee, May 29, 1939 [**117**] b.1876, a.62, resident on Route 1, Sebastopol, hospital #438. <u>BOI, CADI, CAT, DC</u>

HOW, Wing, April 26, 1907, a.72, aka "HAW, Wing." <u>CADI, CC, DC</u>

HOWARD, Edward, June 29, 1907, a.55. <u>CADI, DC</u>

HOWARD, Joseph B., August 13, 1908, a.66. <u>CADI, DC</u>

HOWELL, Louis, June 3, 1934 [515] b.1851, a.82. <u>CADI, CAT</u>

HOWSARE, John, March 22, 1927, b.1848, aka "HOWSER, John H.;" 1900 Census (Cloverdale) T623-114-61, "HOWSARE, John H.," b.December 1848 MD-MD-MD, a.51, single, farmer; family grave marker, "JOHN H. HOWSARE/MAR. 22, 1927/AGED 79 YEARS."

Comment: Mr. Howsare is one of only a few persons in the Chanate Historic

Cemetery to have a privately purchased grave marker and one of only two such markers to have survived undamaged. Mr. Howsare's grave was assigned marker number 705 but no 'soupcan' was actually placed at the grave because of the privately-purchased tombstone. The purchaser of the stone is unknown. The spelling "HOWSER" is from CADI. CADI, CEN, DC, PV

HUBER, John, July 15, 1928, a.79; 1920 Census (Santa Rosa) T625-151-223, a.71, b.Switzerland, single, laborer, emigrated 1890, naturalized 1900. CADI, CEN, DC

HUBER, John, August 9, 1937 [**298**] b.1874, a.63. A five-year resident of the Santa Rosa area, HUBER was survived by a sister, Mrs. John NAKLECTAL, of Santa Cruz. CADI, CAT, DC, NEW

Newspaper records
"Death Claims Ranch Worker," *The Press Democrat*, 8-10-1937.

HUDSON, M. F., June 20, 1908, a.51. CADI, DC

HUEGEL, Julius, May 20, 1942, b.7-31-1883, a.58, mother CORN. Comment: BOI has an unnamed death on 5-20-1942 that may be HUEGEL. There is no other Chanate burial with that date of death. BOI, CADI, DC

HUGHES, David W., April 10, 1915, a.95. BP, CADI, CEN, DC, 1914 GR

Census records
1900 (Sonoma County Farm and Hospital) T623-114-257B, "HUGHES, David W.," b.October 1819 Wales-Wales-Wales, a.80, widowed, emigrated 1874, naturalized, pensioner.
1910 (Sonoma County Farm and Hospital) T624-109-29A, "HUGHS, David," a.90, b.England-England-England, widowed, emigrated 1874.

HUGHES, Thomas, September 21, 1908 (60 Deaths 78) a.60, d.Santa Rosa. CADI, DC, REG

HUGLI, John, March 31, 1935 [**382**] b.12-01-1860 Switzerland, a.74, a resident of Sebastopol, 18 years in California, hospital #3993. CADI, CAT, DC, MIC

HUHTALO, Elis, March 14, 1942, male, b.3-19-1871, a.70. CADI, DC

HUNT, Charles, July 17, 1905, a.66, b.1838 Sweden, beer brewer, died at the county hospital; 1900 Census (Sonoma County Farm and Hospital) T623-114-257B, b.April 1837 Sweden, a.63, single, emigrated 1867, 33 years in USA, patient. CADI, CEN, DC, MIC

* HUST see HAST (1914).

HYDE, Newton, February 1, 1942, a.51, a resident of the "jungles" (a form of homeless encampment, probably on West Third Street just outside the then-city limits of Santa Rosa, today about where Dutton crosses West Third), then moved to the county hospital and died there. BOI, CADI, DC

IDE, Frederick W., November 3, 1888, b.1857 Germany, left $26.60 to the county. DEA, PHY

INMAN, Willoughby W., September 29, 1931 [**553**] b.1872, a.58. CADI, CAT, DC

ISAACS, Enos, November 26, 1919, a.73; 1910 Census (Redwood Township) T624-109-114, "ISAACS, Enoch," a.63, widowed, b.MO-NC-NC. CADI, CEN, DC

ISDELL, William, May 12, 1929, b.1-30-1842 OH, single, miner, father Robert William ISDELL, mother Sarah RAMSAY (both b.OH), 45 years in California, buried 5-14-1929 in the Sonoma County Farm Cemetery. CADI, DC, MIC

IVANS, John E., May 6, 1935 [**447**] b.4-09-1876 CA, a.59, single, father William M. IVANS (b.MO), mother Mary WILSON (b.MO), life in California, 3 months at the county farm, aka "IVANS, John A." CADI, CAT, DC, MIC

IVERSON, Ivit, April 27, 1909, b.Norway, a.76, single, 41 years 10 months in California, hospital #1645; 1906 Great Register of Voters, "IVERSON, Ivers, Lewis Precinct, retired;" aka "IVERSON, Ivin." Comment: Some records have the date of death April 21, 1909. CADI, CC, DC, GR

IVES, Sampson, August 7, 1922, b.1852 TN, a.70, single, laborer, unemployed, father John IVES (b.TN), died at the county hospital, buried in the "County Farm Cem" CADI, CEN, MIC

Comment: Sampson IVES is not in DC. DC lists a "Mr. ONEA" for this date but there is no such person in CADI or MIC. As this is the only documented Sonoma County death on this date, the author concludes Mr. Ives was buried in the county cemetery. The identity of "Mr. ONEA" is unknown.

Census records
1910 (Santa Rosa) T624-109-110, a.64, b.TN-TN-TN, single, laborer.
1920 (Santa Rosa) T625-151-237, a.73, b.TN-TN-TN, single, laborer.

JACK, Amos, October 17, 1899, b.CA, a.2 months, died at 'Spragues' (ranch?), buried at the county farm. DEA, REG

JACK, Mataline, August 14, 1914, a.70. CADI, DC

JACKSON, Amos, September 12, 1894, b.1840 IL, hospital #1259, left $8.10 to the county; 1890 Census Substitute (p.134), b.1842 IL. CS, DEA, PHY

JACOBO, Sabina, September 7, 1937 [**302**] b.1924, a.12, aka "JACOBS, Sabina." Comment: Sabina's father, Juan JACOBO, and his family had come to Healdsburg to work in the harvest. The headline in the following newspaper article refers to two unrelated children, of which Sabina JACOBO is one. No Healdsburg obituary. CADI, CAT, DC

Newspaper records
"Death Claims Two Children," *The Press Democrat*, 9-08-1937.

JACOBS, Eli, December 31, 1889 (County Physician's 1889 Annual Report, p.8); 1880 Census (Sonoma County) T9-0084-147D, a.60, b.PA, farmer. CEN, NEW, PHY

Newspaper records
[No title] *Sonoma County Tribune,* 1-04-1890.

JACOBSEN, Hans, April 13, 1932 [**564**] b.3-07-1853 Germany, a.79, widowed; 1930 Census (Sonoma County Farm and Hospital) T626-222-222B, a.77, b.Germany, single, emigrated 1873. Comment: CADI also lists a "Hans P. JACOBSEN," d.4-16-1935 Sonoma County, a.71, spouse E. JACOBSON. This is evidently a different person. CADI, CAT, CEN, DC

JACOBSEN, Lee, September 21, 1941, b.10-28-1870, a.70, aka "JACOBSON, Lee." CADI, DC

JACOBUS, Arthur Bernard, September 9, 1942, b.2-23-1883 NJ, a.59. CADI, DC

JAMES, Elmer, March 6, 1932 [**562**] b.2-25-1860 IA, a.72 years 10 days, laborer, married, spouse Anna JAMES, a resident of Hilton (a settlement in Sonoma County, along the Russian River near today's Summerhome Park), father Samuel JAMES (b.IA), mother Sarah HUFF (b.IA), 49 years in California, 7 days at the place of death, buried 3-08-1932 in "Santa Rosa;" 1920 Census (Napa County) T625-122-204, a.56, b.IA-IN-OH, tree pruner, wife Anna (a.46, b.IL-TN-IL). CADI, CAT, CEN, MIC

Comment: Here is an example of a person known to have been buried in the county cemetery, but whose death record has only "Santa Rosa" for the place of burial. Since there are four major cemeteries in Santa Rosa (Calvary, Chanate, Odd Fellows/Memorial Park, and Rural) some confusion is inevitable. This also explains why the death records do not provide a complete list of the post-1904 county cemetery burials.

JARBIN, Minnie, November 29, 1923, b.5-28-1921 San Francisco, a.2, d.Santa Rosa, father Nicholas JARBIN. CADI, DC

JOBST, Henry, July 10, 1909, a.69. CADI, DC

JOHNSEN, Edolph, December 23, 1929 [**737**] b.1862, a.67. CADI, CAT

JOHNSON, August, February 12, 1933 [567] b.1854, a.78; 1930 Census (Sonoma County Farm and Hospital) T626-222-222B, b.Sweden, a.75, single, emigrated 1882, alien, inmate. CADI, CAT, CEN

JOHNSON, Baby Boy, November 28, 1906, a.4 hours, Indian, mother Alice JOHNSON (b.CA), father unknown, buried in the Sonoma County Farm Cemetery. CADI, DC, MIC

JOHNSON, Baby Boy, December 25, 1925, stillborn, male, father George JOHNSON (b.CA), mother May MATHEWS (b.ID), buried in the county cemetery. Comment: CC will list him as "JOHNSON, Unnamed" because that is how the death record was written. CADI, DC, MIC

JOHNSON, Bert, January 30, 1934 [**429**] b.6-15-1883 OR, a.50, a resident of Santa Rosa, occupation "pedler," father Charles JOHNSON (b.unknown), mother Mary PETERSON (b.Norway). CADI, CAT, MIC

JOHNSON, Cassie, June 20, 1921, b.1868 IA, a.53, widowed, occupation "domestic," father Charles FARLEY, mother Nancy DAVIS, parents' birthplaces not specified, 3 years 4 months 15 days at the place of death, 45 years in California, died in the county hospital, buried 6-23-1921 at the "County Farm;" 1920 Census (Sonoma County Farm and Hospital) T625-151-12A, a.50, b.IA-U.S.-U.S., married, inmate. CADI, CEN, DC

JOHNSON, Charles, April 18, 1919, b.1834 Sweden, a.85, single, father John JOHNSON, mother Marie CHRISTIANSON (both b.Denmark), no occupation given, a resident of Jackson, Amador County, 32 years in California, 4 years 4 months 21 days at the county farm, died in the county hospital, buried 4-19-1919 in the county farm cemetery. CADI, CEN, DC, 1914 GR, MIC, REG

JOHNSON, Christina, April 17, 1936 [**254**] b.1860, a.75. CADI, CAT, DC

JOHNSON, Edward Franklin, August 26, 1915, b.2-25-1854 San Francisco, a.61, single, laborer, mother born in Cape Cod, Mass., died in the county hospital, #7404, buried 8-30-1915 in the Sonoma County Farm Cemetery. BP, CADI, DC, REG

JOHNSON, Frank, April 23, 1931 [**545**] b.1878, a.52. CADI, CAT, DC

JOHNSON, Henry, March 2, 1909, b.AR, a.63, single, Negro, tailor, hospital #5531. CADI, DC

JOHNSON, Henry, June 22, 1933 [522] b.1878, a.55. CADI, CAT

JOHNSON, Herbert, January 15, 1934 [**399**] b.1892, a.42, died in Napa County, spouse S. JOHNSON. Comment: JOHNSON's death may have been due to tuberculosis; at that time, Sonoma County's tuberculosis patients were sent to a sanitarium in Calistoga. JOHNSON has no Sonoma County death record. No obituary. CADI, CAT

JOHNSON, John, August 28, 1921 [**486**] b.1878 Norway, a.42, single, 15 years in California, 25 in the USA. CADI, CAT, MIC

JOHNSON, Leonard, October 21, 1935 [449] b.1881, a.54. CADI, CAT, DC

JOHNSON, Louis C., September 9, 1929 [**688**] b.1851, a.78. CADI, CAT, CC

JOHNSON, Mahland E., February 18, 1932 [**560**] b.1851, a.80; 1930 Census (Sonoma County Farm and Hospital) T626-222-222B, a.78, b.OH-NY-WI, widowed, patient. CADI, CAT, CEN

JOHNSON, Otto, March 6, 1922, a.80; possible 1910 Census (Santa Rosa Township) T624-109-61, a.60, single, b.Sweden, emigrated 1880, naturalized citizen, painter. CADI, CEN, DC

JOHNSON, Pete, February 2, 1934 [**430**] b.3-07-1851 Sweden, a.83, a resident of Windsor, in California since 1920; 1930 Census (Santa Rosa) T626-222-222B, a.79, b.Sweden, inmate. CADI, CAT, DC, MIC

JOHNSON, Richard Welch, June 22, 1937 [**495**] stillborn, parents Walter Earl JOHNSON and Myrtle Bell SMALL (both b.MI). CADI, CAT, DC, MIC

JOHNSTON, S. D., September 1, 1906, b.MI, a.47, male, single, 3 years in California, hospital #5001, died at the county hospital, buried in the Sonoma County Farm Cemetery. Comment: Not found in CADI under "JOHNSTON/ JOHNSON/ JOHNSEN" with any first name beginning with "S." CADI, DC, MIC

JOHNSTON, William, May 6, 1928, a.82. CADI, DC

JONES, Alfred, September 26, 1887, b.1826 PA, left $0.45 to the county. DEA, PHY

JONES, Charles E., December 14, 1916, b.2-25-1836 ME, a.79 years 9 months 19 days, single, painter, father Luther M. JONES (b.ME), mother A. COPELAND (b.ME), 1 year 10 days at the place of death, 58 years in California, died in the county hospital, #7495, buried 12-18-1916 in the Sonoma County Farm Cemetery. BP, CADI

JONES, Clarence, November 19, 1939, b.10-07-1890 Boulder, CO, a.49 years 1 month 13 days, divorced (wife was Katie JONES), occupation "sheet and iron worker," a resident of Windsor, father Wm. Henry JONES (b.CO), mother Emma DURHAM (b.MO), 12 years in California, 26 days at the place of death, died at the county hospital, date of burial not given, informant Grace WOHLFORD, Klamath Falls, OR. Comment: Jones had worked on the building of the Golden Gate Bridge. The relationship of Grave WOHLFORD to the deceased is unknown. BOI, CADI, DC, MIC, NEW

JONES, Edward J., November 6, 1901, a.60, colored, died at Santa Rosa City Hall, buried in the county farm cemetery; 1900 Census (Pleasanton, Alameda County) T623-81-59, "JONES, Edward J.," Black, b.May 1843 VA-VA-VA, a.57, widowed, occupation "Cleaning & Dying." Comment: Jones was said to have been a Civil War veteran but no proof has been found. CEN, DEA, NEW, REG

JONES, George E., May 8, 1933 [**573**] b.1848, a.84. CADI, CAT

JONES, Harold L., August 8, 1934 [**499**] stillborn. CADI, CAT, DC

JONES, Rodney, May 17, 1916, b.4-03-1882 Cape Vincent, NY, a.34 years 1 month 14 days, single, wine maker, father James JONES (b.Ireland), mother Mary Ann (b.Ireland), 12 years in California, died in the county hospital, #7657, buried 5-20-1916 in the Sonoma County Farm Cemetery. BP, CADI, DC, REG

JONES, Thomas, September 23, 1930, a.74; 1930 Census (Santa Rosa) T626-222-10, a.74, single, b.North Wales, occupation "reborer [?] on farm," emigrated 1890, [naturalization] papers applied for. CADI, CEN, DC

JORGENSEN, Elma, December 19, 1935 [**588**] a.5 hours 15 minutes (premature), parents Richard JORGENSEN (b.IL) and Elma BILL (b.CA), a resident of Santa Rosa. CADI, CAT, DC, MIC

JOYCE, John, December 13, 1905, b.England, a.83, single, laborer, hospital #1914; 1900 Census (Sonoma County Farm and Hospital) T623-114-257B, b.April 1818 England, a.82, single, emigrated 1850, naturalized citizen, pensioner.

Comment: JOYCE was a ward of the county for many years. CADI, CEN, DC, MIC

Newspaper records
"Deaths at the Hospital," *The Press Democrat*, 12-15-1905.

JULIANI, Joseph, August 17, 1939, a.76; 1930 Census (Sonoma County Farm and Hospital) T626-222-222B, a.66, b.Italy, widowed, emigrated 1907, inmate. Comment: The Burial of Indigents says he was a county farm resident since 1936; this appears to contradict the Census data. BOI, CADI, CEN, DC

JUN, Tong, March 11, 1922, a.68. CADI, DC

JUNG, Wong, August 13, 1941, b.1852 China; 1930 Census (Sonoma County Farm and Hospital) T626-222-222B, a.78, b.China, patient. CADI, CADI, CEN, DC

KALLMAN, Andrew, February 9, 1916, b.8-13-1869 Finland, a.46 years 5 months 27 days, married, farmer, a resident of the Town of Sonoma, 3 years 4 months in California, spouse Alfredia KALLMAN, parents Erie [*sic*] Gustav KALLMAN (b.Finland) and Maria PIHL (b.Finland), died in the county hospital, #7403, buried 2-14-1916 in the Sonoma County Farm Cemetery. No *Press Democrat* obituary was found. BP, CADI, DC, REG

KANEKOA, David W., May 8, 1914, a.30, aka "KOA, David." CADI, CC, DC

KARCH, George, January 7, 1936 [**373**] b.1859, a.76. CADI, CAT, DC

KEARNS, John, June 16, 1911, a.56, aka "KERNS, John." CADI, CEN, DC

Census records
1900   (Sebastopol) T623-114-12, b.May 1858, a.42, b.CA-Ireland-Ireland, single, occupation laborer in livery stable.
1910   (Sonoma Township "Foot Hills") T624-109-204, "KERNS, John," a.53, b.CA-Ireland-Ireland, well driller.

KEATING, William, February 6, 1937 [**272**] b.1875, a.61. KEATING was born in New York and came to California in 1890. CADI, CAT, DC, NEW

Newspaper records
"Ill Two Weeks, Dies," *The Press Democrat*, 2-09-1937.

KEE, Charles, October 12, 1934 [**434**] b.1850, a.60. CADI, CAT

KEE, Haw, April 19, 1905, b.China, a.53, female, widow, died on Second Street in Santa Rosa, buried in the county cemetery, aka "KEW, How." CADI, DEA, NEW, REG

Newspaper records
"Chinese Woman Buried," *The Press Democrat*, 4-21-1905.

KEELIN, John, January 28, 1905, b.1827 England, a.78, single, laborer, died at the county hospital (Dr. S. S. BOGLE), buried in the "County Plot." KEELIN had been a resident of the county hospital since 1894. CADI, CEN, CS, DC, MIC, NEW

Census records
1880 (Cloverdale) T9-84-180, a.48, b.England, laborer.
1890 (Cloverdale) Census Substitute, laborer.
1900 (Sonoma County Farm and Hospital) T623-114-257B, "TELLING, John," b.March 1826 England, a.74, widowed, emigrated 1865, 34 years in USA, naturalized citizen, pensioner.

Newspaper records
"The Hand of Death is Laid on These," *The Press Democrat*, 1-29-1905.
[No title] *Healdsburg Tribune*, 2-09-1905.

KEISER, Nicholas, November 17, 1908, b.Switzerland, a.64, hospital #7141, possible 1900 Census (Solano County) T623-113-265, "KAISER, Nicholas," b.1840 Germany, a.60, single, emigrated 1860, naturalized citizen, farm laborer. CADI, CEN, DC

KEITH, Louis, January 18, 1916, b.6-09-1847 IN, a.68 years 7 months 2 days, single, farmer, father E. KEITH (b.OH), mother Manda M. THERNBERG (b.U.S.), 6 years in California, 1 month 9 days at the place of death, died in the county hospital of disease contracted at Red Bluff, California, hospital #7525, buried 2-17-1916 in the Sonoma County Farm Cemetery; 1900 Census (Lassen County) T623-88-97, "KEITH, Louis T.," b.June 1849 IN-OH-IN, a.51, single, farm laborer. BP, CADI, CEN, DC, REG

KEITH, Richard Edward, February 28, 1922, b.11-03-1921 AZ, a.3 months 25 days, father Edward G. KEITH (b.AZ), mother Pearl E. HOPKINS (b.WI), a resident of Santa Rosa, 23 days in California, 3 days in the hospital, died at the Mary Jesse Hospital, Santa Rosa. CADI, DC, MIC

KELLEY, John, May 24, 1913, a.71, aka "KELLY, John," hospital #6677. CADI, DC, MIC

KELLY, Charles Herbert, "found dead" April 19, 1938 [**149**] b.3-29-1869 Buffalo, NY, a.69 years 1 month ? days, suicide (gunshot), had been dead about a week when found, widowed, spouse was "KELLY, Ida May," parents unknown, died at home on 2nd Street in Santa Rosa, buried 4-20-1938 in the county cemetery, aka "KELLEY, Charles." CADI, CAT, MIC, NEW

Newspaper records
"Ill Health Given Blame for Suicide of C. H. Kelly, 70," *The Press Democrat*, 4-20-1938.

KELLY, John, June 19, 1918, age "over 40," 9 days in the county hospital, buried in the "County Hospital Cemetery." CADI, DC, REG

KELLY, Joseph, December 2, 1937 [**315**] b.1883, a.54, a resident of route 6, Santa Rosa, aka "KELLEY, Joseph." Comment: Kelly was burned in a house fire and died soon afterwards. BOI, CADI, CAT, NEW

Newspaper records
"Farm Hand Trapped In Fire Near Death," *Santa Rosa Press Democrat*, 12-02-1937.
"Kelly Rites Today," *Santa Rosa Press Democrat*, 12-03-1937.

KELLY, Michael, January 15, 1919, b.1856 Ireland, a.62, single, farm laborer, father John KELLEY, mother Annie COSGROVE (both b.Ireland), 35 years in California, 11 months in the county hospital, #74, buried 1-22-1919 in the county farm cemetery, aka "KELLEY, Michael." Comment: The death certificate has a hand-written correction to the name, "KELLEY," but CADI uses "KELLY" as originally written. CADI, DC, REG

KEMP, John, October 1, 1909, a.65. CADI, DC

KENNEDY, William, January 17, 1944, b.10-03-1866 Michigan, single, 2½ years at the county hospital and died there, buried in the "Co. Cemetery." BOI, CADI, DC

KEYS, Frank B., August 3, 1940, b.10-06-1868 Pittsburgh, PA, a.71 years 9 months 27 days, retired (had been at Mare Island), widower, veteran status unknown, parents unknown, 50 years in California, 1 year local, died at his residence on Garden Street in Santa Rosa, buried 8-8-1940 in the county cemetery, informant Mrs. GARIHAN (landlady?), aka "KEIP, Frank." CADI, CEN, DC, MIC

Comment: CADI also lists the death of Mrs. Phoebe M. KEYS, who died 3-14-1930 in Solano County.

Census records
1910 (143B York Street, Vallejo, Solano County) T624-108-117, wife Airmeda [Almeda?] P., a.50, second marriage for both, married 15 years.
1920 (929 Tennessee Street, Vallejo, Solano County) T625-149-163, "KEYS, Frank B.," a.48, b.PA-U.S.-U.S., illiterate, machinist's helper in navy yard, wife Phoebe, a.59, b.NY-PA-CT.

KILL, James M., January 29, 1919, b.NY, a.78, married, laborer, father James M. KILL (b.NY), mother unknown, a resident of Santa Rosa, 40 years in California, 6 days in the county hospital, #457; 1910 Census (San Mateo County) T624-104-174, a.70, b.NY-U.S.-U.S., married 42 years, carpenter, spouse Elizabeth, a.66, b.IL. Comment: No *Press Democrat* obituary was found. CADI, CEN, DC, REG

KIMBALL, William, April 23, 1927, b.1870, age 57, 10 days in hospital (had a stroke, fell, fractured skull); 1920 Census (Russian River Township) T625-150-243, a.65, b.ME-ME-ME, poultry farm laborer, wife Ella M. (a.50, b.MA-NH-MA). CADI, CEN, DC

KING, Charles, May 23, 1903, Chinese, cook, died in the county hospital, "indigent." Comment: Before 1905, county authorities were not required to state the place of burial on death certificates, and did not so state for Mr. KING. However, since he was indigent, Chinese and died in the county hospital, it is safe to conclude he was buried in the county cemetery. DEA, REG

KING, James, July 8, 1910, a.73. CADI, DC

KIRBY, Julius, October 24, 1936 [207] b.1853, a.83. CADI, CAT, DC

KIRK, Harry, December 18, 1917, b.2-27-1867 England, a.50 years 9 months 21 days, widowed, farm laborer, residence Petaluma, father Edwin KIRK, mother Sarah CHAPLAM (both b.England), 8 days at the place of death, 30 years 5 months 6 days in California, died in the county hospital, buried 12-21-1917 in the Sonoma County Farm Cemetery. No obituary. CADI, DC

KITTZ, Adam, March 1, 1920, b.2-01-1851 Germany, a.69 years 1 month, single, laborer, father Franz R. KITTZ, mother Gerbaida SCHLEY (both b.Germany), 49 years 7 months 12 days in USA, 49 years 2 months 11 days in California, 4 days in the hospital, disease [pneumonia] contracted at "Sonoma [town of?], Cal.," buried "Apr. 2" [March 2 intended?] at the "Co. Farm." CADI, CEN, DC, MIC

Census records
1900 (Cloverdale Township) T623-114-62, b.April 1845 Germany, a.55, single, emigrated 1874, naturalized citizen, wine maker.
1910 (Sonoma Township) T624-109-205, "KEITZ, Adam" a.59, b.Germany, single, farm laborer. *Heritage Quest* Census index error "KEIT, Adam."

KLEINMAN, Rheinholt, September 14, 1933 [519] b.1856, a.76, aka "KLEINMAN, Pheinholt." CADI, CAT

KLENWORTH, Henrich, May 13, 1914, a.60. CADI, DC

KNECHT, Fredrick, December 17, 1916, b.5-28-1839 Switzerland, a.77 years 6 months 20 days, widowed, residence "Meletia" [Melita, east of Santa Rosa on the Sonoma Highway], laborer at the "Hefthy Winery," father Johannas KNECHT (b.Switzerland), name of mother not given (b.Switzerland), 1 year 6 months 4 days at the place of death, died in the county hospital, #7355, buried 12-18-1916 in the Sonoma County Farm Cemetery. BP, CADI, REG

KNOTT, Jane, May 12, 1911, a.79. CADI, DC

KNUDSEN, Healma, October 13, 1907, b.1-18-1855 "Norway-Sweden," a.52, married, housewife, father "Matthew OLSEN," mother "Hannah KNUDSEN," informant "Conrad KNUDSEN" of Valley Ford, aka "KNUDSEN, Healina," died at the county hospital, #5194, buried in the Sonoma County Farm Cemetery; 1900 Census (Bodega Township) T636-114-44, "Knudsen, Yelina," b.January 1855 Norway, a.45, spouse of Conrad KNUDSEN (b.June 1855 Norway). Comment: Between 1814 and 1905, Sweden and Norway were united. CADI, CEN, DC, MIC

KOENIG, Ernest, November 27, 1916, b.9-09-1853 WI, a.53 years 2 months 18 days, widowed, farm laborer, father Charles KOENIG, mother Minnie GREIF (both b.WI), 9 months at the place of death, 32 years in California, died in the county hospital, #7589, buried 11-29-1916 in the Sonoma County Farm Cemetery. BP, CADI, DC, REG

KOHLER, Earnest, November 14, 1930 [**736**] b.1857, a.72, aka "KOHLER, Ernest;" 1930 Census (Analy Township) T626-221-2A, "KOHLER, Ernest W.," a.72, b.Germany, poultry farm laborer, emigrated 1893, alien. CADI, CAT, CEN, DC

KONG, Chow, December 28, 1901, b.China, a.50, a resident of Sebastopol, buried in the "S.R. County Cemetery." DEA, REG

KORPONYA, Joseph, July 24, 1936 [**224**] b.1886, a.49, spouse A. KORPONYA, aka "KORBONYA, Joseph." CADI, CAT, DC

KOSKI, Matt, July 13, 1917, a.55, buried 7-14-1917. Comment: DC has date of death July 18, 1917 in error. BP, CADI, DC

KOSTER, Frank J., June 23, 1929 [**694**] b.7-21-1852 NY, single, laborer, father Henry KOSTER, mother Dora MILLER (both b.Germany), informant Ed KOSTER of Englewood, NJ; aka "FOSTER, Frank" (CAT error); possible 1910 Census (Napa County) T624-90-35, a.57, b.NY-Germany-Germany, single, farm laborer. CADI, CAT, CEN, DC, MIC, NEW

Newspaper records
"Aged Man Hit by Tree Near Death," *The Press Democrat*, 2-27-1929.
"Death of Man Hit By Log Accidental," *The Press Democrat*, 6-27-1929.

KRACHOWITZ, Alexander, February 14, 1905, b.1846 Hungary, a.59, butcher, cause of death was dropsy (congestive heart failure), aka "KOEROZ, Alexander;" possible 1880 Census (Colusa County) T9-64-458, "KRACHOWITZ, Alex," a.41, b.Hungary, widowed, laborer. CADI, CEN, DC, MIC, NEW

Newspaper records
[No title] *Healdsburg Tribune*, 2-23-1905.

KROLL, Frank, March 16, 1938 [**145**] b.11-11-1865 Germany, a.72 years 4 months 5 days, single, laborer, father August KROLL, mother Amelia MELINSKI (both b.Germany), a resident of Cotati, 52 years in USA, 10 years in Sonoma County, died at the county hospital, buried 3-18-1938 in the county cemetery. Comment: Not found in the 1900-10-20 Census. BOI, CADI, CAT, CEN, DC, MIC, NEW

Newspaper records
"Ranch Worker Dies," *The Press Democrat*, 3-17-1938.

KUHL, Fritz, May 22, 1930, a.87; 1930 Census (Sonoma County Farm and Hospital) T626-222-222B, a.87, b.Germany, widowed, emigrated 1900, naturalized citizen, patient. CADI, CEN, DC

KUMATH, Paul, February 25, 1941, b.2-15-1867, a.74. CADI, DC

KURCH, Otto, June 5, 1938 [**159**] b.7-09-1875 Germany, a.62, father Ferdinand KURCH, mother Anastasia THIHL (both b.Germany), 15 years in Santa Rosa, 25 years in California, 35 years in U.S., laborer; BOI lists him as a "hobo" with an "unknown" home address. BOI, CADI, CAT, MIC, NEW

Newspaper records
"Otto Kurch Dead," *The Press Democrat*, 6-07-1938.

* LACENSTINA see LORENTINO (1912)

LAGARETTI, Joseph, February 24, 1937 [**277**] b.1882 Italy, a.55, a ranch worker in Kenwood, 27 years in California, aka "LAGARETTE, Joseph." CADI, CAT, DC, NEW

Newspaper records
[No title] *The Press Democrat*, 2-25-1937.

LAGO, Manuel, March 7, 1937 [**278**] b.1884 Spain, a.53, a ranch worker, lived in Decker Street. CADI, CAT, DC, NEW

Newspaper records
"Ranch Worker Passes," *The Press Democrat*, 3-09-1937.
"Funeral Held," *The Press Democrat*, 3-11-1937.

LAING, Peter M., January 9, 1939 [**104**] b.1869, a.69, a resident of Windsor; 1920 Census (Alameda County) T625-91-164, a.50, b.Scotland, emigrated 1884, carpenter, wife Jemima A. LAING (a.50, b.Scotland). BOI, CADI, CAT, CEN, DC

LAIRD, Samuel Wilson, May 20, 1918, b.5-19-1872 OH, a.46, widower, farmer, father B. LAIRD (b.Loydsville, Blair County, PA), mother Jennie WILSON (b.PA), residence Sebastopol, 14 years in California, 12 days at the county hospital, #135. CADI, DC, REG

LAMBERT, George, February 8, 1935 [**436**] b.1859, a.75. CADI, CAT, DC

LANDQUIST, Iven [*sic*], November 20, 1933 [**407**] b.9-06-1882 Sweden, a.51, single, laborer, father William LANDQUIST, mother Betty (both b.Sweden), 27 years in California, died at the county hospital, buried in the county cemetery, aka "LANDQUIST, Ivea." CADI, CAT,

LANSING, Edward D., January 20, 1886, b.1836 NY, left $5.00 to the county. DEA, PHY

LARANDE, John, July 31, 1886, left $2.60 to the county. Comment: Not found in the 1880 Census. CEN, PHY

LARSON, Henry, March 16, 1930, a.69. CADI, DC

LARSON, Josephine, November 25, 1896, b.Finland, a.27, died in the county hospital, #168, buried at the county farm. DEA, REG

LASSEN, Marcus, April 25, 1918, b.10-08-1852 Germany, a.65 years 6 months 17 days, single, fisherman, father Peter LASSEN, mother Mary CORSTENSEN (both b.Germany), residence Bodega, 20 years in California, 1 month 10 days at the county hospital, #15, buried in the county farm cemetery; 1920 Census (Bodega Precinct) T624-109-101, a.58, b.Germany, single, emigrated 1881, laborer. CADI, CEN, DC, REG

LATON, Harry, August 23, 1916, a.40, aka "WAGNER or WAGONER or WAGGONER, Harry." Comment: CADI has both WAGNER and LATON, with the same state index number (27293). LATON/WAGGONER died in custody at the county jail from a "stroke of apoplexy." BP, CADI, CC, DC, NEW

LAUGH, Harry, August 10, 1888, left $10.00 to the county. Comment: Not found in the 1880 Census. CEN, PHY

LAURANCE, James B., November 17, 1922 [871] b.1844, a.78, aka "LAURENCE, James R." CADI, CAT

LAW, Jack E., June 11, 1936 [263] a.33, died in Napa County, probably a tuberculosis patient. CADI, CAT

LAWRANCE, Thomas, March 29, 1933 [571] b.8-03-1858 MA, a.74 years 7 months 26 days, single, lumberman, a resident of Healdsburg, father Isaac LAWRANCE (b.MA), mother Adeline SLOCOMB (b.MA), 50 years in California, 3 days in the hospital, buried 3-31-1933 in "Santa Rosa," aka "LAURENCE or LAWRENCE, Thomas;" 1920 Census (Knights Valley) T625-159-129, a.62, b.MA-MA-MA, single, wood chopper. Census note: *Heritage Quest* index "LAWRENCE" but image clearly is "LAURENCE." CADI, CAT, CEN, MIC

Comment: A few Sonoma County death records have incomplete information, in that the place of burial is given only as "Santa Rosa." This could be in any one of four cemeteries: Calvary, Chanate, Odd Fellows, or Rural (which includes Fulkerson, Moke, Stanley, and "Old Rural"). Because of this, Mr. Lawrance does not appear in the 1988 DC list, since the compiler was told to record only burials in the "county cemetery" or similar entries.

Newspaper records
[No title] *Healdsburg Tribune*, 1-02-1929.
[No title] *Sotyome Scimitar*, 1-03-1929.

LAWRENCE, Tillie (Matilda?), April 10, 1907, b.CA, a.12, female, white, schoolgirl, parents unknown, county hospital #5036, buried in the Sonoma County Farm Cemetery. Comment: Not in CADI under the common variations of her last name; not in the 1900 Census. CADI, DC, MIC

LAWSON, John, July 21, 1941, b.1850, a.91, a resident of the county hospital for three years. BOI, CADI, DC

LEA, A. E., June 10, 1899, b.Norway, a.60, buried in the county cemetery. DEA, REG

LEANDER, Charles E., April 29, 1917, b.1-02-1853 Scotland, a.66, single, cabinet maker, father Charles LEADER [*sic*], died in the county hospital, #7155, buried 5-03-1917 in the Sonoma County Farm Cemetery. BP, CADI, DC, REG

LECUYER, Gus, January 15, 1935 [**390**] b.1891, a.43. Comment: Probably French-Canadian. CADI, CAT, DC

LEE, Bing, August 6, 1934 [**506**] b.1848, a.86. CADI, CAT

LEE, John, January 1, 1898 (42 Deaths 77) b."America," a.54, indigent, buried in the "County Grave Yard." REG

LEE, Kim, July 22, 1940, born "about 1845" in China, a.95, marital status and parents unknown, resident on 2nd Street in Santa Rosa, no occupation, 60 years in California, died in the county hospital, #3946, buried 7-25-1940 in the county cemetery, aka "MOK, Kim." BOI, CADI, DC, MIC

LEE, Tom, January 2, 1932 [746] b.1856, a.76. CADI, CAT, DC

LEICHNER, Jacob, October 19, 1908, a.48 aka "LEICHNES, Jacob." CADI, DC

LEMMON, Helen, January 8, 1939 [**587**] b.7-01-1932 NE, a.6 years 6 months 7 days, a resident of Prospect Street, Petaluma, father Daniel LEMMON (b.Fairbury, NE), mother Elsie WATTS (b.Hebron, NE), 2 years in California, buried 1-10-1939 in the "Sonoma Co. Cem." Comment: Helen, a sister of James Thomas LEMMON, died of pneumonia. BOI, CADI, CAT, DC, MIC

LEMMON, James Thomas, April 25, 1938 [**454**] b.12-18-1937 Petaluma, a.4 months 7 days, father Daniel LEMMON (b.Fairbury, NE), mother Elsie WATTS (b.Hebron, NE), residents of Prospect Street in Petaluma, buried 4-27-1938 in the county cemetery, aka "LEMON, James." Comment: A brother of Helen LEMMON, James died of marasmus, a form of severe protein-energy malnutrition that especially strikes infants under one year of age. For a discussion of this subject see John Steinbeck, *The Grapes of Wrath*. BOI, CADI, CAT, DC, MIC

LENNOX, James, May 4, 1914, a.73. CADI, DC

LEONARD, Patrick, November 1, 1905, b.1841 Ireland, a.64, single, laborer. CADI, DC, MIC

LEUPELLONI, Frank, January 31, 1912, b.Italy, a.40, widowed, a resident of the City of Sonoma, father George LEUPELLONI, mother Katrina GOUDATI (both b.Italy), 7 years 6 months in California, 1 month at the county hospital, hospital #6354, buried in the county farm cemetery, aka "LENPELLONI, Frank." CADI, DC, MIC

LEURASKY, Joseph, February 5, 1921, a.81; 1920 Census (Sonoma County Farm and Hospital) T625-151-13A, a.80, b.Italy, illiterate, inmate. CADI, CEN, DC

LEWIS, Fred, July 30, 1940, b.10-01-1859 Indiana, a.80 years 9 months 29 days, single, "timber worker," resident on 4th Street in Santa Rosa, not a veteran, father Elias Smith LEWIS (b.NY), mother Jane MOORE (b.OH), 51 years in California, 3 years local, 9 months 20 days in the hospital and died there, buried 8-02-1940 in the "County Burial Grounds." BOI, CADI, DC, MIC

LEWIS, James H., December 1, 1918, b.1841 IN, a.77, widowed, barber, father Evermont LEWIS, mother Harriet CAMPBELL (both b.IN), a resident of Petaluma, 66 years in California, 15 days in the hospital, buried in the county farm cemetery; 1910 Census (21 Washington St., Petaluma) T624-109-42, a.66, b.IN-IN-IN, divorced, barber, mother Harriet LEWIS, a.86, widowed, b.IN-SC-NC. No newspaper obituary was found. CADI, CEN, DC, REG

Comment: See Evermont LEWIS in the 1880 Census for Sonoma County (T9-84-131). Harriet Elizabeth LEWIS, a daughter of James, died 8-17-1896, a.2 years 6 months 7 days. Harriet LEWIS, mother of James, a.88, d.12-25-1911 in Sonoma County.

LIGHTHOLDER, Charles H., July 12, 1933 [523] b.1864, a.69. CADI, CAT

LILLARD, Newton Abraham, June 8, 1930 [671] b.12-17-1853 Benton, Polk County, TN, a.77. Comment: Newton LILLARD is one of only a few persons in the Chanate Historic Cemetery for whom living family members are known. The birthdate and birthplace information is from a granddaughter, V. Jeanne HARRIS. CADI, CAT, CEN, DC, FAM, GR

Census records
1860   (Polk County, TN) M653-1268-382, "Newton LILLARD," a.7, b.TN.
1900   (Santa Rosa Township) T623-114-326, "LILLARD, Newton," a.46, b.TN.
1930   (Sonoma County Farm and Hospital) T626-222-222B, "LILLAND, Newton," a.84, b.TN-TN-TN, widowed, patient.

LIN, Ah, April 22, 1896, b.China, a.47, died at 630 2nd St., Santa Rosa, buried at the county farm. DEA, REG

LIND, John, March 31, 1937 [282] b.1870, a.66. CADI, CAT, DC

LINDEN, Samuel, December 8, 1925, a.69. CADI, DC

LINGO, Margaret E., April 14, 1942, b.2-19-1942 CA, a.1 month, 25 days, father James LINGO, mother Leota STOKER (b.OK), resident on the "Venado Route" [?] out of Healdsburg, died at the county hospital, buried 4-16-1942 in the "County Cemetery." BOI, CADI, DC, MIC

LINN, Charles, July 12, 1931 [665] b.6-12-1836 Sweden, a.95 years 1 month, single, laborer, parents unknown but born in Sweden, 44 years 7 months 27 days in the U.S., 40 years 9 months 20 days in California, 22 years 8 months 11 days at the place of death (Sonoma County Farm), died in the county hospital, #116, buried 7-14-1931 in the "County Farm Cemetery," aka "SINN, Charles." CADI, CAT, CEN, DC, MIC

Comment: This person's name is almost certainly "LINN," not "SINN." In the Census records the name is clearly "LINN." His name must have been put down as "SINN" on the death certificate (it is very clear) and then copied by CADI, CAT, and DC. The duration of LINN's residence at the county farm suggests he was there for the 1910 Census but this cannot be confirmed. A German-born "Charles LINN" is in Healdsburg for the 1910 Census but he is 20 years too young.

Census records
1920 (Sonoma County Farm and Hospital) T625-151-204, "LINN, Charles," a.83, white, b.Sweden, language German, marital status and citizenship unknown, parents b.Sweden (language German).
1930 (Sonoma County Farm and Hospital) T626-222-222B, "LINN, Charles," a.94, single, inmate, b.Sweden-Sweden-Sweden, emigrated 1890, alien.

LIVINGSTON, William, October 25, 1942, b.1882, a.60. CADI, DC

LOANING, Thomas, August 30, 1930 [**740**] b.1856, a.73. CADI, CAT, DC

LONG, Baby Girl, July 31, 1930 [**364**] a.1 day (premature, 6-1/2 months), father Clarance [sic] LONG (b.ID), mother Tiny May BABB (b.ID), buried 8-02-1930 in the Sonoma County Farm Cemetery. Comment: The person who filled out the death record wrote "Infant daughter of Mr. and Mrs. Tiny Long." CADI lists the infant as "LONG, ZZ." CADI, CAT, DC, MIC

LOOK, Lee, November 27, 1922, a.68. CADI, DC

LOOK, Yep, June 10, 1906, a.57, aka "LOOK, Yeh." CADI, DC

LOPEZ, Enos, October 27, 1936 [**206**] b.1876, a.57. CADI, CAT, DC

LOPEZ, Michael, July 20, 1938 [**124**] b.1892, a.46, resident on Route 2, Santa Rosa. BOI, CADI, CAT, DC

LORENTINO, Larry, October 30, 1912, b.CA, a.32, Indian, single, laborer, father Lorenzo LORENTINO, mother Santa WYANA (both b.CA), life in California, died in Santa Rosa at the Northwestern Pacific Railroad Depot when struck by a train, inquest by Coroner Blackburn, aka "LACENSTINA, Larry." No *Press Democrat* obituary was found. DC, CADI, MIC

LOTT, Frank, October 22, 1927, b.10-24-1859 WI, a.67 years 11 months 28 days, laborer, 15 years in California, 9 months 25 days in the hospital, #606, buried in the "Sonoma Farm Cemetery;" 1920 Census (Sonoma County Farm and Hospital) T625-151-12B, a.6 [sic], b.WI-OH-PA. Comment: Age in CADI looks like "47." CADI, CEN, DC

LOTTREVZ, Ferdinand T., August 8, 1911, a.50. CADI, DC

LOUI, Ah, April 18, 1906, died at the St. Rose Hotel (earthquake), b.China, a.40, married, male, "yellow," cook. CADI, CC, DC, MIC

LOUSTALOF, Louis, November 14, 1909, b.France, a.54, laborer, father b.France, 28 years in California, died at the county hospital, #5701, buried in the Sonoma County Farm Cemetery, aka "STALOF, Louis Lou." CADI, DC, MIC

LOVELAND, Albert O., February 13, 1938 [**139**] a.85, aka "LOVLAND, Albert;" possible 1900 Census (Cloverdale) T623-114-65, "LOVELAND, Emmet A., b.October 1854, a.45, b.IA-IA-IA, married 9 years to wife Mary E., railroad section man. Comment: See also the 1910 (Healdsburg: Emmet A.) and 1920 (Healdsburg: Albert) Sonoma County Census. CADI, CAT, CEN, DC

LOY, Wong, November 9, 1892, a.40, killed on Second Street in Santa Rosa (coroner Blaney), buried at the county farm. The coroner's inquest found the deceased, an employee of the Ning Yung Company, was shot and killed by Wong FONG. Comment: The newspaper records suggest the defendant in the murder trial was framed by enemies in San Francisco. COR, DEA, REG

Newspaper records
"Charge of Murder," *The Press Democrat*, 1-21-1899.
"After His Head," *The Press Democrat*, 1-25-1899.
"A Hot Legal Battle," *The Press Democrat*, 1-25-1899.
"Chinese Murder Case Continued To Monday," *The Press Democrat*, 1-28-1899.
"Must Stand Trial," *The Press Democrat*, 2-01-1899.
"Ah Loy's Murder," *The Press Democrat*, 2-11-1899.
"Fifty Thousand," *The Press Democrat*, 2-15-1899.
"In Superior Court," *The Press Democrat*, 2-22-1899.
"The Legal World," *The Press Democrat*, 3-01-1899.
"The Jury Secured," *The Press Democrat*, 3-15-1899.
"Great Sensation," *The Press Democrat*, 3-18-1899.
"The Murder Trial," *The Press Democrat*, 3-18-1899.
"In Superior Court," *The Press Democrat*, 3-22-1899.
"The Murder Trial," *The Press Democrat*, 3-22-1899.
"The Murder Trial," *The Press Democrat*, 3-25-1899.
"Ong Fong Set Free," *The Press Democrat*, 3-25-1899.

LUCAS, Emma, Mrs., November 20, 1905, b.Germany, a.33, married, cook, died at the Sonoma County Hospital, buried in the "Hospital Cemetery." CADI, DC, MIC

LUCHESE, Placido, May 23, 1911, a.63. CADI, DC

LUCIANO, Theodore, September 26, 1938 [**184**] b.1900, a.38. CADI, CAT, DC

LUCIFER, Joseph, February 16, 1920, a.35. CADI, DC

LUHRS, Henry, March 16, 1915, a.86. BP, CADI, DC, 1914 GR

LUNG, Lee, February 19, 1890, a.58, male, single. REG

LUONI, Emelio M., May 2, 1939 [**113**] b.1877 Italy, a.62, employed by the BERTOLINI family, aka "LUONI or LUONIO, Amelio." CADI, CAT, DC, NEW
Comment: The Bertolini farm family lived at the end of Trowbridge Street, along Santa Rosa Creek in what was then a rural area just west of Santa Rosa. Today, this area is midway between Dutton Avenue and Stony Point Road.

Newspaper records
"Amelio Luonio Passes," *The Press Democrat*, 5-03-1939.

LUSSO, Gioccomo, January 20, 1942, b.3-29-1873, a.68, a resident of Boyes Hot Springs (near Sonoma), father LUSSO, aka "LUCCO, Giacomo." BOI, CADI, DC

LYNCH, John, January 28, 1937 [**271**] b.1875, a.61. CADI, CAT, DC, NEW

Newspaper records
[No title] *The Press Democrat*, 2-02-1937.

LYNCH, William, July 22, 1942, b.1881, a.61, father LYNCH. CADI, DC

LYNN, Charles, November 8, 1905, b.1869 NY, a.36, single, parents b.England, occupation "sewer work." CADI, DC, 1914 GR, MIC

LYNSKY, Patrick, December 2, 1905, b.1824 Ireland, a.81, single, laborer, buried in the "Hospital Cemetery." CADI, DC, MIC

MAATTI, Charles M., March 9, 1918, b.3-24-1849 Finland, a.68, single, farmer, father Andrew MAATTI, mother unknown (both b.Finland), 40 years in California, 1 year 5 months 13 days in the county hospital, hospital #7805, buried 3-20-1918 in the county farm cemetery. CADI, DC, REG

MACCARIO, George, April 18, 1921, b.2-20-1921, a.1 month 29 days, died at 454 South E Street, Santa Rosa, parents unknown, 23 days at the county hospital ("congenital debility"), buried in the county farm cemetery, aka "MOCCARIO, George." CADI, CEN, DC, MIC
Comment: There are three Maccario families in the 1920 Census (Santa Rosa) T625-151-264 and -266. The three men, Anthony (a.28, spouse Christina), Joseph (a.35, spouse Rosie), and Lawrence (a.41, spouse Rosie), probably brothers, were proprietors of a bakery. Any one couple could have been the parents of George although Lawrence is less likely as he and his family are older.

MacKARTY, Helen, April 15, 1931, b.1861. Comment: Not found in CADI. CADI, CAT, DC

MacKARTY, Robert, May 25, 1930 [**673**] b.1864, a.66; 1930 Census (Sonoma County Farm and Hospital) T626-222-222B, a.66, b.WI-OH-IN, single, patient, aka "McKARTY, Robert." CADI, CAT, CEN, DC

MacRAEAL, Augostine, September 23, 1913, a.46, aka "MacREAL, Augostine." CADI, DC

MacWHITE, Edward, February 28, 1934 [**232**] b. 12-18-1877, a.56. CADI, CAT, DC

MADARELLI, Venzenzo, March 15, 1929 [**699**] b.1879 Italy, a.50, male, widower, laborer, 15 years in California, father Francisco MADARELLI, hospital #7136, buried 3-18-1929, aka "MADARPLLI, O." CADI, CAT, CC, DC, MIC

MADSEN, Martin Olavez, September 13, 1937 [**306**] b.10-14-1866 Norway, a.70, unmarried, ranch worker, a resident of Healdsburg. No Healdsburg obituary. CADI, CAT, DC, MIC, NEW

Newspaper records
"Long-Time Resident Dies," *The Press Democrat*, 9-14-1937.

MAGRINI, Frank, March 28, 1935 [387] b.1896, a.39. CADI, CAT, DC

MAGUS, John, July 7, 1940, b.1880, a.60, residing in the Western Hotel, Santa Rosa. BOI, CADI, DC

MAHONEY, John, January 19, 1919, b.Ireland, a.48, single, wood chopper, father Florance [*sic*] MAHONEY, mother unknown (both b.Ireland), a resident of Santa Rosa, 15 years in California, 1 year 1 month 2 days in the county hospital, #420, buried in the county farm cemetery. CADI, DC, REG

MAKELA, Henry, February 7, 1939 [**106**] b.1886, a.52, a resident of Cotati. A native of Finland, Mr. MAKELA had been in California 32 years, 10 of them in Cotati. BOI, CADI, CAT, DC, NEW

Newspaper records
"Ranch Worker Dies," *The Press Democrat*, 2-09-1939.

MALONE, Patrick J., May 17, 1936 [258] b.1873, a.63, aka "MATONE, Patrick." CADI, CAT, DC

MAN, You O., July 20, 1913, b.1842, a.71, male, cook, in California 30 years, aka "MAN, Yon Don or You Won." CADI, DC, MIC

MANASSI, John, August 25, 1886, left $0.40 to the county. PHY

MANCINI, Peter, March 14, 1935 [**441**] b.1876, a.59, aka "MANGINI, Peter." CADI, CAT, DC

MANDERSON, Thomas, March 10, 1938 [**144**] b.1877, a.60, died in the county hospital. BOI, CADI, CAT, DC

MARBLE, Archibald, June 26, 1939 [**107**] b.1869, a.68, a resident of Bay (today's Bodega Bay); 1920 Census (East D Street, Petaluma) T625-151-39, "MARBLE, Archie," a.49, single, b.NY-NY-Ireland, laborer. BOI, CADI, CAT, CEN, DC, NEW

MARBLE, Thomas, February 3, 1940, b.5-09-1870 California, a.69, a resident of Bay (today's Bodega Bay), father MARBLE, mother BURKE; 1920 Census (East D Street, Petaluma) T625-151-39, "MARBLE, Thomas," a.49, single, b.U.S.-NY-Ireland, laborer. CADI, CEN, DC, NEW

Newspaper records
"Man Found Dead," *The Press Democrat*, 2-04-1940.

MARCHAM, Harry, August 17, 1928, a.65; 1920 Census (Sonoma County Farm and Hospital) T625-151-12B, a.56 or a.64, b.PA-France-PA, widowed (two entries for this person). Comment: The age in CADI suggests the Census entry with age 56 is the correct one. CADI, CEN, DC

MARCUS, Joseph, September 10, 1943, b.3-18-1863 Austria, a.80, a resident of Petaluma, 40 years in the U.S., 25 years in California. CADI, DC

MARIANI, Emilio, July 14, 1923, a.33. CADI, DC

MARIN, James, December 20, 1922, a.74; 1920 Census (Sonoma County Farm and Hospital) T625-151-12A, age unknown, single, b.Ireland, no emigration information. CADI, CEN, DC

MARINI, George, February 1935 [**438**] b.1888. Comment: Not in CADI, no obituary. The exact date of death is unknown (CAT gives only the year), probably mid- to late February based on the sequence of marker numbers. He may have died out of Sonoma County (e.g., a Napa County tuberculosis patient, the time frame is correct). CADI, CAT, NEW

MARION, Louis, September 2, 1920, a.12, Indian, schoolboy, b.1908 Healdsburg, father Henry MARION (b.CA), mother unknown, 1 month 17 days in the hospital, buried at the county farm. No Healdsburg obituary. CADI, DC, MIC

MARKHAM, John, October 6, 1911, a.71. CADI, DC

MARKLEY, John G., June 17, 1900, b.PA, a.35, died in the county hospital, buried at the county farm; 1900 Census (Sonoma County Farm and Hospital) T623-114-258A, a.45, b.PA, single, patient. CEN, DEA, REG

MARKY, George, January 15, 1934 [**398**] b.7-04-1859 Denmark, a.74, widowed, laborer, father Peter MARKY, mother Sarlna [*sic*] MELSLING, aka "MACKY, George." CADI, CAT, DC, MIC

MARQUEZ, Benita, March 29, 1935 [**384**] a.39, died of tuberculosis at the Silverado Sanitarium in Calistoga, Napa County (spouse Trinidad). CADI, CAT, NEW

Newspaper records
"Devoted Mexican Spouse Bereaved At Wife's Death," *The Press Democrat*, 3-31-1935.

MARSHALL, Richard, March 18, 1906, b.U.S. [?], a.85, laborer; 1900 Census (Santa Rosa Township) T623-114-319, b.January 1817 Ireland, a.82, widowed, naturalized citizen, prisoner in county jail. CADI, CEN, DC, MIC

MARTELL, Sarah, October 28, 1912, a.76. CADI, DC

MARTIN, Harry, August 11, 1928, a.69. CADI, DC

MARTIN, John, October 5, 1910, a.64; 1910 Census (Sonoma County Farm and Hosp.) T624-109-29B, a.76, b.U.S.-Ireland-Ireland, widowed. CADI, CEN, DC

MARTIN, Manuel, October 29, 1941, b.1-22-1881, a.60, resident on the Chisholm Ranch, Santa Rosa, father MARTIN, mother DUARTE. BOI, CADI, DC

MARTIN, Mr. (Indian), April 30, 1900, died in the county jail of an alcohol overdose, Coroner PIERCE (file missing), buried at the county farm. DEA, NEW, REG

MARTINES, Amelio, September 16, 1926, a.45, aka "MARTINEZ, Amelio." CADI, DC

MARTINEZ, William F., November 23, 1927, a.54. CADI, DC

MARTINIS, Joseph, December 7, 1913, a.22. CADI, DC

MASON, Ada, Mrs., December 7, 1941, b.10-15-1867 California, a.74, a resident of the county hospital. BOI, CADI, DC

MASON, Baby Boy, July 27, 1916 (stillborn at the county hospital) b.Cloverdale, parents Irwin MASON and Lucy ANDREW, buried 8-05-1916 in the Sonoma County Farm Cemetery. BP, CADI, DC, REG

MASSA, Joseph, December 8, 1909, a.45. CADI, DC

MASSERO, Mose, October 8, 1920, a.37. Comment: Not found in 1920 Census. CADI, CEN, DC

MATHERS, John, September 2, 1912, a.81. CADI, DC

MATTOS, Louis, February 20, 1934 [**230**] b.1875, a.48. CADI, CAT, DC

MAURELLI, Lawrence, January 21, 1941, b.11-01-1869 Switzerland, a.71 years 2 months 20 days, single, farm laborer, not a veteran, residence address General Delivery, Bloomfield, father Joe MAURELLI, mother Joana MARIE (both b.Switzerland), 46 years in the USA, California, and local, 3 months in the hospital, buried 1-24-1941 in the county cemetery. BOI, CADI, DC, MIC

MAYER, Sebastian, March 19, 1915, a.68; 1910 Census (Santa Rosa) T624-109-135, a.63, b.Germany, laborer, divorced, emigrated 1880, naturalized citizen. CADI, BP, CEN, DC

McCAFFERTY, Michael, September 17, 1935 [**377**] b.1868, a.67. CADI, CAT, DC

McCARTEN, Daniel, November 20, 1939, b.9-26-1865 Ireland, a.74 years 1 month 24 days, single, laborer, a resident of Petaluma, father Daniel McCARTEN, mother Mary DEMPSEY (both b.Ireland), 70 years in USA, 33 years in California, 18 years local, buried 11-22-1939 in the county cemetery, aka "McCARTAN, Daniel." Comment: The death certificate and BOI (residence Petaluma) conflict with the obituary (residence Santa Rosa). No Petaluma obit was found. BOI, CADI, DC, MIC, NEW

Newspaper records
"Daniel McCarten Claimed by Death," *The Press Democrat*, 11-22-1939.

McCARTHY, John H., July 26, 1887, b.1845 Canada, a resident of Santa Rosa, left $10.30 to the county. Comment: McCarthy is not in the 1880 Census in Sonoma County. The name is otherwise too common to find without research beyond the scope of this book. CEN, PHY, REG

McCARTHY, Martimer [Mortimer?], February 10, 1929, a.50. CADI, DC

McCLOSKEY, Gale F., June 15, 1934 [**513**] b.1870, a.65. Comment: An error in CAT caused [**512**] to be duplicated, see FERRARA [**512**]. CADI, CAT

McCOY, Walter F., May 6, 1939 [**114**] b.1862 CA, lumberman. Comment: Walter McCoy is one of the few in Chanate with known living family members. Although authorities conducted an investigation following McCoy's death, the death certificate never made it to the county clerk's office so if you were to ask, you would be told no such person is in the records. Lacking a death certificate, McCoy is not listed in CADI. A bronze plaque for McCoy's grave has been purchased with a contribution from the family. CAT, FAM, NEW

Census records
1870 (Bodega Twp.) M593-91-262 "McCOY, Walter," a.7, b.CA, living with two younger sisters in an unrelated household.
1910 (Hydesville Twp., Humboldt Co.) "McCOY, Walter F.," a.47, single, b.CA-KY-Unk, occupation "chopper, logging woods."

Newspaper records
"Dying Man Slashes Throat To Avoid Entering Hospital Here, Life Ended With Razor As Protest," *The Press Democrat*, 5-06-1939.
"Walter McCoy Rites," *The Press Democrat*, 5-10-1939.

McCRERY [*sic*], Alexander, January 15, 1931 [745] b.1859, a.71. CADI, CAT, DC

McCUNE, Samuel, February 5, 1912, a.81; 1910 Census (Sonoma County Farm and Hospital) T624-109-29B, a.80, b.Ireland, single, inmate. CADI, CEN, DC

McDANIELS, Oliver, November 3, 1918, b.1854 AR, a.64, widowed, laborer, father John McDANIELS (b.unknown), mother Minerva St. CLAIR (b.AR), 60 years 4 months 14 days in California, 11 months 4 days in the hospital, #81; 1900 Census (Trinity County) T623-115-23, a.45, b.AR-AR-AR, widowed, laborer. CADI, DC, MIC

McDONALD, Alex, March 5, 1917, b.1872 Ireland, a.45, single, carpenter, father Alex McDONALD (b.Ireland), died in the county hospital, #7951, buried 3-24-1917 in the Sonoma County Farm Cemetery. BP, CADI, DC, REG

McDONALD, Patrick, May 24, 1905, b.1830 Ireland, a.75, single, laborer, a resident of Occidental, died at the county hospital. CADI, DC, MIC

McDONALD, William, September 20, 1938 [**172**] b.1902, a.36. CADI, CAT, DC

McELLIOTT, John, May 19, 1931 [**548**] b.1883, a.48, "wanderer," died at the Mary Jesse Hospital, informant Petaluma Police Department, aka "McELLEOTT, John." Comment: No obituary. CADI, CAT, DC, MIC

McFADDEN, John, January 8, 1936 [**243**] b.1881, a.55. CADI, CAT, DC

* McFARLANE, D. L. see McLEAN, Duncan McFarlane (1930).

McGOWAN, Michael, November 18, 1910, b.Ireland, a.86, widowed, farm laborer, parents unknown (both b.Ireland), 50 years 7 months in California, 14 years 4 months at the place of death (county poor farm), died in the county hospital, #59, buried 11-19-1910 in the Sonoma County Farm Cemetery. Comment: The 1988 volunteer missed this name. CADI, CEN, MIC

Census records
1900 (Sonoma County Farm and Hospital) T623-114-258A, "McGOWEN, Mac," b.September 1857, a.62, widowed, b.Ireland, parents b.Ireland, emigrated 1840, 60 years in the USA, emigration status not indicated, pensioner.
1910 (Sonoma County Farm and Hospital) T624-109-29A, "McGOWAN, M.," a.78, widowed, b.Ireland, parents b.Ireland, emigrated 1874.

McKEE, Edwin, May 26, 1930 [**672**] b.1848, a.82; 1930 Census (Sonoma County Farm and Hospital) T626-222-223A, a.81, b.PA-PA-PA, single, inmate. CADI, CAT, CEN, DC

McKEE, George, April 24, 1938 [**151**] b.1846, a.91, a resident of Guerneville. BOI, CADI, CAT, DC

* McKESSON see MIKKELSON (1937).

McKNIGHT, Matt, June 25, 1918, b.10-31-1887 Ontario, Canada, a.30, single, locomotive fireman, father Matt McKNIGHT (b.Dublin, Ireland), formerly a resident of Rainy River, Ontario, Canada, 8 months 25 days in the U.S., 3 months 19 days at the county hospital, buried 7-03-1918 in the county farm cemetery. CADI, DC, REG

McLAUGHLIN, Hubert, September 9, 1908, a.32. Comment: Not found in the 1900 Census. CADI, DC

McLEAN, Allen, May 16, 1927, a.54. CADI, DC

McLEAN, Donald, March 6, 1898, b.Scotland, a.70, married, died in the county hospital, #19, interred at the county farm. DEA, GR, REG

McLEAN, Donald, January 16, 1933 [**526**] b.1863, a.69, buried 1-17-1933. CADI, CAT, DC, REG

McLEAN, Duncan McFarlane, May 15, 1930 [**676**] b.1856 Australia, age "about 74," single, laborer, parents unknown, 41 years in the U.S., 40 years in California, 3 years 4 months 11 days at the place of death (308 4th St., Santa Rosa), buried 5-17-1930 in the Sonoma County Farm Cemetery. Comment: The *Catalogue of Grave Markers* (CAT) has the name listed as "McFARLANE, D. L." in error. CADI, CAT, CEN, DC, MIC

Census records
1910 (Santa Rosa) T624-109-61, "McLEAN, Duncan McF."
1920 (Santa Rosa) T625-151-157, "McLEAN, Duncan," a.61, b.Australia-Scotland-Scotland, emigrated 1895, naturalized 1904, farm manager.

McNEIL, Andren, December 3, 1917, b.11-08-1840 Scotland, a.77, widowed, laborer, a resident of Sebastopol, father John McNIEL [*sic*] (b.Scotland), mother Mary SLOAN (b.Scotland), 16 days at the place of death, 30 years in California, died in the county hospital, buried 12-06-1917 in the Sonoma County Farm Cemetery, aka "McNIEL, Andrew." CADI, DC, MIC, REG

McNEIL, John, September 27, 1920, a.72; 1920 Census (Sonoma County Farm and Hospital) T625-151-12B, a.82 b.Ireland, single, emigrated 1868, naturalized 1873. CADI, CEN, DC, 1914 GR

McPHERSON, Edward, April 27, 1910, a.69; 1910 Census (Sonoma County Farm and Hospital) T624-109-29B, a.69, b.U.S.-Scotland-U.S., widowed. CADI, CEN, DC

McSHAY, James, January 16, 1926, a.75. CADI, DC

McVEY, William, August 17, 1934 [**505**] b.1862, a.72, aka "VEY, William M." CADI, CAT, CC, DC

MEADOWS, "Texas," September 27, 1937 [**312**] b.1887, a.50, "wanderer." CADI, CAT, DC, MIC, NEW

Newspaper records
"Itinerant Succumbs," *The Press Democrat*, 9-28-1937.

MELTON, Jesse, January 2, 1934 [**424**] b.12-13-1883 Petaluma, a.50, male, single, a resident of Santa Rosa, life in California, father Comte DeROIN (b.CA), mother Elizabeth DeROIN (b.CA). Comment: The handwritten names in the death certificate are hard to read. No obituary. CADI, CAT, DC, MIC

MELTON, Newton, September 15, 1906, a.48. Comment: Not found in the 1900 Census. CADI, DC

MENDOSA, Eli, January 16, 1930, a.50; 1920 Census (Santa Rosa) T625-151-132, a.43, b.CA-Mexico-CA, single, farm laborer. CADI, CEN, DC

MERRILL, Wallace, November 12, 1911, a.48. CADI, DC

MERRITT, Carl. H., March 23, 1933 [**525**] b.1869, a.63. CADI, CAT

MERRITT, Edward, September 25, 1916, b.4-14-1845 KY, a.71 years 5 months 11 days, single, cigar maker, father John MERRITT (b.KY), mother Sophia WATSON (b.KY), 2 months 2 days at the place of death, 20 years in California, died in the county hospital, #7721, buried 10-21-1916 in the Sonoma County Farm Cemetery. BP, CADI, DC, REG

MESOT, Joseph, January 6, 1911, a.44. CADI, DC

* MEY, Fung see FUNG, Moy (1917).

MEYER, Baby Boy, March 28, 1922, father Frank FITZGERALD (b.unknown), mother Hazel MEYER (b.Healdsburg), stillborn at the county hospital; 1920 Census (Healdsburg) T625-150-179, "Hazel MEYER," a.16, b.CA-CA-CA, single. CADI, CEN, DC, MIC

MEYER, Joseph, January 20, 1916, b.Germany, a.50, single, wood chopper, died "about 2 miles northwest of Cloverdale," buried 1-29-1916, in the Sonoma County Farm Cemetery; 1910 Census (Embarcadero Road, Sonoma Township) T624-109-191, a.47, b.Germany, single, hay farm laborer, emigrated 1884, naturalized citizen. BP, CADI, CEN, COR, DC, REG

MEYERS, Antonio, January 21, 1938 [**137**] a.70. CADI, CAT, DC

MEYERS, William, June 6, 1936 [**261**] a.70. CADI, CAT, DC

MICKELSON, John, December 8, 1913, a.55. CADI, DC

MICKLITCH, John, December 16, 1940, b.1891, a.59. CADI, DC

MIKKELSON, John, November 17, 1937 [**317**] b.1860 Finland, a.77, single, a resident of the Stewarts Point area, aka "McKESSON, John." Comment: MIKKELSON was survived by three brothers in Minnesota. CADI, CAT, DC, NEW

Newspaper records
"Ranch Worker Dies," *The Press Democrat*, 11-18-1937.

MILES, Emery M., February 6, 1935, a.62. CADI, DC

MILES, Paul, June 1885 (exact date unknown), left $35.00 to the county; 1880 Census (Mendocino Township) T9-84-197, a.47, b.TN-TN-TN, single, miner. CEN, PHY

MILLER, Alpharetta, December 20, 1899, a.4 years 6 months, born in Napa County, died on Adams Street in Santa Rosa, buried at the county farm, aka "MILLER, Alpha Etta." Comment: Alpharetta is a town in Georgia; perhaps the parents had some connection with that part of the nation before coming to California. DEA, NEW, REG

Newspaper records
"Death Of A Child," *Daily Republican*, 12-21-1899.
"Local," *The Press Democrat*, 12-23-1899.

MILLER, Antonio, April 24, 1912, a.65; 1910 Census (Sonoma County Farm and Hospital) T624-109-30A, a.82, b.France, single, emigrated 1856. CADI, CEN, DC

MILLER, Charles Peter, September 17, 1918, b.1843 Sweden, a.75, a resident of Petaluma, laborer, 53 years 7 months 14 days in California, 6 months in the hospital. No obituary. CADI, DC, REG

MILLER, Garnet, March 18, 1926, b.9-16-1861 IN, a.63 years 6 months 2 days, male, white, laborer, spouse "MUELLER, Minnie," father John MUELLER (b.IN), mother Nancy HUTCHINSON (b.IN), 4 months 1 day at the place of death, died in the county hospital, buried 3-20-1926 in the county cemetery. Comment: Not found (as a head of household) in the 1920 Census. CADI, CEN, DC, MIC

MILLER, John, November 24, 1934. Comment: This name was not found in CADI, not found on the microfilm of original death records or in the county's computer index. There is no John MILLER with that date of death anywhere in California. The spelling MILLAR was also checked. CADI, DC

MILLER, Peter Henry, November 14, 1916, b.5-24-1864 Germany, a.52 years 5 months 21 days, single, miner, father Nicholas MILLER (b.Germany), mother Regina MILLER (b.Germany), 3 days at the place of death, 2½ years in California, died in the county hospital, #7832, buried 11-15-1916 in the Sonoma County Farm Cemetery. BP, CADI, DC, REG

MILLER, Robert, February 14, 1926, a.75. CADI, DC

MINOR, Benjamin, September 4, 1936, a.86. CADI, DC

MINTER, Frank A., October 18, 1911, a.58. CADI, DC

MIRCONOLO, Anabale [sic], February 4, 1912, a.25. CADI, DC

MIRONE, Andrew, November 2, 1941, b.12-16-1871, a.70, a resident of Polk Street in Santa Rosa, father MIRONE, mother PALMARY, aka "MARONE, Andrew." BOI, CADI, DC

MITCHELL, George W., March 24, 1913, a.62. CADI, DC

MITCHELL, Levi, June 22, 1938 [**162**] b.1866, a.72, farm laborer, a resident of Penngrove (or Petaluma?), spouse "Alice MITCHELL," aka "MITCHEL, Levi." BOI, CADI, CAT, NEW

Newspaper records
"Petaluman Dies," *The Press Democrat*, 6-23-1938.

MITCHELL, William R., September 18, 1936 [**212**] b.1850, a.85; 1930 Census (Sonoma County Farm and Hospital) T626-222-222B, a.79, b.IN-IN-KY, widowed, patient. CADI, CAT, CEN, DC

MOLINI, John, February 12, 1912, a.36. CADI, DC

MOLLER, Peter, March 3, 1932 [**561**] b.1868, a.63. CADI, CAT

MOLOOF, Baby Girl, August 10, 1909, stillborn, daughter of Charles MOLOOF (b."Mt. Lebanon, Servia") and Camalina PANINA (b.Italy), residents of Decker Street, Santa Rosa, buried 8-12-1909 in the Sonoma County Farm Cemetery, aka "MOOLOF, Baby." Comment: Dr. STUART delivered the stillborn infant in the parents' home. DC has "Baby Boy" but the death record is clear: female. The family seems to have settled on "MALOOF" as most of the vital records are in that spelling. CADI, CEN, DC, MIC
Several other possible MALOOF (MOLOOF) family members (Abraham, John, and Michael) are in Sonoma County in the 1910 Census, all Turkish born. At this time, and until after World War I, Turkey included much of modern Iraq including Baghdad and Basra as well as the entire eastern shore of the Red Sea. The place of birth is variously spelled, for example (in the 1920 Census) "Mont Labann" in Syria. An examination of the Census records for the (possible) other MALOOF family members suggests they settled first in the

---

states of Washington and Oregon before coming further south to California just before 1900. This family may be distantly related to the MALOOF family who are the owners of the Sacramento Kings and Monarchs basketball teams and the Las Vegas Palms hotel-casino.

Census records

1910 (Decker Street, Santa Rosa) T624-109-166, "MALOOF, Charles, a.38, b."Turkey in Asia" (language: Syrian), married 6 years, emigrated 1887, alien, laborer (odd jobs), wife Carmela (a.39, b.Italy, emigrated 1900, 3 children born, 1 alive), daughter Regina, b.CA, a.3, and mother Ella, b.Turkey, a.62, emigrated 1894(?).

MONI, Antonio, August 14, 1913, a.29; 1910 Census (Ocean Township) T624-109-258, a.24, b.Italy, single, emigrated 1901, alien, woodsman for mill company. CADI, CEN, DC

MONTGOMERY, William, August 24, 1916, a.40, Negro, bootblack, 9 years in California, died in Santa Rosa, buried 8-28-1916 in the Sonoma County Farm Cemetery. BP, CADI, DC, NEW, REG

Newspaper records

"Man Horribly Mangled Under Wheels Of Train," *The Press Democrat*, 8-25-1916.
"Inquest Held Here Yesterday Afternoon," *The Press Democrat*, 8-26-1916.

MONZAGA, Edward, January 3, 1925, a.22. CADI, DC

MOORE, Tom, January 27, 1933 [**566**] b.1867, a.65, aka "MOORE, Thomas," buried 1-30-1933. CADI, CAT, DC

MORA, Elija, August 26, 1906, a.25. CADI, CC, DC

MORELLI, Joseph, January 20, 1942, b.2-17-1871, a.71, a resident of Laguna Road in Santa Rosa, father MORELLI, hospital #5818. BOI, CADI, DC

MORGAN, Edward, January 2, 1897, a.83, b.England, marital status unknown, died in the county hospital, #1805, interred at the county farm. DEA, REG

MORLEY, Joseph, June 1, 1935 [**235**] b.1892, a.42. CADI, CAT, DC

MORRIS, Joseph, October 25, 1909, a.76. CADI, DC

MORRISON, Delta May, February 22, 1938 [**140**] b.6-17-1893 Indianapolis, IN, a.44 years 8 months 5 days, female, housewife, married, spouse "MORRISON, Benjamin Franklin," father Eli MAXWELL (b.unknown), mother Estella FETTERS (b.Oaklandson, Indiana), resident on Route 3 (Mountain View Avenue), Santa Rosa, 12 years in California, 1 year 5 months local, found dead (fractured skull) on Petaluma Hill Road "near Santa Rosa," buried 2-25-1938 in the county cemetery, aka "MORRISON, Pelta May." Comment: Nothing has been found in Sonoma County records to suggest charges were brought against her husband or anyone else. BOI, CADI, CAT, CRT, DC, MIC, NEW

MORROW, James A., August 1, 1917, b.6-14-1860 TN, a.57, single, occupation cook, father William H. MORROW (b.TN), mother Mattie ATTOWAY (b.TN), 21 days at the place of death, died in the county hospital, buried 8-15-1917 in the Sonoma County Farm Cemetery. CADI, DC, REG

MORTON, William Sidney, March 30, 1922, b.4-04-1838 MI, a.83 years 11 months 26 days, widowed, laborer, father Philan MORTON (b.NY), mother Polly GREEN (b.NY), 7 months 21 days at the place of death, died at the county hospital, buried 4-03-1922 in the "Co. Farm Cem," aka "MORTON, William Sydney." Comment: Not found in Census. Not found in CADI. CADI, CEN, DC, MIC

MOZZOLINE, Joe, February 17, 1940, b.7-16-1862, a.77, father MOZZOLINE, mother ALBINI, at death a resident of the county hospital. BOI, CADI, DC

MUDGET, Arthur J., January 11, 1930, a.49, spouse "MUDGET, M." CADI, DC

MUELLER, Minna, August 5, 1928, a.72. CADI, DC

MULHOLLAND, Michael, May 11, 1933 [**524**] b.1854, a.79, spouse "K. MULHOLLAND;" 1920 Census (Mendocino County) T625-121-10A, "Michel MULHOLLAND," a.65, b.Canada-Ireland-Ireland, single, house carpenter, emigrated 1873, naturalized 1896. CADI, CAT, CEN

MULVEHILL, Jerry, January 6, 1925, b.NY, age "about 69," male, single, father John MULVEHILL (b.Ireland), mother Suzan [*sic*] RAFFERTY (b.VA), 42 years in California, 6 years 7 months 26 days at the place of death, died in the county hospital, buried in the county cemetery, aka "MULLEHILL, Jerry." CADI, DC, MIC

MURPHY, Michael, July 29, 1936 [**223**] b.1902, a.34. CADI, CAT, DC

MURPHY, Patrick, November 9, 1897, b.Ireland, a.70, widower, died at the county hospital, #1996, interred at the county farm. REG

MURPHY, Peter, July 28, 1930 [**668**] b.1862, a.68. CADI, CAT, DC

MURRY, Michael, November 26, 1916, b.10-20-1845 Ireland, a.71 years 1 month 6 days, single, laborer, father Thomas MURRY (b.Ireland), mother Mary McCONNIK (b.Ireland), 15 days at the place of death, 40 years in California, died in the county hospital, #7833, buried 11-29-1916 in the Sonoma County Farm Cemetery. BP, CADI, DC, REG

MYERS, Charles Benjamin, July 26, 1933 [**520**] b.8-28-1871 CA, a.61, wife Anna MYERS, parents Andrew MYERS and Anna GIBSON, died at the Silverado Sanitarium in Calistoga, Napa County, aka "MEYERS, Chas. B." CADI, CAT, DC, FAM, MIC

Comment: At this time, Sonoma County did not have a facility for treating patients with tuberculosis. Consequently, tuberculosis patients were sent out of the county. When they died (and most did), they were returned to Sonoma County for burial. Mr. Myers is one of only a few Chanate burials for whom living relatives have been located. No *Press Democrat* obituary was found.

MYGREN, Charles, February 26, 1920, a.84; 1910 Census (Sonoma County Farm and Hospital) T624-109-29A, "MYGRIN, Carl," a.77, b.Sweden, widowed, emigrated 1860. CADI, CEN, DC

NASH, Michael, October 2, 1936 [**211**] b.1-12-1877, a.58, resident at 321 K Street, Sacramento, 2 months in Santa Rosa, life in California, parents Patrick NASH, b.Ireland, and Mary DOLLAR, b.unknown, died at the Sonoma County Hospital. CADI, CAT, DC, MIC

NATRONI, Louis, May 6, 1912, a.82, aka "NATRON, Louis." Comment: "NATRONI" not found in the 1910 U.S. Census. CADI, CEN, DC

NAVARRO, Marcos, February 7, 1918, b.2-02-1877 Mexico, a.41, single, laborer, father Yenes NAVARRO, mother Juagina PULIDA (both b.Mexico), a resident of Petaluma, 15 years in California, 1 month 1 day in hospital, died in the county hospital, #8404, buried 2-08-1918 in the county farm cemetery. No obituary. CADI, DC, REG

NAVARRO, Sotero Charles, May 20, 1933 [**574**] b.4-22-1861 CA, father Charles NAVARRO (b.Spain), mother Soledad BADILLA [PADILLA?] (b.CA), buried 5-22-1933 in "Santa Rosa." Comment: The obituaries suggest a San Francisco burial but the death record and the *Catalogue of Grave Markers* are more reliable. Not in DC due to "Santa Rosa" burial. CADI, CAT, CEN, MIC, NEW

Census records
1900   (Almaden Township, Santa Clara County) T623-110-4, b.April 1861 CA, a.34, married 15 years, day laborer, with wife Virginia and four children.
1910   (Berkeley, Alameda County) T624-72-234, NAUARRO, Charles, b.CA, a.49, widowed, laborer, living with daughter Victoria CHRISTIANA.

Newspaper records
"Novarro Funeral In San Francisco," *Santa Rosa Republican*, 5-22-1933.
"Charles Novarro's Body Sent To S. F.," *The Press Democrat*, 5-23-1933.

NAVONI, Beniamino, December 4, 1906, a.40; 1900 Census (Santa Rosa) T623-114-270, "NAVONI, Beniamino," b.May 1867 Switzerland, a.33, single, emigrated 1882, 17 years in USA, alien, day laborer. Comment: Another boarder in the same household was "NAVONI, Batista," b.August 1826 Switzerland, a.73, widowed, emigrated 1882, possibly Beniamino's father. CADI, CEN, DC

NAYLEN, Patrick, January 21, 1888, left $15.00 to the county, aka "NAGLER, Patrick." Comment: The 1880 Census does not list this person in California. Further research is beyond the scope of this book. CEN, PHY

NEILSON, Adolph, October 3, 1886, left $1.50 to the county. PHY

NEKERVIS, Jane Moore, May 24, 1941, b.11-29-1912 CA, aka "NEKERUIS, Jane." CADI, DC

NELL, John, March 8, 1923, b.1850 Switzerland, age "about 73," single, farm laborer, father Peter GAUSCH, mother Catherine WALKER (both b.Switzerland), 53 years in California and USA, 1 month 19 days at the place of death, died in the county hospital, buried 3-13-1923 in the "Co. Farm Cem." Comment: This person was not found in California Census records. CADI, DC, MIC

NELS, Philip, January 26, 1928, a.63. CADI, DC

NELSON, Herman, May 26, 1900, a.60, died in the county hospital, buried at the county farm. DEA, REG

NELSON, Louis, December 6, 1910 [1305] b.Sweden, a.60, single, farm laborer, father Louis NELSON, mother Betty JOHNSON (both b.Sweden), 28 years in California, died in the county hospital, #6021, buried 12-12-1910 in the county farm cemetery; 1910 Census (Santa Rosa Township) T624-109-37, a.60, b.Sweden, single, wood chopper. CADI, CAT, CEN, DC, MIC

NESTER, Patrick, December 31, 1918, b.1869 NJ, a.49, single, farm laborer, father Patrick NESTER, mother Bridget CLARK (both b.Ireland), 20 years in California, 8 months 16 days in the hospital, died at the county hospital, #40, buried 1-30-1919 at the Sonoma County Farm; 1910 Census (Placer County) T624-91-154, a.40, married, b.NJ-Ireland-Ireland, occupation quarry man in granite quarry. CADI, CEN, MIC, REG
Comment: Duplicate records exist in REG, one in 1918, one in 1919; 1918 is correct. This may be because he died in 1918 but was buried in 1919. No information has been found as to why it took a month to bury him; perhaps it was too wet for the grave diggers. CADI notes the death was not officially recorded in Sacramento until 1919. Not in DC. *Heritage Quest* has this man indexed in the 1910 Census as "Nestor" but this author reads the name as "Nester" and CADI also has "Nester." The Census record shows Nester as married but does not list a spouse for him.

NEVAREZ, Julio, February 17, 1939 [108] b.1896 NM, a.44, married, spouse Mary NEVAREZ, laborer, parents unknown, 20 years in California, 3 years local, died in the county hospital, buried 2-20-1939 in the county cemetery. Comment: The death certificate gives his age as 42. BOI has "Petaluma, General Delivery," as his address. BOI, CADI, CAT, DC, MIC

NEWELL, Hershel V., May 17, 1940, b.12-17-1873 MN, a.66, father NEWELL, mother FLOCK, a resident of Sebastopol, aka "NEWELL, Hershall." BOI, CADI, DC

NEYCE, J. H., March 10, 1910, a.93. CADI, DC

NICHOLS, Sylvester, January 11, 1932 [**558**] b.11-21-1852 PA, a.79 years 1 month 20 days, single, laborer, 50 years in California, 17 years at the place of death, died in the Lone Redwood School District of Santa Rosa, buried 1-13-1932 in the "County Farm Cemetery, S.R.," aka "NICHOLSON, Sylvester." Comment: No relation to the author. CADI, CAT, DC, MIC

* NICHOLSON, Grover, April 13, 1929. DC error: the 1988 volunteer misread the death record. Grover was buried in Mountain Cemetery, Sonoma, California. On April 16, the Reverend MOORE officiated at Grover's funeral service, which was held at the Bates Funeral Parlor in Sonoma. CADI, DC, DM, MIC

NIEDRUSGHANE, Harry, December 14, 1916, b.5-26-1831 Germany, a.85 years 6 months 19 days, widowed, retired cabinet maker, father Fred NIEDRUSGHANE, mother Henrietta KLOBUS (both b.Germany), 7 months 21 days at the place of death, 30 years in California, died in the county hospital, buried 12-18-1916 in the Sonoma County Farm Cemetery. BP, CADI, CC, REG

NIELSON, Marinus, January 16, 1942, b.3-03-1864, a.77, father NIELSON. CADI, DC

NILES, Clyde Ancil, September 11, 1943, b.5-02-1887, wife Inez, 9 years in California, 7 years in Santa Rosa, died at home, buried "County Cemetery." CADI, DC

NIVEN, Francis J., February 18, 1939 [**101**] b.1869, a.70. CADI, CAT, DC

NOREEN, Albert O., February 14, 1929, a.79, spouse "NOREEN, W. O." CADI, DC

NORTON, Harry, July 17, 1939 [**100**] b.1872, a.66, a resident of English Street in Petaluma. BOI, CADI, CAT, DC

* NORTON, William Sidney see MORTON, William Sidney (1922).

* NOVARRO see NAVARRO (1933)

NOTT, Edith, September 27, 1926, a.40, spouse "NOTT, N." Comment: Not in the 1920 Census of California. No "NOTT" in 1920 Sonoma County. CADI, DC

NUGENT, Ambrose, February 19, 1908, a.24. Not in the 1900 Census. CADI, DC

OBERMEIER, Frank, October 8, 1938 [**174**] b.1876, a.62, a resident of Cloverdale, a "hospital case." Not in the 1920 California Census. BOI, CADI, CAT, CEN, DC

O'BRIEN, Joseph, January 11, 1937 [**192**] b.1860, a.76; 1930 Census (Sonoma County Farm and Hospital) T625-222-223A, a.69, b.N.Ireland, single, inmate, emigrated 1889, alien. Comment: CAT lists both Joseph O'BRIEN and Dominico AQUISTAPACE in [**193**] and no one in [**192**]. Based on the dates of death, Joseph O'BRIEN is most likely to have been buried in [**192**]. Additionally, the volunteer who created DC made an error, putting 1936 as O'BRIEN's year of death. CADI, CAT, CEN, DC

* O'BRIEN, Patrick or Thomas see SPARKS, Charles O. (1937).

OCACIO, Carmilio, August 17, 1930, b.1-04-1930 CA, female, Hawaiian, a.7 months 13 days, father Joseph OCACIO (b."Porta Rico"), mother Mary PEREIVA (b.Honolulu, HI), buried 8-19-1930 in the "County Farm Cemetery," aka "OCACIO, Carmilda or Carmilida." CADI, DC, MIC

O'CONNELL, James, August 14, 1939, a.51. CADI, DC

O'CONNOR, John, January 26, 1936 [**246**] b.1861, a.74. CADI, CAT, DC, NEW

Newspaper records
"Geyserville Man Dies in Hospital," *The Press Democrat*, 1-27-1936.

O'DELL, Simpson George, September 27, 1897 (40 Deaths 99) b.OH, a.75, white, county hospital #1906, buried in the county farm cemetery. Comment: Simpson O'DELL is one of a few persons in Chanate for whom living family members have been located. The 1860 Census suggests the move from Iowa to California occurred after Mary's birth in 1852 and before John's birth in 1853. CEN, DEA, FAM, GR, NEW, REG

Census and voter registration records
1850 (Moscow, Muscatine, IA) "ODLE, Simpson," a.27, b.OH, wife Susanna, a.20, b.IN, son Sylvester, a.8 months, b.IA.
1860 (Washington Township, Geyserville PO) M653-69-666, "O'DELL, S. G.," a.38, b.OH, farmer, wife and five children, first two b.IA, last three b.CA.
1870 (Washington Township, Healdsburg PO) M593-91-465, "O'DELL, Simp. G.," a.48, b.OH, farmer, wife and eight children.
1880 (Washington Township) T9-84-165, "O'DELL, Simpson G.," a.58, b.OH-VA-VA, wife and nine children.
1890 (Washington Township) Great Register of Voters, "O'DELL, Simpson George, a.65, b.OH, farmer."

Coroner's records
9-20-1875, death of Mrs. Mary BOGGS at the "house of S. Odell near Geyserville." Witnesses: Amanda and Sarah O'DELL, granddaughters of Mrs. BOGGS.
9-07-1877, death of Charles HUMPHRIES at the "Old Doc ELY place, Geyserville," due to an overdose of strychnine. Witness: S. G. O'DELL.
9-03-1885, death of Lincoln G. O'DELL in Cloverdale Township at the age of 25 due to an accidental self-inflicted gunshot wound. Witness: Sylvester O'DELL.

Newspaper records
"Death of S. F. O'Dell," *The Sonoma Democrat*, 10-02-1897.

ODEN, Baby Girl, October 13, 1928 [368] stillborn at the county hospital, #2244, father Ernest ODEN (b.OR), mother Grace CLARNS (b.OR), buried 10-17-1928 in the Sonoma County Farm Cemetery. CADI, CAT, MIC

O'DOWN, George, July 31, 1925, a.46. CADI, DC

O'HARA, Peter, March 31, 1887, left $1.35 to the county. PHY

OHIE, Wong, February 21, 1921, b.2-03-1921 Santa Rosa, a.1 year 18 days, female, father WONG, Kouck Shun, mother YEE, Shee (both b.China), 1 year 18 days in California and local, informant WONG, Tan, 642 2nd Street, Santa Rosa, buried 2-22-1921 in the "County Farm Cem." CADI, CEN, DC, MIC

Comment: Either the date of birth or the age and length of residence is in error. The baby does not appear in the Census, suggesting she was not yet born. The family name is clearly WONG but CADI and the death record list OHIE.

Census records
1920   (642 2nd Street, Santa Rosa) T625-151-237

O'LEARY, Dennis, October 3, 1941, b.4-20-1880 MA. CADI, DC

O'LEARY, Thomas, May 8, 1916, b.3-25-1842 Queenstown (now Cobh), County Cork, Ireland, a.74 years 1 month 13 days, single, laborer, father Thomas O'LEARY (b. Queenstown, Ireland), mother Nora ALLEN (b. Ireland), 4 days at the place of death, 30 years in California, died in the county hospital, #7644, buried 5-10-1916 in the Sonoma County Farm Cemetery. BP, CADI, DC, REG

OLHSON, Henry, July 17, 1920, a.63; possible 1900 Census (Sonoma County Farm and Hospital) T623-114-258A, "OLSON, Henery," a.36, b.Germany. CADI, CEN, DC

OLLINI, John, December 9, 1924, a.43. CADI, DC

OLSEN, Elak, January 13, 1938 [136]   a.75, "transient hobo" (BOI). No Press Democrat obituary was found. BOI, CADI, CAT, DC

OLSEN, Julia, September 11, 1940, b.7-05-1877 Grantsburg, WI, a.63 years 2 months 7 days, widow of Martin OLSEN, a resident of Jeffery's Auto Camp, Sebastopol, housewife, father Charles WESTER (b.Sweden), mother Bertha OLSEN (b.Norway), 15 years in California, 11 years local, 4 months 8 days in the county hospital and died there, hospital #4348, buried 9-16-1940 in the "County Cemetery." BOI, CADI, DC, MIC

OLSEN, Thevorld, January 18, 1937 [269] b.1853 Norway, a.83, a resident of Petaluma. CADI, CAT, DC, NEW

Newspaper records
"Thevorld Olsen, Ill Three Years, Dies," The Press Democrat, 1-19-1937.
"Thevorld Olsen At Rest In S. Rosa," Petaluma Argus-Courier, 1-21-1937.
"Olsen Rites Held," The Press Democrat, 1-21-1937.

OLSON, Jacob, March 31, 1936 [253] b.1859, a.76; 1930 Census (Sonoma County Farm and Hospital) T626-222-223A, a.70, b.Germany, single, inmate, emigrated 1887, alien. CADI, CAT, CEN, DC

OLSON, Martin, November 26, 1926, b.Norway, age "about 69," sailor. CADI, DC

ON, Yee, November 20, 1942, b.5-13-1868 California. CADI, DC

* ONEA, Mr. see IVES, Sampson (1922). Although listed in DC, no such person exists in Sonoma County records or in CADI. The only death on August 7, 1922 was Sampson IVES, who was indeed buried in the Sonoma County Farm Cemetery although he is not in DC.

O'NEILL, Harry, January 23, 1943, b.1888, a.55. CADI, DC

ORSTROM, James, November 25, 1911, a.85. CADI, DC

ORTIZ, Ustocia, January 14, 1934 [**425**] b.1856 Yountville, Napa County, a.78, male, Spanish, single, a resident of Davis Street in Santa Rosa, father Joe ORTIZ (b.Mexico), mother Margrete VALEJO (b.CA), aka "ORTIZ, Ustocha." Comment: He had a brother, Jesus ORTIZ. CADI, CAT, DC, MIC, NEW

Newspaper records
"Funeral is Held," *The Press Democrat*, 1-18-1934.

OSBORN, Henry, May 11, 1913, a.85; 1910 Census (Sonoma County Farm and Hospital) T624-109-29A, a.86, b.U.S.-Unknown-Germany, single. CADI, CEN, DC

O'SHAUGHNESSY, Edward, May 22, 1930 [**674**] b.1851, a.79; 1930 Census (Sonoma County Farm and Hospital) T626-222-223A, a.79, b.Ireland, single, emigrated 1900, alien, patient. CADI, CAT, DC

OSTRAKANT, Henry, November 12, 1907, a.87. Comment: This person could not be found in the 1900 Census. CADI, DC

OSTRAND, John, November 4, 1936 [**204**] b.1871, a.65. Comment: Transcribed in error, "STRAND, John O.," from the hospital records to CAT. CADI, CAT, DC

OTTI, Ali, July 23, 1939 [**195**] b.1888, a.50, a resident of Sonoma, hospital #3388. Comment: CAT has "ALIO, no first name," obviously a misreading of "Ali O." BOI, CADI, CAT, CC, DC

OTTMER, Frank J., November 24, 1933, b.9-05-1870 CA, a.63, single, laborer, a resident of San Francisco, father John OTTMER (b.Ireland), mother unknown (b.Germany), life in California, 7 days in the hospital, buried in the county cemetery. CADI, CC, CEN, DC, MIC

Comment: This person is listed in DC as "CHERMER, John, November 24, 1933," but there is no such person in any Sonoma County record searched. For this date, CC and MIC have only Frank OTTMER. A comparison of DC (which used the old paper registers) with MIC (which is on microfilm) shows the names in this time period are in the same order in both databases except that OTTMER somehow becomes CHERMER. This is a strange error but error it has to be. Also note Frank OTTMER of Sonoma County appears in CADI whereas the name CHERMER is not listed at all. Although there is an OTTMER family in Sonoma County, according to Census records, Frank is not among them.

OUELLET, J. C., March 20, 1915, a.76. BP, CADI, DC

OUER, Paulina, September 15, 1907, a.59, aka "OVER, Pauline." This person was not found in the 1900 Census under either spelling. CADI, CEN, DC

OVERMAN, Chas., December 18, 1928 [**731**] b.1854, a.74; 1920 Census (Russian River Township) T625-150-243, "OVERMAN, C. F.," a.65, single, b.IN-Portugal-NC, wood cutter. CADI, CAT, CEN

OWENS, William, July 1, 1939 [**118**] b.1865, a.74; 1920 Census (Salmon Creek Road, Bodega Township) T625-150-80, "OWENS, William A.," b.CA-Canada-NH, a.38, single, farm laborer, "working out." CADI, CAT, CEN, DC

OY, Hoy, April 14, 1937 [**286**] b.1854, a.83. CADI, CAT, DC

PALM, Charles W., April 23, 1906, a.43, divorced, occupation "traveling man," died at 741 Humboldt St., [due to] "delirium tremens (2 days) and shock from earthquake." CADI, CEN, DC, MIC

PALMER, Capt. Jacob, October 23, 1916, b.4-28-1843 Portland, ME, a.73 years 5 months 25 days, widowed, submarine diver, father Capt. Stephen PALMER, mother Jane CAME (both b.Portland, ME), 5 days in the county hospital and died there, buried 11-03-1916 in the Sonoma County Farm Cemetery. BP, CADI, DC, REG

PALOMA, Enos, January 7, 1930, a.55; 1920 Census (Coleman Valley Road, Bodega Township) T625-150-78, "PALAMO, Enos," a.49, single, b.Guam, race "T" (Filipino?), wood chopper. CADI, CEN, DC

PANKATOLINO, Peter, December 22, 1924, a.45. CADI, DC

PAPERA, Andrew, June 1, 1936 [259] b.1847, a.89; 1930 Census (Sonoma County Farm and Hospital) T626-222-223A, a.83, single, b.Italy, emigrated 1877, alien, inmate. CADI, CAT, CEN, DC

PARREN, Frank, August 20, 1939, born in Spokane, Washington, a.63, a transient fruit worker, spouse "Myrtle PARREN." Comment: The obituary lists many surviving relatives. BOI, CADI, DC, NEW

Newspaper records
"Rancher Dies of Heart Ill," *The Press Democrat*, 8-22-1939.

PARRY, Thomas O., February 8, 1934 [**229**] b.1863, a.70, aka "PERRY, Thomas C." CADI, CAT, DC

PATACK, Bert, July 27, 1927, b.8-20-1876 Austria, a.50 years 11 months 7 days, single, laborer, a resident of Cloverdale, father Bernard PATACK, mother Catherine REGLER (both b.Austria), 16 years in California, died in the county hospital, #7167, buried 7-29-1927 in the "Sonoma Co. Cemetery." CADI, DC, MIC

PATERSON, William W., November 24, 1912, b.NY, a.67, single, farm laborer, father unknown (b.NY), mother unknown (b.England), 28 years 10 months in California, 15 years 7 months local, died in the county hospital, #48, buried 11-27-1912 in the "Sonoma Co. Farm Cem;" 1900 Census (Sonoma County

Farm and Hospital) T623-114-257B, "Patterson, William W.," b.July 1855 IN-England-England, a.44, single, pensioner. Comment: Not found in CADI. Other CADI listings for Sonoma County: "PATTERSON, William, a.80, d.5-14-1912;" "PATTERSON, William W., a.29, d.11-04-1918;" "PATTISON, William, a.69, d.5-29-1906." CADI, CEN, DC, MIC

PATTERSON, Frank, March 30, 1942, b.10-08-1867 PA, a.74, a resident of the county farm, mother LANGFORD, father PATTERSON. BOI, CADI, DC

PATTERSON, William, March 14, 1913, a.66, aka "PATERSON, William." CADI, DC

PATTON, Charles J. or T., May 23, 1927, a.70. CADI, DC

PEARSON, Peter H., August 26, 1941, b.12-04-1883, a resident of the county hospital. BOI, CADI, DC

PEASLEE, Ibyllys [sic], February 9, 1925, a.67. CADI, DC

PEDREGEN, Urbano, October 21, 1921, a.55, aka "PEDROGEN, Urbano." Comment: This person was not found in a search of the 1920 U.S. Census. CADI, CEN, DC

PEDROCK, Peter, February 7, 1910, a.60. CADI, DC

PELLANDO, Ubaldo, November 2, 1942, b.3-19-1867, "transient." BOI, CADI, DC

PELLEGEINE, Augusto, December 29, 1914, a.53, aka "PELLEGEINE, Augusta." Comment: This person was not found in a search of the 1920 California Census. CADI, CEN, DC

PENZ, Charles, November 24, 1925, a.51. Comment: This person was not found in a search of the 1920 California Census. CADI, CEN, DC

PEPE, Barteo M., December 19, 1933 [422] b.1864, aka "PEFE, Barteam." CADI, CAT, CC, DC

PERACCA, Rudolph, April 6, 1937 [284] b.12-22-1883 Italy, a.53, single, laborer, died in the county hospital, father Andrew PERACCA (b.Italy), mother Margaret NARRA (b.Italy), 17 years in Santa Rosa and in California, 30 years in the USA, buried 4-08-1937 in the "Co. Cemetery." CADI, CAT, DC, MIC

PERASSO, Giacoma, February 2, 1912, a.34. CADI, DC

PEREZ, Julian, December 25, 1939, b.Mexico, a.64, died at the home of his son, Jesus PEREZ, 403 Hewitt Street, Santa Rosa; possible 1920 Census (Mendocino County) T625-121-81, a.41, b.Mexico, rancher, emigrated 1910, alien, wife Lucy. CADI, CEN, DC, NEW

Newspaper records
"Julian Perez," The Press Democrat, 12-26-1939.

PERRING, Leo, September 9, 1917, b.4-16-1863 Germany, a.54 years 4 months 24 days, single, laborer, father Antone PERRING (b.Germany), mother Virginia VAGERY (b.Germany), residence Caliente Springs, 12 years 6 months 8 days in California, hospital #8293, buried 9-11-1917 at the county farm. CADI, DC, REG

PERRY, Henry, September 23, 1937 [**311**] b.1887, a.50, Negro, transient, "fell from train, fractured skull." CADI, CAT, DC, MIC, NEW

Newspaper records
"Fall From Train Proves Fatal To Negro," *Petaluma Argus-Courier*, 9-23-1937.
"Itinerant Falls From Train Near Petaluma, Killed," *The Press Democrat*, 9-24-1937.
"Itinerant Dies In Fall From Train," *Santa Rosa Daily Republican*, 9-23-1937.

* PERRY, Thomas <u>see</u> PARRY, Thomas (1934).

PERSONS, Clark C., September 20, 1934 [**393**] b.1858, a.76; 1930 Census (Sonoma County Farm and Hospital) T626-222-223A, a.72, b.WI-NY-U.S., widowed, patient. CADI, CAT, CEN, DC

PETERSEN, Anker Daune, July 23, 1934 [**498**] b.7-22-1934 in the county hospital, a.20 hours 40 minutes, "dual sex," father Anker E. PETERSEN (b.Denmark), mother Elzada PETERSEN (b.Cloverdale), buried 7-26-1934 in the "Sonoma Co. Cem." Comment: In the 'cause of death' section of the death record, the doctor noted the baby had "congenital deformities." CAT listed this infant as "PETERSON, Baby" with no date of death. CADI, CAT, MIC

PETERSEN, Charles, October 8, 1928 [**724**] b.1863, a.65, aka "PETERSON, Charles." CADI, CAT

PETERSEN, Christopher, March 5, 1922, a.77, aka "PETERSON, Christopher;" 1920 Census (Petaluma) T625-151-3, "PETERSEN, Chris," a.74, single, b.Schleswig-Holstein (overwritten "Denmark," by a Census compiler, perhaps because his mother tongue was Danish rather than German), emigration status unknown, laborer on poultry farm. CADI, CEN, DC

PETERSON, John, August 15, 1915, b.12-22-1837 Sweden, a.78 years 7 months 21 days, single, father Andrew PETERSON (b.Sweden), mother Carrie OLSEN (b.Sweden), 20 years in California, died in the county hospital, #7395, buried in the Sonoma County Farm Cemetery. BP, CADI, DC, REG

PETERSON, John P., April 8, 1886, b.1854 Sweden, left $5.60 to the county. Comment: The 1880 Census does not list this person in Sonoma County. CEN, DEA, PHY

PETERSON, P. A., July 27, 1923, a.81. CADI, DC

PETRI, Jacob, October 17, 1906, a.60. Comment: Jacob PETRI is not found in the 1900 Census. CADI, CEN, DC

PETRI, Norisco, January 22, 1934 [**397**] b.5-07-1862 Italy, a.71, cook, father John PETRI, mother Katherine GENETTI, in California since 1889, a resident of Healdsburg. No Healdsburg obituary. CADI, CAT, DC, MIC

PETTY, James E., December 3, 1916, b.3-25-1840 MA, a.75 years 8 months 8 days, single, farm laborer, father Ephraine PETTY (b.MA), mother unknown, 22 days at the place of death, died in the county hospital, buried 12-11-1916 in the Sonoma County Farm Cemetery; 1910 Census (River Road, Monte Rio area, Ocean Township) T624-109-255, a.66, b.MA-U.S.-U.S., married, laborer (odd jobs). BP, CADI, CC, CEN, REG

PHILBRICK, Charles C., October 23, 1938 [**175**] b.1882, a.56, a "hospital case." BOI lists him as "transient—no home." BOI, CADI, CAT, DC

PHILLIPS, Frank, March 29, 1895, b.NY, a.49, died at the county hospital (#1402), buried at the county farm. DEA, REG

PHILLIPS, William, October 8, 1914, a.56. BP, CADI, DC

PICASSO, Alfred, May 27, 1913, b.CA, age "about 14," single, father Manuel PICASSO (b.unknown), mother unknown, died at the county hospital of septicemia due to an "exploded appendix," buried 6-05-1913 in the "Sonoma Co. Farm Cem," aka "PICASSA, Alfred." CADI, CEN, DC, MIC

Census records
1900 (819 Vallejo Street, San Francisco) T623-107-42, Emanuel (a.41, b.Italy) and Mary (a.40, b.Italy, 9 children) PICASSO and their seven children including "Alfredo," b.February, 1900 in California.
1910 (St. Vincent Orphan Asylum, San Rafael Township, Marin County) T624-88-101, "PICASSO, Alfred," a.11, parents born in Italy.

PICKLE, Thomas B., September 5, 1925, a.73. CADI, DC

PIERCE, Louis, May 24, 1920, a.57; 1920 Census (Santa Rosa) T625-151-162, a.50, single, b.CA-U.S.-[illegible], laborer. CADI, CEN, DC

PING, Ah, January 13, 1917, b.1817 China, a.99, male, married, laborer, father Su PING (b.China), 46 years in California, died in the county hospital, buried 1-16-1917 in the Sonoma County Farm Cemetery. BP, CADI, CEN, REG

PINOLA, Minnie, June 12, 1917, b.7-17-1901, a.15 years 10 months 25 days, Indian, single, schoolgirl, father Joe PINOLA (b.CA), mother Susan PHILLIPS (b.CA), a resident of Healdsburg, died in Bodega Township, buried 6-23-1917 in the Sonoma County Farm Cemetery, informant Roy PHILLIPS, Bodega. BP, CADI, CC, REG

PITTS, Arthur, September 12, 1935 [**378**] b.1883, a.51. CADI, CAT

PLATT, Henry, May 11, 1942, b.4-07-1878 MI, a.64, a resident of the county hospital, mother PLATT, father PLATT. BOI, CADI, DC

PLENN, Walter, June 4, 1931 [**549**] b.1865, a.66. Comment: CAT spells the name "PLUM" in error. CADI, CAT, CC, DC

PLUBELLINI, John, April 24, 1938 [**152**] b.1873, a.65, a resident of Hewitt Street, Santa Rosa, aka "PINBELLINI, Geo." BOI, CADI, CAT, DC

POLAND, Josiah, December 4, 1911, a.82, aka "POLAND, Joseph." CADI, DC

PONTANELLI, Pedro, January 23, 1910, a.26. CADI, DC

PORTER, William, January 16, 1914, a.42; possible 1910 Census (532 1st St., Santa Rosa) T624-109-134, a.39, b.CA-Norway-CA, laborer, wife Lulu and four children by her two previous marriages to BARRY and MEYER. CADI, CEN, DC

POWELL, Frank, December 30, 1925, a.85. CADI, DC

POWERS, Maurice Vincent, March 11, 1916, b.11-24-1872 Oakland, a.43 years 3 months 16 days, single, occupation lineman, father David POWERS (b.Ireland), mother Mary WHITE (b.Waterford, Ireland), died in the county hospital, #7542, buried 3-15-1916 in the Sonoma County Farm Cemetery. BP, CADI, DC, REG

POZZI, Angela, November 29, 1933 [**405**] b.1881, a.52, male, aka "POZZI, Angelo." CADI, CAT, DC

PREFUME, Charles, July 29, 1941, a.50. CADI, DC

PRESBY, Elijah, August 15, 1887, b.1810 NH, left $0.30 to the county. Comment: The earliest-born person in Chanate is not in 1880 Census. CEN, DEA, PHY

PRESBY, Myron, July 31, 1930, a.75; 1930 Census (Sonoma County Farm and Hospital) T626-222-223A, a.75, b.NY, inmate. CADI, DC, CEN

PRETI, Giovanni, October 22, 1936 [**208**] b.1861, a.75. CADI, CAT, DC

PRICE, Charles, July 17, 1940, b.11-03-1858 NY, a.81. CADI, DC

PRYOR, Owen, June 5, 1937 [**290**] b.1860, a.67. CADI, CAT, DC

QUARRY, Jack Pete, August 26, 1940, b.3-07-1884 TX, a.56 years 5 months 19 days, wife Jannette QUARRY, a.53, a resident of Wright Road, Santa Rosa, farmer, not a veteran, father George QUARRY (b.AR), mother Nannie LEPER (b.TX), 8 months in California, 6 days local, 3 hours in the hospital (and died there), buried 8-29-1940 in the county cemetery, the informant was Mrs. QUARRY. CADI, CEN, DC, MIC

Comment: No Texas-born QUARRY is head of a household in any 20th century U.S. Census. CADI lists the wife as "Jeanette QUARRY, b.09-27-1887 Arkansas, mother MORSE, father THOMAS, d.09-06-1952 in Kern County, California."

QUARTAROLI, Frank, April 25, 1943, b.4-23-1865, a.78, father QUARTAROLI. CADI, DC

QUAY, Edward, May 21, 1938 [**127**] b.6-30-1863 PA, a.74, father Lloyd QUAY (b.PA), mother Mary FLEMING (b.PA), a resident of Boyes Springs, 15 days in Santa Rosa, 31 years in California, aka "GUAY, Edward;" 1930 Census (Sonoma Township) T626-222-245, a.67, widowed, b.PA-PA-PA, owns a radio, plumber. Comment: Census records show most of the QUAY family living in Pennsylvania. BOI, CADI, CAT, CC, CEN, DC, MIC, NEW

Newspaper records
"Edward Quay Dies," *The Press Democrat*, 5-24-1938.
"Quay Funeral Held," *The Press Democrat*, 5-25-1938.
"Boyes Springs Old Timer Crosses Divide," *Sonoma Index-Tribune*, 5-27-1938.

QUISENBERRY, Walter, December 24, 1933 [**423**] b.1876, a.57, aka "Walter GUINSENBERRY." CADI, CAT, CC, DC

QUONG, Wong, November 29, 1914, a.58. Comment: DC error, "QUONG, Jwong." BP, CADI, CC, DC

RADER, John Forster, February 27, 1907, a.20. CADI, DC

RADFORD, Fred, September 12, 1937 [**303**] b.2-01-1900 Texas, a.37, transient working as a hop picker, run over by train. CADI, CAT, DC, MIC, NEW

Newspaper records
"Hop Picker Slips Under Train, Dies," *The Press Democrat*, 9-12-1937.

RAMONA, Baby Boy, November 4, 1936 [**370**] stillborn (premature, 8 months), Indian, parents Anthony and Barbara RAMONA (both b.California), a resident of Santa Rosa, buried 11-12-1936 in the Sonoma County Cemetery. CADI, CAT, DC, MIC

RAPKA, Dorette, April 26, 1911, a.76. Comment: No *Press Democrat* obituary was found. Also see county records for August RAPKA (husband?), d.9-16-1913, a.70, in Sonoma County, buried elsewhere. CADI, DC

RATTO, Louis, July 3, 1910, a.72; 1910 Census (Sonoma County Farm and Hospital) T624-109-29A, "RATO, Louis," a.74, b.Italy, widowed, emigrated 1890, aka "RATLO or RATO, Louis." CADI, CEN, DC

RAVETTO, Secondo, July 1, 1930 [**670**] b.1875, a.54, aka "BAVETTO, Unnamed." CADI, CAT, DC

RAY, Edward, January 3, 1919, b.1847 Ireland, a.72, single, laborer, father George RAY (b.Ireland), mother Mary McGUIRE (b.Ireland), a resident of Santa Rosa, 4 years in California, 3 months 21 days in the county hospital, #371, buried 1-23-1919 in the county farm cemetery. Comment: The delay between death and burial may have been due to an exceptionally wet winter. CADI, DC, MIC, REG

RAYBURN, Wayne, August 17, 1912, a.79, aka "RAYBRIAN, Wayne;" 1910 Census (Sonoma County Farm and Hospital) T624-109-29, "REYBOURNE, Wayne," a.77, b.U.S., single, inmate. CADI, CEN, DC

RAYMOND, Donald, November 15, 1928 [**726**] b.1882, a.46. CADI, CAT

REBSTACH, John, August 1, 1885, left $7.00 to the county. Comment: "REBSTACH" may be a misspelling (the 1880 Census has no such name anywhere in the USA. PHY

REDCLEFF, Michael, September 14, 1913, a.56. CADI, DC

REDMOND, John, March 7, 1922, a.42. CADI, DC

REDMOND, Levi, March 21, 1917, a.59. BP, CADI, DC

REED, William D., November 6, 1907, a.81. CADI, DC

REEDER, William, April 22, 1937 [**287**] b.1858, a.79. CADI, CAT, DC

REGIS, John, September 20, 1937 [**308**] b.10-02-1877, a.59, a resident of Windsor. CADI, CAT, DC, MIC, NEW

Newspaper records
"Windsor Man Dies," *The Press Democrat*, 9-21-1937.
"John Regis, Windsor Rancher, Dies Here," *Santa Rosa Daily Republican*, 9-21-1937.

REID, Anthony, December 21, 1922, a.65; 1920 Census (Sonoma County Farm and Hospital) T625-151-12B, a.65, b.Ireland, single, naturalized citizen. CADI, CEN, DC

REID, Oscar, September 15, 1938 [**171**] b.1859, a.79, resident on Route 4, Santa Rosa. Comment: BOI lists him as a "hospital case." BOI, CADI, CAT, DC

RELYEA, Bert Garfield, March 16, 1938 [**453**] a.4 hours, father Fred RELYEA (b.CA), mother Hazel WALTON (b.OR), resident on 1st Street, Healdsburg, died at the county hospital, buried 3-18-1938 in the county cemetery, aka "RALYEA, Baby" or "GARFIELD, Bert." BOI, CADI, CAT, DC, MIC

RENALDS, Benjamin George, June 23, 1921, b.9-04-1895, a.25 years 9 months 19 days, single, Mexican, laborer (ranch), father Jesus RENALDS (b.Mexico), mother Florence OZONA (b.Mexico), 8 months at the place of death, suicide (gunshot), buried 6-25-1921. MIC, NEW

Comment: On June 24, 1921, newspaper headlines screamed the story of Benjamin Renalds' murder of Bob MILLS and his young wife. After quarreling with Mr. MILLS over his work, RENALDS shot both the 65 year old MILLS and his (MILLS's) 19 year old wife, Virginia, wrote out a note, and then shot himself.

Although the death record gives Moke's Cemetery as the place of burial, this has to be an error. H. H. Moke was a Santa Rosa undertaker who had his own cemetery on land adjacent to (and now part of) the Santa Rosa Rural Cemetery. Moke's Cemetery was considered to be a very high class place in which to lay the remains of your loved ones, which can still be seen today in the large, expensive monuments that decorate the graves. Individual graves sold for ten dollars or more and would not have been provided to a man who was an indigent, much less a murderer.

Although contemporary newspapers played the story as a murder-suicide, some neighbors thought otherwise and stories still circulate in the mountain neighborhood east of Santa Rosa. One alternate explanation is that Renalds was involved with Virginia. Bob Mills shot them both, wrote a note incriminating Renalds, and then killed himself.

Newspaper records
"Bob Mills, Young Wife Murdered By Spaniard," *The Press Democrat*, 6-24-1921.
"Divine Hand Saves Lives of Children of Tragedy," *The Press Democrat*, 6-24-1921.
"Death Cycle Visits City Three Times," *The Press Democrat*, 6-24-1921.
"Getting The News Under Difficulties," *The Press Democrat*, 6-24-1921.
"County To Bury Body Of Killer," *The Press Democrat*, 6-25-1921.
"Funeral Services Murder Victims 2 O'clock Today," *The Press Democrat*, 6-26-1921.

REYES, Antonia, January 24, 1910, a.31, male, aka "REYS, Antonia," or "REYES, Antone." CADI, DC, NEW

Newspaper records
"Sleeps In Storm and Death Comes," *The Press Democrat*, 1-25-1910.

* REYNOLDS, Roy, March 14, 1937, b.10-04-1894 Hart County, KY, a.42 years 5 months 10 days, single, laborer, transient, residence unknown, father Edward REYNOLDS (b.Hart County, KY), mother Sarah Frances MURRAY (b.Hart County, KY), buried 3-16-1937 in the county cemetery, reburied 4-19-1937 in the Santa Rosa Odd Fellows Cemetery, informant Toney REYNOLDS, Stockton, California.

Comment: Reynolds' death certificate has two sheets; the second sheet records the reburial. Evidently Reynolds was buried before the relative in Stockton could be notified. The reburial has been confirmed by Santa Rosa Memorial Park, which manages the adjacent Odd Fellows Cemetery. CADI, DC, MIC, NEW

Newspaper records
"War Vet Killed At Bellevue By Eureka Express," *The Press Democrat*, 3-16-1937.
"Train Victim Is Identified From Fingerprint Card," *The Press Democrat*, 3-18-1937.

RHINE, Baby Boy, September 9, 1931 [458] age 4 hours, twin, son of M/M Leland Rhine. Comment: One entry in CADI for both twins. CADI, CAT, DC

RHINE, Baby Girl, September 9, 1931 [458] age 4 hours, twin, daughter of M/M Leland Rhine. Comment: One entry in CADI for both twins. CADI, CAT, DC

RHODES, William, May 28, 1908, a.68. CADI, DC

RHUDART, Richard, January 27, 1939 [105] b.1885, aka "RHUDDARD" or "RHUDAT." Comment: CADI has both "RHUDART" and "RUDAT" with the same state file number, 7059. CAT has "RUDAT." CADI, CAT, DC

RICE, David P., June 8, 1917, b.3-12-1839 TN, a.77 years 2 months 27 days, single, laborer, residence Graton, father Spincer [*sic*] RICE (b.TN), mother Miss NOIL, 4 months 20 days at the place of death, 59 years in California, died in the county hospital, #7943, buried 6-15-1917 in the Sonoma County Farm Cemetery; 1910 Census (Green Valley Road, Analy Township) T624-109-72, a.71, b.MO, single. Comment: No *Press Democrat* obituary was found. BP, CADI, CEN, MIC, REG

RICE, Ernest E., January 7, 1931 [744] b.1847, a.83; 1930 Census (Sonoma County Farm and Hospital) T626-222-223A, a.82, b.OH-OH-NY, single, patient. CADI, CAT, DC

RICHARD, George, November 18, 1907, age "about 38," single, died in the "Santa Rosa Hospital" [Santa Rosa General], buried in the Sonoma County Farm Cemetery, aka "RICHARDS, George." Possible 1900 Census (Napa State Insane Asylum, Napa County) T623-95-84, a.37, b.Germany, single, patient. CADI, CEN, DC, MIC

RICHARDS, Eliza, September 28, 1897, b.CA, a.30, died at the county hospital, #1956 (40 Deaths 109) "Interred at Farm;" possible 1880 Census (Fourth Street, Petaluma) T9-84-79, "McFARLAN, Eliza," a.12, b.CA-TN-FL, black, daughter of Alexander (a.73) and Levinia (a.52) McFARLAN. No Petaluma obit. CEN, DEA, NEW, REG

RICHINA, Bart, August 8, 1942, b.7-20-1878 Other (rest of the world), a.64, father RICHINA. CADI, DC

RIDOLFI, Attibus, December 10, 1917, b.5-09-1849 Italy, a.68, single, farm laborer, father Vincent RIDOLFI (b.Italy), mother Margaret BISUSI (b.Italy), 1 month 1 day at the place of death, 42 years 1 month 4 days in California, died in the county hospital, buried 12-14-1917 in the county farm cemetery. CADI, DC, MIC, REG

RIGNELL, Gus, August 22, 1916, b.Sweden, a.60, single, wood chopper, 5 years in California, died "4 miles from Geyserville," buried 8-24-1916 in the Sonoma County Farm Cemetery, aka "BIGNELL" or "RINGELLI." Comment: Coroner Frank Phillips reported Mr. RIGNELL died of "accidental injuries . . . received by having a butt of a tree he was sawing up roll upon him." BP, CADI, CC, DC, MIC, NEW, REG

Newspaper records
"Falling Tree Crushes Man," *The Press Democrat*, 8-24-1916.

RILEY, George, January 19, 1905, b.1847 MA, a.58, occupation "naval employee," widowed, died at the county hospital. CADI, DC, MIC

RINGER, Arthur, November 24, 1921, a.51. CADI, DC

ROACH, Charles, September 12, 1930 [738] b.1856, a.74. CADI, CAT, DC

ROACH, Robert, February 15, 1937 [**276**] b.1886, a.50. CADI, CAT, DC, NEW

Newspaper records
"Dies at Hospital," *The Press Democrat*, 2-16-1937.

ROBATTO, May, November 23, 1896, b.CA, a.24, died at the county hospital, #1769, "Interred at Farm." DEA, REG

ROBERTS, Sydney, April 9, 1935 [444] b.1850, a.84, aka "ROBERTS, Sidney." CADI, CAT

ROBERTSON, Bertie, April 23, 1933 [**572**] b.1874, a.58. CADI, CAT

ROBERTSON, William, July 17, 1909, a.64. CADI, DC

ROBINSON, William, September 30, 1926, b.12-07-1837 PA, a.88 years 9 months 23 days, single, laborer, father William ROBINSON, mother Mary HUNTER, 67 years in California, 10 months 3 days at the place of death, died in the county hospital, buried in the county cemetery. CADI, CEN, DC, MIC

ROCHAT, Louis S., December 18, 1935 [**374**] b.1869, a.68. CADI, CAT, DC

RODANDO, Francisco, August 30, 1921, a.73; 1920 Census (Sonoma County Farm and Hospital) T625-151-12B, a.72, b.Mexico, emigrated 1872, naturalized in 1905, aka "RODAUDO, Frasisco." CADI, CEN, DC

RODGERS, Joseph, July 22, 1936 [**226**] a.72. CADI, CAT, DC

RODRIQUEZ, Isabel Palacio, September 17, 1937 [**493**] b.5-09-1937 Pescadero, San Mateo County, a.4 months, a resident of the "Blosi Ranch," Windsor, parents Ausencio RODRIGUEZ and Inez PALACIO, aka "RODRIQUES, Isabel." CADI, CAT, DC, MIC, NEW

Newspaper records
"Death Claims Infant," *The Press Democrat*, 9-18-1937.

RODRIGUEZ, Manuel, September 11, 1937 [**494**] b.1-01-1937, a.8 months, a resident of the Miller Ranch, parents Joseph RODRIGUEZ and Victoria RAYS (REYS?), aka "RODRIQUES, Manuel." CADI, CAT, DC, MIC, NEW

Newspaper records
"Infant Son Dies," *The Press Democrat*, 9-12-1937.

ROGERS, Morton, October 11, 1931 [**532**] b.1862, a.69, spouse "ROGERS, E. M." CADI, CAT, DC

ROGERS, William, June 19, 1935 [**236**] b.1880 HI, a.55, ranch worker. CADI, CAT, DC, NEW

Newspaper records
"William Rogers, 55, Of Sebastopol, Dies," *The Press Democrat*, 6-20-1935.

ROMONA, Manuel, May 14, 1906, b.Central America, a.30, single, laborer, died in Sebastopol, run over by an electric trolley car while drunk. Comment: Due to the earthquake, this time period had limited Santa Rosa newspaper coverage and there are no surviving Sebastopol newspapers. The accident was covered in Petaluma, where the newspaper article said Romona, an Indian, was sleeping on the tracks "not far from McCauley's station." The historical community of McCauley was located near Sebastopol and Wright roads, an area now part of Santa Rosa. CADI, MIC, NEW

Newspaper records
"Briefs," *Petaluma Daily Courier*, May 15, 1906.

RONCONI, Frank, August 19, 1940, b.2-1876 Italy, a.64 years 6 months, widowed, former wife's name unknown, laborer, parents names unknown, veteran status blank, a resident of Upham Street in Petaluma, 35 years in the USA, 22 years in California, entered the hospital 8-25-1938, died in the county hospital, buried 8-22-1940 in the "Co. Burial Grounds," aka "RANCONI, Frank." BOI, CADI, DC, MIC, NEW

Newspaper records
"Petaluma Man Dies In S. R.," *Petaluma Argus-Courier*, 8-20-1940.

ROOT, Daniel, July 7, 1932 [**415**] b.2-2-1852 PA, a.80, single, 42 years in California, a resident of Glen Ellen, relatives in New Holland, PA, died at the county hospital. CADI, CAT, DC, MIC, NEW

Newspaper records
"Daniel Root Dies in Local Hospital," *The Press Democrat*, 7-08-1932.

ROSANDER, Viven, July 9, 1921, b.6-12-1901 WA, a.20, male, single, laborer, father Otto ROSANDER (b.Sweden), mother unknown (b.Sweden), 7 months 24 days in California, 3 months 24 days in the county hospital, buried in the county farm cemetery. CADI, DC, MIC

ROSS, Frances S., August 13, 1936 [**221**] b.1846 Sausalito, Marin County, female, a.90, Indian, widowed, 8 years in Santa Rosa, spouse "ROSS, J.," aka "ROSS, Francis." CADI, CAT, DC, MIC

ROSSETTA, Martin, June 4, 1918, b.Italy, age "about 73," single, laborer (wood chopper), father Martin ROSSETTA (b.Italy), mother unknown (b.Italy), a resident of Sebastopol Avenue, Santa Rosa, 40 years in California, 7 months at the county hospital, #133, buried in the county farm cemetery. CADI, DC, MIC, REG

ROSSI, Celso, November 9, 1940, b.4-14-1895, a.45, a resident of Petaluma, mother CROPLER, father ROSSI. BOI, CADI, DC

ROSTAN, James, February 7, 1937 [**273**] b.1848 NY, a.89, marital status unknown, occupation miner, father John ROSTAN (b.unknown), mother Marie BRISCOL (b.England), 62 years in California, 22 years at the place of death, died in the county hospital, buried 2-10-1937 in the "county plot," aka "ROSTON, James." Comment: In the newspaper article, ROSTAN claimed to have been raised on an island in the English Channel and to have crossed the channel to fight for France, presumably in the Franco-Prussian War of 1870–71. ROSTAN's presence in the hospital was said to have been due to hop poisoning, which blinded him. CADI, CAT, CEN, DC, MIC, NEW

Census records
1900   (Yolo County) T623-116-14, a.62, b.August 1838 NY-NY-NY, miner.
1910   Not found.

1920   (Sonoma County Farm and Hospital) T625-151-12B, a.68, single, b.NY-NY-NY, inmate.
1930   (Sonoma County Farm and Hospital) T626-222-223A, a.82, single, b.NY-U.S.-England, inmate.

Newspaper records
"'Blind Jim,' in County 62 Years, Dies At 89; In Hospital Here Since 1915," *The Press Democrat*, 2-09-1937.

ROTHENBERGER, Ranis, December 11, 1933 [**517**] a.67, aka "RATHENBERGER, Rauis." CADI, CAT

ROUSSEAU, George F., November 17, 1930 [**742**] b.1854, a.76, aka "ROUSSEAN, Geo. F." or "ROUSSEAU, George S." CADI, CAT, DC

ROY, Harry E., September 4, 1908, b.NJ, a.54, parents b.NJ, laborer, died at the county hospital. CADI, DC, MIC

ROYCE, George, May 10, 1925, a.72. CADI, DC

RUGEN, John, January 3, 1942, b.7-03-1855, a.86, a resident of Webster Street in Petaluma, mother OTTEN, father RUGEN, hospital #4512. BOI, CADI, DC

RUGG, Josua, June 30, 1934 [**511**] b.1851, a.83; 1930 Census (Sonoma County Farm and Hospital) T626-222-223A, "RUGG, Jeshua," a.78, single, b.Canada, emigrated 1866, alien, patient. CADI, CAT, CEN, DC

RUGG, Wm., October 20, 1929 [**687**] b.1852, a.77. CADI, CAT, CC

RULAND, Joseph, January 27, 1916, b.1-25-1844 France, a.72 years 2 days, single, laborer, father Louis RULAND, mother Catherine RADER (both b.France), 8 months 9 days at the place of death, 27 years in California, died in the county hospital, buried 1-29-1916 in the Sonoma County Farm Cemetery. BP, CADI, DC, MIC, REG

RYAN, Frank, July 3, 1921, b.11-05-1864 PA, a.56 years 7 months 26 days, widowed, laborer, transient, father William RYAN (b.Ireland), mother Margaret LUCAS (b.England), 2 months at the place of death, 15 years in California, buried July 1921 [exact date not specified] in the "county farm cemetery;" 1920 Census (Healdsburg) T625-150-141, a.53, b.U.S., single, occupation wood cutter. Comment: No Healdsburg obituary. CADI, CEN, DC, MIC

RYAN, Mathew, September 27, 1938 [**173**] b.1869, a.69, transient, a "hospital case" [indigent?]. BOI, CADI, CAT, DC

SAABECLEA, Augustine, April 21, 1921, b.Mexico, a.38, parents b.Mexico, married, spouse Rosie SAABECLEA, laborer for C. W. WILSON, a resident of Windsor, 13 years in U.S., 12 years in California, 5 days at the place of death, aka "SAABEDA or SAABEDEA, Augustine." CADI, DC, MIC

SAINTTI, Antonio, April 20, 1912, b.Italy, a.61, parents b.Italy, divorced, farm laborer, 10 years in California, county hospital #5806, buried at the Sonoma County Farm, aka "SANSETTI or SAIUTTI, Antonio;" 1910 Census (Sonoma County Farm and Hospital) T624-109-30, a.59, divorced, b.Italy, emigrated 1895. Comment: The name may be SANSETTI. CADI, CEN, DC, MIC

SAIS, Angela, February 4, 1910, b.4-02-1909 in Sonoma County, a.10 months 2 days, male, Indian, father Gabriel SAIS, mother Rachel [Raphiel?] CRUISE (both b.CA), a resident of Healdsburg, buried in the Sonoma County Farm Cemetery. No Healdsburg obituary. CADI, DC, MIC

SAIS, Raphel C., Mrs., February 18, 1910, b.Sonoma County, a.18, female, Indian, married, housewife, parents b.CA, buried in the Sonoma County Farm Cemetery; 1910 Census (Sonoma County Farm and Hospital) T624-109-30A, a.18, married, Indian, b.U.S., mother of one child, one child living. Comment: Might this be the mother of Angela SAIS? If Mrs. SAIS really died in February 1910, she should not have been in the 1910 Census. However, the enumerator wrote on the Census form that he worked from the monthly hospital reports so he might have got out-of-date information. CADI, CEN, DC, MIC

SAKIL, No, August 6, 1907, b.Japan, a.35, male, parents b.Japan, laborer, 2 years in California, died at the county hospital, #5126, buried in the Sonoma County Farm Cemetery. CADI, CC, DC, MIC

SALES, Henry, July 13, 1915, age "about 67," single, laborer, died at the county hospital, #7377, buried in the Sonoma County Farm Cemetery. Comment: The age at death was hard to determine as the CADI image was hard to read and so was the handwritten death record. The death record is "about 6—" while the CADI entry is "—7." Therefore, "about 67" is chosen as the most likely correct age. BP, CADI, DC, MIC

SALIMINA, Augustino, October 19, 1924, a.50. CADI, DC

SALVI, Andrew J., March 7, 1913, a.34, aka "SALVI, Audrew J.;" 1910 Census (Pleasanton, Alameda County) T624-72-79, a.32, b.Italy, emigrated 1890, status "pa" (naturalization papers applied for), occupation "barkeeper in saloon." CADI, CEN, DC

SANDERSON, John, March 13, 1933 [570] b.1862, a.71. CADI, CAT

* SANSETTI see SAINTTI (1912).

SANTIAGO, Levandro, May 28, 1911, a.53, aka "SANTIAGO, Levanclro." CADI, DC

SATHER, Peter, January 19, 1943, b.3-11-1879, a.63, a resident of Route 2, Sebastopol, mother OREN, father SATHER. BOI, CADI, DC

SAUNDERS, Jessie T., August 31, 1934 [504] a.55, a resident of Piper Street in Healdsburg. No Healdsburg obituary. CADI, CAT, DC, NEW

Newspaper records
"Saunders' Rites Scheduled Today," *The Press Democrat*, 9-01-1934.

SCHAEFFER, Oscar Barry, November 29, 1940, b.4-28-1867 Missouri, a.73. CADI, DC

SCHARA, Frederick, February 20, 1931 [538] b.1868, a.62. CADI, CAT, DC

SCHARFENBERG, John C., September 9, 1937 [**305**] b.1856 Germany, a.81, retired cooper. CADI, CAT, DC, NEW

Newspaper records
"Scharfenberg, 81, Dies at Hospital," *The Press Democrat*, 9-10-1937.
"Scharfenberg Rites Today," *The Press Democrat*, 9-14-1937.

SCHLEIMANN, Carle, March 20, 1906, b.Germany, a.65, married, laborer. CADI, DC, MIC

SCHLOBOHM, Guse, June 4, 1917, b.4-14-1836 Germany, a.84 years 1 month 14 days, single, occupation baker, father Harry SCHLOBOHM, mother Rebecca MANGELS (both b.Germany), 3 months 17 days at the place of death, 50 years in California, died in the county hospital, buried 6-11-1917 in the Sonoma County Farm Cemetery. Comment: Not found in the 1910 Census. CADI, CC, CEN, MIC, REG

SCHMIDT, Carl, January 7, 1916, b.Germany, age 95, parents b.Germany, barber and watchmaker, died in the county hospital, #3007, buried 1-08-1916 in the Sonoma County Farm Cemetery. BP, CADI, DC, 1914 GR, REG

SCHMIDT, Gottfried, December 21, 1938 [**178**] b.1-04-1869 Switzerland, a.69, a resident of Monte Rio, 15 years in California, died at the county hospital, aka "SCMIDT, Gottfried" or "SCHMID, Goettfeld." BOI, CADI, CAT, DC, MIC

SCHMIDT, John M., November 4, 1934 [**580**] b.1867, a.67, spouse "C. V. SCHMIDT." Comment: Not in the 1910 or 1920 Census. CADI, CAT

SCHOPP, Fritz, January 25, 1934 [**428**] b.3-08-1868 Germany, a.65, single, a resident of Petaluma, father Lendick SCHOPP, mother Elizabeth BOLERLE (?), in the U.S. since 1897, in California since 1918, aka "SCHOFF or SCHUFF, Fritz." Comment: The handwritten death record was hard to read; the spelling "SCHOPP" is from CADI. No obituary. CADI, CAT, DC, MIC

SCHULTE, Frank, September 19, 1938 [**170**] b.3-27-1860 MI, a.78 years 5 months 22 days, single, laborer, father John SCHULTE, mother Josephine SCHULTE, parents place of birth unknown, length of residence unknown, died at 15 South Main Street, buried 9-21-1938 in the county cemetery, aka "SCHUITZ, Frank." Comment: Not found in the 1920 Census for California. BOI, CADI, CAT, CEN, DC, MIC, SAN

Comment: The Sanborn fire map shows Schulte's residence at 15 South Main Street to be "sleeping rooms in loft" over a business on the first floor. This brick building, which somehow survived the 1906 earthquake, was originally Frank McGregor's "Fashion Stables." It later became a 'garage' devoted, like so much of modern Santa Rosa, to the care and feeding of the automobile. BOI has the Frank Schulte residence at 9 Main Street, which shows on the map as a blacksmith's shop in the Fashion Stables building.

SCHULTZ, Fritz, February 16, 1908, a.62. Comment: Not found in the 1900 Census. CADI, DC

SCHULTZ, John, February 4, 1944, b.4-18-1856, a.87. CADI, DC

SCHUMICHEAL, John, April 2, 1911, a.74. Comment: Not found in the 1900 or 1910 U.S. Census. CADI, CEN, DC

SCOTT, Clyde, August 21, 1936 [**220**] b.1878, a.58. CADI, CAT, DC

SCOTT, Della, December 24, 1899, a.25, birthplace unknown, died at the county hospital, buried in the county farm cemetery. No *Press Democrat* obituary was found. DEA, REG

SCOTT, Owen Gregg, October 13, 1906, a.42, single, laborer, died in the county hospital, buried in the Sonoma County Farm Cemetery. CADI, DC

SEE, Haw, March 12, 1888, a.62, male, "died at Santa Rosa." DEA, REG

SEE, Leong, December 1, 1906, a.65. Comment: Leong SEE was not found in the 1900 Census. CADI, CEN, DC

SEN, Wong, November 25, 1926, age "about 64," single, died at 620 2nd Street, Santa Rosa. CADI, DC

SERINI, Jim, August 9, 1935 [**240**] b.1883, a.52. CADI, CAT, DC

* SEVEN, Chung see CHUNG, Seven (1887).

SHAMOAN, Joseph, April 26, 1911, a.5 hours, father Anthony SHAMOAN, mother Lennie (?) SHAMOAN (both b."Beirut Jerusalem"), buried in the Sonoma County Farm Cemetery; possible parents 1910 Census (Santa Rosa) T624-109-167, "SHAMON, Jo. A.," a.27, male, white, b.Turkey, wife Mary, a.25, b.Turkey (spoken language Syrian). Comment: These people may have been from what contemporary atlases called "Modern Palestine," although Beirut and Jerusalem are miles apart. CADI, CEN, DC, MIC

SHANNON, Erwin V., July 13, 1925, a.64. CADI, DC

SHARP, Daniel, July 21, 1928 [**717**] b.1862, a.66. CADI, CAT

SHAW, William, July 26, 1934 [**508**] b.1-21-1864 MI, a.70 years 6 months 5 days, a resident of Geyserville, single, laborer, unemployed, father Lester SHAW, mother Letitia BARROUGHS (both b.MI), 42 years in California, 8 days in the hospital, buried 7-27-1934 in the Sonoma County Cemetery; possible 1920 Census (Marysville, Yuba County) T625-153-269, a.55, single, b.MI-MI-NY, ranch laborer. CADI, CAT, CEN, MIC

Comment: The *Catalogue of Grave Markers* (CAT) has duplicated [**508**] in error. The other listing is Jerry DEVINE, who actually is buried in [**503**].

SHEEPERS, James, April 20, 1927, b.4-01-1849 Belgium, a.78, single, 41 years in California, 10 years at the county hospital. CADI, DC, MIC

SHEPARD, Margin [Martin], December 14, 1905, b.NY, a.77, single, farmer, hospital #2053; 1900 Census (Eighth St., Petaluma) T623-114-194, b.December 1828, a.71, single, b.NY-NY-Wales, peddler. Comment: The spelling "Margin" is an error but it is used by both the county death record and CADI and so is included here for consistency. The 1870, 1880, 1890 [substitute] and 1900 Census records and the *Argus* all spell the name "Martin." Only the

---

Democrat, copying the death record, spells the name "Margin." In the 1870 Census (Analy Township) is a third brother, Caleb, age 37; Caleb later went back east and in 1900 was in St. Joseph County, Indiana. Martin, the elder brother, was listed in the 1900 Census as "head" of the family, with Morris as "brother." CADI, CEN, DC, MIC, NEW

SHEPARD, Morris, December 27, 1905, b.OH, a.75, single, farmer, father M. SHEPARD (b.NY), aka "SHEPHERD, Morris;" 1900 Census (Eighth St., Petaluma) T623-114-194, b.October 1830, a.69, single, b.OH-NY-Wales. Comment: Morris died two weeks after his older brother Martin. The cause in part, according to notes made by hospital staff on the death certificate, was "exhaustion from grief." The brothers were buried side by side. Unfortunately, their graves are unidentified. CADI, CEN, DC, MIC, NEW

Newspaper records
"Passed Away At The Hospital," *Petaluma Argus*, 12-15-1905.
"Death at the Hospital," *The Press Democrat*, 12-15-1905.
"Follows His Aged Brother," *Petaluma Argus*, 12-28-1905.
"Brothers Are United Again," *The Press Democrat*, 12-29-1905.

SHIELDS, Thomas, March 1, 1938 [**142**] b.1897, a.40. BOI, CADI, CAT, DC, NEW

Newspaper records
"Relief Worker Dead," *Santa Rosa Republican*, 3-01-1938.
"Thomas Shields Dies," *The Press Democrat*, 3-02-1938.

SHINN, Casswell, April 11, 1916, b.2-23-1855 IL, a.61 years 1 months 19 days, widowed, painter, father William SHINN (b.VA), mother Susan CUNNINGHAM (b.IL), 8 days at the place of death, 6 years in California, died in the county hospital, buried 4-12-1916 in the Sonoma County Farm Cemetery. BP, CADI, DC, REG

SHIRE, George, December 18, 1913, a.52; 1910 Census (East Windsor Precinct) T624-109-140, a.47, single, b.NY-Germany-Germany, hired man on Adam BARTH farm. CADI, CEN, DC

SHOCK, Edward, December 17, 1902, b.LA, a.90, a resident of the county farm, aka "SCHOCK, Edward." DEA, CEN, GR, NEW

Census records
1880 (Mendocino Township) T9-84-196, a.65, b.LA-MD-MD, carpenter (10 months unemployed), wife Elizabeth (a.62, b.PA-NY-NY).
1900 (Sonoma County Farm and Hospital) T623-114-257, b.September 1815 LA-MD-PA, a.84, widowed, pensioner.

Newspaper records
"Funeral of a Nonagenarian," *The Press Democrat*, 12-19-1902.
"Old Resident Dead," *Healdsburg Enterprise*, 12-20-1902.
"Over the Hills to the Poor House," *Healdsburg Tribune*, 12-25-1902.

* SHROM see STROM (1908).

SIEGLER, Casper, December 19, 1931 [**557**] b.1891, a.40, aka "SIEGLER, Caspar." CADI, CAT, DC, NEW

Newspaper records
"Found Lying Unconscious," *Petaluma Argus-Courier*, 12-16-1931.
"Petaluma Laborer Found Injured In Locked Room Dies," *The Press Democrat*, 12-20-1931.

SILSBEE, Bert R., October 31, 1936 [**205**] b.1874, a.62. Comment: Not in the 1920 California Census. CADI, CAT, DC

SIMONI, Louis, September 25, 1931 [**552**] b.1864, 67. CADI, CAT, DC

SIMPSON, Charles A., September 19, 1941, b.11-27-1865 CA, a.75, mother BLAZER, father SIMPSON. CADI, DC

SING, Lee, March 11, 1892, b.China, a.45, died in Santa Rosa, buried at the county farm. DEA, REG

SING, Lung, October 8, 1900, a.50, male, a resident of Sebastopol, buried in the county cemetery. DEA, OLE

SING, Wong, June 25, 1931 [823] b.1881, a.49. CADI, CAT, DC

SING, Wong, November 25, 1941, b.6-16-1847 China, a.94, male, a resident of 2nd Street, Santa Rosa. BOI, CADI, DC

SING, Wong Tong, January 9, 1927, a.70, single, known as "Wong the chairmaker," died at the county hospital, inquest (hit by car). Comment: This person was missed when the records were searched in 1988. CADI, COR, MIC, NEW

Newspaper records
"Aged Chinese Hit By Auto Here, May Not Survive, Fear," *The Press Democrat*, 12-23-1926.
"Chinese Dies From Injury By Machine," *The Press Democrat*, 1-11-1927.

SING, Yup Ah, August 29, 1912, b.China, a.72, male, "farm laborer, ranch work," father SING Young of "6th Company," mother unknown (both b.China), 30 years in California, 10 years local, died at 628 2nd Street, Santa Rosa, buried 8-31-1912 in the county farm cemetery, aka "SIN, Yup Ah." Comment: The Rural Cemetery book lists "YUP, Ah Sing" and the correct information but there is no tombstone. Given the existing prejudice against the Chinese at that time, his burial there is unlikely although not impossible. CADI, DC, MIC, RUR

*SINN see LINN (1931).

SKOK, Joseph, September 27, 1940, b.3-19-1872 Austria, a.68 years 6 months 8 days, single, chair maker, parents unknown, a resident of Guerneville, 33 years in the USA, 25 years in California and local, 9 days in the hospital and died there, buried 10-01-1940 in the "County Cemetery." BOI, CADI, DC, MIC

SLATTERWHITE, William C., October 28, 1913, a.53. CADI, DC

SMITH, Charles, December 16, 1913, a.74; 1910 Census (Sonoma County Farm and Hospital) T624-109-29A, a.79, b.U.S.-U.S.-U.S., widowed. CADI, CEN, DC

SMITH, Charles, June 16, 1931 [**550**] b.1850, a.81. CADI, CAT, DC

SMITH, Charles, October 6, 1937 [**313**] b.1860, a.77, living with Mr. and Mrs. S. BOURRAS of Healdsburg. CADI, CAT, DC, NEW

Newspaper records
"Healdsburg Resident Dies," *The Press Democrat*, 10-07-1937.
"Charles Smith Died Wednesday," *Sotoyome Scimitar*, 10-07-1937.

SMITH, Derian Warren, March 12, 1914, b.MA, a.69, single, male, laborer, father Harry SMITH, mother Amanda MITCHELL (both b.MA), a resident of Healdsburg, 30 years in California, died at the county hospital, #6971, buried at the Sonoma County Farm. Comment: The death certificate has age 59. DC has "Dlrian," an error caused by the death record writer, who made the "e" in "Derian" with a big loop later misread as an "l." CADI, DC, MIC

SMITH, Dora, December 1928 [**732**] Comment: There is no record of this person in Sonoma County beyond mention in the *Catalogue*. The order of dates in the grave marker sequence suggests a death in mid-to-late December 1928. The death could have occurred in another county, such as San Francisco. Checked alternate first names "Dorothy," "Eudora," and "Theodora," and alternate last names "Smeith" and "Smyth[e]." No obituary. CADI, CAT, CC, DC

SMITH, Elmer, February 8, 1931 [**540**] b.1875, a.56. CADI, CAT, DC

SMITH, Emma, October 8, 1911, a.54. CADI, DC

SMITH, Frank, September 19, 1934 [**431**] b.1856, a.78. CADI, CAT, DC

SMITH, Harry, December 26, 1925, a.41. CADI, DC

SMITH, Henry, May 27, 1920, a.66. Comment: SMITH's family was from Alsace-Lorraine, which 'moved' after World War One from Germany to France, hence the different birthplaces in the Census records. CADI, CEN, DC

Census records
1910 (Sonoma County Farm and Hospital) T624-109-29B, a.56, b.Germany, single, emigrated 1869.
1920 (Sonoma County Farm and Hospital) T625-151-12B, a.67, b.France, emigrated 1874, naturalized 1881.

SMITH, James T., December 3, 1929 [**686**] b.1862, a.67. CADI, CAT

SMITH, John, September 13, 1937 [**304**] b.1847 Potter Valley, Mendocino County, a.90, Indian, widowed (spouse was Nora SMITH), aka "SMITH, John Sr.," informant John SMITH, Jr. CADI, CAT, DC, MIC

SMITH, L. J., January 10, 1897, b.KY, a.35, county hospital #1345, "interred at farm." DEA, REG

SMITH, Robert, March 24, 1944, b.1884, a.60, died in the county hospital. BOI, CADI, DC

SMITH, Thomas G. [J.], January 5, 1918, b.11-17-1861 OR, a.56 years 1 month 19 days, widowed, laborer, a resident of Petaluma, father Alexander SMITH (b.Scotland), mother Catherine DEPE (b.Canada), 2 years 5 months in California, died in the county hospital, #8441, buried 1-09-1918 in the Sonoma County Farm Cemetery. ARCH, CADI, DC, MIC, NEW, REG

Comment: The Sacramento newspaper articles refer to this subject as "John Smith," but this may simply have been a form of his full name, "Thomas John Smith." A search of the *Sacramento Bee* for this time period failed to turn up anyone else who could have been the man sentenced to prison for grand theft. The records of Folsom Prison, now in the state archives, show Smith, a 64 year old teamster, was sentenced to four years for grand larceny and was paroled on August 7, 1917, having served about nineteen months. The records noted he "died on parole 1/6/18" [*sic*]. The use of the initial "G." in the death record appears to have been an error.

Newspaper records
"Theft Opens Jail; Crime Story Failed," *Sacramento Bee*, 12-15-1915.
"Man Who Tried To Break Into Jail Gets 4 Years," *Sacramento Bee*, 12-21-1915.
"Passed Away At Hospital," *Petaluma Argus*, 1-08-1918.

SNELL, Baby Girl, July 2, 1938 [**502**] a.4 hours (premature), father Forest A. SNELL (b.Frankford, MI), mother Mary DOTO (b.MS), residents of Monte Rio, buried 7-06-1938 in the county cemetery. CADI, CAT, DC, MIC

SNELSON, John, January 26, 1916, b.MO, age "about 83," widowed, parents b.MO, farmer, 6 years at the county farm, buried 1-29-1916 in the Sonoma County Farm Cemetery; 1910 Census (Sonoma County Farm and Hospital) T624-109-29A, "NELSON, John," a.79, single, b.U.S.-U.S.-U.S. BP, CADI, CEN, DC, 1914 GR, MIC, REG

SNIDER, Albert, February 22, 1908, b.CA, age 19 years 10 months, single, laborer, parents unknown, died at the county hospital, #5270, buried in the Sonoma County Farm Cemetery. Comment: Not found in the 1900 Census under SINDER/SNIDER/SNYDER. No *Press Democrat* obituary was found. CADI, DC, MIC

SNOW, James Leonard, August 8, 1920, a.64; 1920 Census (Sonoma County Farm and Hospital) T625-151-12B, a.63, b.KY-KY-KY, widowed. CADI, CEN, DC

SNUGG, Gus, February 24, 1936 [**250**] b.1852, a.77. CADI, CAT, DC

SOMARNO, Rose Marie, September 1, 1938 [**584**] a.4 months. CADI, CAT, DC

* SONORA, Lapislado, March 8, 1939, b.Mexico, a.59, single, laborer, resident on Route 1, Sebastopol, parents unknown, aka "SONORA, Albert." Comment: DC error, buried in "Catholic Cemetery." BOI, CADI, DC, MIC

Newspaper record
"Albert Sonora Dies," *The Press Democrat*, 3-09-1939.

SOTO, Mary, June 22, 1917, age "about 50," Indian, single, born in Sonoma County, 27 days at the place of death, life in California, died in the county hospital, #8061, buried 6-23-1917 in the Sonoma County Farm Cemetery. BP, CADI, REG

* SOULE, Andrew Jackson, December 5, 1899, b.NJ, a.70, died at the county hospital, buried (according to the death record) at the county farm; 1880 Census (T9-84-208) "SOULE, A.J., b.NY-NY-NY, a.51, single, farmer." Comment: Andrew Soule is also listed as being buried in Santa Rosa Rural Cemetery and does have a tombstone there. Although no records indicating removal have been found, it is possible someone paid to have his body exhumed and re-interred. The Healdsburg obituary said he was buried "by his friends." If so, the Rural Cemetery grave may have been purchased by one of them. That would suggest the Register of Deaths is in error. [The Andrew Soule, b.NY, age 47, with wife and family in the 1880 Census of Siskiyou County is a different person; he is still there in 1900 and 1910.] CEN, DEA, NEW, REG, RUR

Newspaper records
[no title] *Petaluma Argus*, 12-08-1899. [The *Argus* gave his birthplace as NY.]
"Death of a Pioneer," *Healdsburg Tribune*, 12-14-1899.

SOUSA, Wayne Donald, April 15, 1939 [**586**] age 9 days and hence born about 4-06-1939, son of Mr. and Mrs. Manuel SOUZA, died in San Francisco. BOI, CADI, CAT, MIC, NEW
Comment: Wayne Sousa confounded this author for several years because the "*Catalogue of Grave Markers*" listed only his name, the year 1939, and the grave number [**586**]. There was no Wayne Sousa/Souza or [unknown first name] Sousa/Souza in the Sonoma County records for 1939.
Eventually, the name "Baby Sousa" was found in the "Burial of Indigents" with a 4-15-1939 date of death and a note that $10.00 was paid for "Trans[portation]." With the exact date of death in hand, a Wayne Sousa, age 9 days, was found in the California Death Index for San Francisco on that date. One may conclude the infant Sousa was born in Sonoma County and sent to San Francisco for neonatal care. Dying in that county, the baby was returned to Sonoma County for burial, hence the "transportation" charge. This was confirmed by the newspapers, which also noted the baby died of "exfoliative dermatitis."
Finally, a birth record for "Wayne Donald Sousa" was found in VitalSearch <http://www.vitalsearch-ca.com/> with a birthdate of 4-06-1939, the

mother's last name of DRYSVALE [*sic*], and the place of birth as Sonoma County.

Newspaper records
"Baby Here Sheds Skin," *The Press Democrat,* 4-15-1939.
"Baby Rushed To S.F. Dies Of Rare Malady," *The Press Democrat,* 4-16-1939.

SOUTHARD, Walter, July 5, 1931 [**534**] b.1857, a.74. <u>CADI, CAT, DC</u>

SOW, Wong, February 3, 1924, age "about 71," died in the Mary Jesse Hospital, Santa Rosa. <u>CADI, DC, MIC</u>

SOWERS, Orlando, September 19, 1905, b.1827 PA, a.78, laborer, a resident of the Sonoma County Farm, aka "SOWERS, Orlande." <u>CADI, DC, MIC</u>

SPAGNOLA, Robert, March 1, 1938 [**143**] b.12-25-1896 Italy, age 41, occupation merchant (shoe store), married, spouse Louise SPAGNOLA, father Alphonso SPAGNOLA (b.Italy), mother Pasqualina SPAGNOLA (b.Italy), 20 years in USA and California, 1½ years local, died at the county hospital, buried 3-04-1938 in the county cemetery. <u>BOI, CADI, CAT, DC, DIR, MIC, NEW</u>

Comment: The 1924 *Press Democrat* directory of Petaluma lists on page 405 "Spagunolo, Roberto, shoemaker, r[esidence] 515 Washington;" the 1939 Polk directory of Petaluma lists on page 128 "Spagnolo, Louise (wid Robt) h[ome] 112 Fair." BOI lists his residence at the time of his death as 112 Fair St, Petaluma.

Newspaper records
"Petaluman Dies," *The Press Democrat,* 3-03-1938.
"Hobert Spagnola Dies In S. R. Hospital," *Petaluma Argus-Courier,* 3-04-1938.

SPARKS, Charles O., September 17, 1937 [**310**] born "about 1877" in Iowa, a.60, transient, a resident of the University Hotel in Palo Alto (Santa Clara County), died at 422 Wilson Street, Santa Rosa; coroner's inquest (noted on death certificate) indicates death was a homicide due to gunshot wounds. <u>CADI, DC, MIC, NEW</u>

Comment: The newspaper articles of September 1937 identified this man as "Thomas O'Brien," "Tom Owens," and "Pat Sullivan." The *Catalogue of Grave Markers* lists "Sullivan or O'Brien, Patrick, died 1937, grave 310." However, there is no death record or entry in the California Death Index (1930-1939) for these names and this date in Sonoma County. The *Catalogue* was based upon hospital records and may have been in error, since Sparks was not correctly identified until later, by the Sonoma County Coroner.

The Coroner's report lists the man as 'Charles O. Sparks' and does not mention his aliases. The *Catalogue* does not list the decedent by the name 'Sparks' even though his death record clearly shows him being buried in the "County Cemetery." Since there <u>is</u> a death record for Sparks which matches the known facts of the case, he is likely the person in grave number 310. Further, Sparks' date of death fits the sequence of dates in which marker 310 belongs.

Newspaper records
"Man Mistaken For Burglar, Killed Here," *Santa Rosa Daily Republican*, 9-17-1937.
"Seek Identity Of Man Killed In Bakery Here," *Santa Rosa Daily Republican*, 9-18-1937.
"Prowler Shot To Death When He Ignores Orders To Halt," *The Press Democrat*, 9-18-1937.

SPARKS, Russel, September 15, 1908, b.AR, a.27, single, occupation clerk, hospital #5345. Comment: Russel SPARKS was not found in California for the 1900 Census. Due to his birth in Arkansas, 146 "SPARKS" entries in the 1900 Arkansas Census were searched but no "Russel" was found. CADI, DC, MIC

SPENCER, John A., May 27, 1911, b.KY, a.39, single, laborer, parents b.KY, 6 years in California, died at the county hospital, #6175, buried in the county farm cemetery; possible 1910 Census (Big River Township, Mendocino County) T624-88-93, "SPENSER, John A.," a.26, b.KY-KY-KY, single, lumberman. CADI, DC, MIC

SPILLANE, Jerry, January 26, 1917, b.4-13-1849 Ireland, a.66, widowed, occupation foreman, father Jerry SPILLANE, mother Margaret CALAHAN (both b.Ireland), 45 years in California, died at the county hospital, #7272, buried 1-30-1917 in the Sonoma County Farm Cemetery; 1910 Census (Tomales, Marin County) T624-88-311, a.62, b.Ireland, married 13 years, no children, wife's name not given, emigrated 1870, naturalized citizen, railroad foreman. BP, CADI, CEN, MIC, REG

SPINETTI, Henry, October 26, 1918, b.1878 Italy, a.40, single, farm laborer, father Louis SPINETTI, mother Carola TRUMBELLA (both b.Italy), a resident of Cloverdale, 11 years 4 months 26 days in California, 8 days in the hospital, #348. CADI, DC, REG

SPRUNK, Henry, December 16, 1931 [663] b.1848, a.83, aka "SPUNX, Henry;" the *Indigent Records* show him to be a resident of Windsor, a widower with no children, a.79, owns a house and lot, has income from the eggs of 50 chickens, for reason of old age he requested $10 per month on 8-18-1917 and received $8 per month on 11-13-1917. CADI, CAT, CC, DC, IND

SPURR, Leonora (Nora), December 20, 1928, b.CA, age "about 62," parents "no record," 37 years in the hospital, life in California, hospital #123. Comment: Most of the death certificate information is in error. Nora SPURR was developmentally disabled; she spent 50 years, her entire adult life, at the Sonoma County Farm and at her death was almost 74 years old. CADI, CEN, DC, FAM, MIC, NEW

Comment: Nora Spurr was born in Bellvue [*sic*], Jackson County, Iowa, the third child and first daughter of attorney Daniel Francis Spurr and his first wife, the former Miss Sarah A. KIRKPATRICK of Illinois. Daniel Spurr appears to be a descendant of Captain Richard Spurr, Loudon County (VA) Militia. Nora's birthdate is most probably in late 1854 or early 1855 based on her age of 5 in the 1860 U.S. Census. This agrees reasonably well with the special schedule "3D" (Defective, Delinquent, and Dependent) of the 1880 Census, which states Nora was admitted to the county farm at age 22 in September, 1878.

Nora may have been a twin: a sibling, Daniel F. Spurr, "son of D. F. and S. A. Spurr," died on June 29, 1855 at the age of 5 months and 7 days and was buried in Iowa. If so, Nora and Daniel's birthdate would have been January 22, 1855. [Source: Iowa Gravestone Photo Project http://iowagravestones.org/gs_view.php?id=219848 accessed 4-23-2007.]

Newspaper records
"Woman Inmate of Hospital for 37 Years Is Dead," *The Press Democrat*, 12-21-1928.

STAHL, John, May 19, 1938 [**156**] b.6-09-1855 Denmark, a.82, father John STAHL, mother Anna FRAU, a resident of the county farm since 1926, 40 years in Santa Rosa, 68 years in California and U.S., aka "STIHL, John;" 1930 Census (Sonoma County Farm and Hospital) T626-222-223A, a.74, single, b.Denmark, emigrated 1870, inmate. BOI, CADI, CAT, CEN, DC, MIC, NEW

Newspaper records
"John Stahl Passes," *The Press Democrat*, 5-20-1938.
"Graveside Service," *The Press Democrat*, 5-21-1938.

STALCUP, Joseph, January 1, 1938 [**135**] b.1863 (CAT error "1963"), a.74, a resident of Sebastopol. BOI, CADI, CAT, DC

STALDER, Peter, July 22, 1934 [**509**] b.1884, a.49. CADI, CAT

STALKER, Julius, February 14, 1936 [**248**] b.1861, a.74. CADI, CAT, DC

* STALOF see LOUSTALOF (1909).

STANLEY, Harry E., October 25, 1906, a.81. Comment: The "Harry E. Stanley," a.39, in the 1900 Census (Riverside County) is too young. CADI, CEN, DC

STANOFF, Richard, May 9, 1931 [**536**] b.1891, a.40. CADI, CAT, DC

STARK, Frank, August 24, 1897, b.CA, a.10, died at the Talmadge Ranch, buried in the county farm cemetery. DEA, REG

STARK, Julia Ann, April 15, 1887, b.CA, a.4 years 3 months 14 days, white, female, single, died at the county farm. DEA, REG

STEIN, Charles R., October 13, 1893, b.1859 OH, hospital #1055, left $1.00 to the county; possible 1880 Census (Jasper County, IA) T9-346-195, "STEIN, Charles R.," a.22 (b.1857) OH-MD-PA, farmer. CEN, DEA, PHY

STEVENSON, John, June 25, 1930 [**541**] b.1834, a.96; 1930 Census (Sonoma County Farm and Hospital) T626-222-223A, a.94, b.CA, Indian, "Full Blood Capella," patient. CADI, CAT, CEN, DC

STEVENSON, Wallace, December 16, 1936 [**198**] b.1857, a.79. CADI, CAT, DC

STIEPAN, John, September 2, 1941, b.5-05-1894, mother EIBEN, father STIEPAN. CADI, DC

STOCKIN, August, November 1, 1905, b.1832 Switzerland, a.73, married, farmer, aka "STACKIN, August." CADI, DC, MIC

STONE, Baby Boy, May 23, 1938 [**455**] stillborn at the county hospital, parents were residents of Graton, father Oransby STONE, mother Pearl WAGGINS (both b.OK). BOI, CADI, CAT, MIC

* STRAND see OSTRAND (1936).

STRANG, Henry, July 7, 1931 [**551**] b.1881, a.50. CADI, CAT, DC, NEW

Newspaper records
"Inquests Into 3 Deaths Held," *The Press Democrat*, 7-09-1931.

STRAUTIN, Hans, March 21, 1938 [**147**] b.1889, a.48, died in the county hospital. BOI, CADI, CAT

STROHMEIER, William H., April 12, 1912, a.81, husband of Johanna, aka "STOHMUIER or STROMIER, William A." Comment: Mr. STROHMEIER's wife, Johanna (q.v.), was also buried in Chanate. CADI, DC

STROM, Andrew, May 3, 1908, b.Sweden, a.72, single, carpenter, 23 years in California, 8 months in the Sonoma County Hospital and died there, #5129, buried in the Sonoma County Farm Cemetery, aka "SHROM, Andrew." CADI, DC, MIC

STROMIER, Johanna, January 5, 1919, b.1822 England, a.96, widow of William H. STROMIER (STROHMEIER), occupation domestic, residence Graton, 64 years in California, 6 years 1 month 21 days in the county hospital, buried in the county farm cemetery. Comment: Mrs. STROMIER's husband, William STROHMEIER (q.v.), was also buried in Chanate. CADI, DC, REG

SUEY, Hue L., April 3, 1909, b.China, a.58, single, died at 632 2nd St., Santa Rosa, aka "LOYE, Suey Hue." Comment: This person was missed in the 1988 search of the records. CADI, REG

SULLIVAN, Patrick, June 6, 1915, b.3-21-1861 Ireland, a.54 years 2 months 15 days, single, laborer, father John SULLIVAN, mother Maria HURLEY (both b.Ireland), 25 years in California, died at the county hospital, #7334, buried in the Sonoma County Farm Cemetery. BP, CADI, DC, MIC

* SULLIVAN, Patrick see SPARKS, Charles (1937).

SUNG, Wong Yup, February 6, 1909, a.61, married, died at 632 2nd Street, Santa Rosa CADI, DC

SUTTON, Henry, March 20, 1923, b.1842 Switzerland, age "about 81," father Martin SUTTON (b.Switzerland), mother unknown, 9 years in California, 8 months at the place of death, died in the county hospital, buried in the county farm cemetery, aka "SUTTER, Henry." CADI, DC, MIC

SWAMP, Lester, April 20, 1928, b.6-25-1892 WI, a.35, Indian, single, farm laborer, a resident of Guerneville, father Paul SWAMP, mother Elizabeth DOUBATO (both b.WI), 4 years in California, hospital #3031, died at the county hospital (tuberculosis), buried in the Sonoma County Farm Cemetery; International Genealogical Index, b.6-25-1892 (Oneida, Brown County, WI), parents Paul SWAMP (b.1866) and Elizabeth DOXATATOR (b.1870) who married 11-06-

---

1891; 1910 Census (Hobart, Brown County, WI) T624-1701-138, Lester SWAMP, a.18, living with parents (Paul and Minnie) and siblings (Minnie is Paul's second wife and not Lester's mother); 1920 Census (Military and Naval, Philippines, Cartel De Espana, Co-K, 27th Infantry) T625-2040-368, a.27, b.WI-WI-WI, single, residence Oneida, WI, occupation soldier. CADI, CEN, DC, IGI, MIL, NPRC

Military service record. WWI draft card <www.ancestry.com> Born 6-25-1892 in Hobart, Brown County, Wisconsin, unemployed, living at home, no previous military service. Physical description: height medium, build medium, dark brown eyes, black hair, no disabilities. Service with the U.S. Army, Infantry, Private, WWI. Service dates: 9-19-1917 to 5-26-1923. Entered service at Jefferson Barracks, Missouri. Separated at the Presidio of San Francisco. Decorations and awards: World War I Victory Medal, World War I Victory Button.

Comment: The SWAMP family of Wisconsin is made up primarily of Oneida Indians from New York. Lester's mother was descended from a DOCHSTADER family that emigrated to New York from Germany around 1800. The Oneidas were members of the Six Nations (Mohawk, Oneida, Onondaga, Cayuga, Seneca and Tuscarora), sometimes called the Civilized Tribes. Known historically but incorrectly as the Iroquois, these nations are the Haudenosaunee, the People of the Longhouse.

SWAN, Edward, September 6, 1926, a.51. CADI, DC

SWANSON, John, August 29, 1929 [**689**] b.1864, a.65. CADI, CAT

SWEATMAN, Solomon J., June 20, 1937 [**293**] b.8-30-1860 TN, a.76, parents Samuel SWEATMAN and Fanny TUCKER (both b.TN), widowed, spouse was Fanny SWEATMAN, a resident of Healdsburg, 17 years in California. No Healdsburg obituary. CADI, CAT, DC, MIC, NEW

Newspaper records
"Sweatman Rites Held," *The Press Democrat*, 6-22-1937.
"Sweatman Funeral," *The Press Democrat*, 6-23-1937.

SWED, Frank, October 3, 1938 [**182**] b.1893, a.45, laborer, death occurred on "Hiway 101 North of S. R.," residence "X Transient," marital status unknown, parents unknown, buried 10-19-1938 in the "Co. Cemetery," informant "Friends," aka "FRANKS, Charles." CADI, CAT, CC, DC, MIC, NEW

Comment: Both names are listed in CADI with the same state file number (63889) so there must have been some question of identification. The death certificate has "Frank Swed or Charles Franks."

Helen WEST (q.v.), who died in the same accident, is buried next to Frank Swed in [**183**].

Newspaper records
"Haub Blamed For Causing Fatal Crash," *The Press Democrat*, 10-14-1938
"Woman Still Unconscious From Crash," *The Press Democrat*, 10-15-1938

SYKES, Joseph, March 13, 1907, a.89; 1900 Census (Sonoma County Farm and Hospital) T623-114-257B, b.October 1822 England, a.77, widowed, emigrated 1842, naturalized citizen. CADI, CEN, DC

TABBERS, Benjamin, November 26, 1912, a.55. CADI, DC

TAIT, George, October 31, 1921, a.84. CADI, CEN, DC

Census records
1910   (Sonoma County Farm and Hospital) T624-109-30A, "TATE, George," a.70, b.U.S.-Ireland-Ireland, widowed.
1920   (Sonoma County Farm and Hospital) T625-151-12B, "TATE, George," a.83, b.IL-Ireland-KY, widowed.

TARACHINI, B. T., January 12, 1943, b.1888, a.55. Comment: We owe our knowledge of this man to an error. When Mr. TARACHINI died, he was given a "county burial" by the firm of Hampton and Eggen, the firm that had the contract to bury the county's indigent dead. TARACHINI's last salary check was to be paid to Hampton and Eggen for the burial but was instead paid to the Sonoma County Hospital, in compensation for medical benefits received. When the error was discovered, a resolution correcting the problem was passed by the Sonoma County Board of Supervisors (39 Minutes 404, 5-08-1944). CADI, MIN

TARTAR, Chris, October 6, 1925, a.64. CADI, DC

TAYLOE, James P., July 3, 1939 [**119**] b.1873, a.65, resident on Webster Street in Petaluma, aka "TAYLOR, James P." Comment: Chanate has two markers numbered "**119**." Either one could mark Mr. Tayloe's grave. BOI, CADI, CAT, DC

TAYLOR, Edward James, April 20, 1936, a.81. CADI, DC

TELLES, Charles C., January 30, 1907, a.33. CADI, DC

TELO, August, April 18, 1930 [**678**] b.1857; 1930 Census (Sonoma County Farm and Hospital) T626-222-223A, a.72, single, b.France-Italy-Italy, speaks Italian, emigrated 1881, alien, patient. CADI, CAT, CEN

TERAO, Tadaichi, February 20, 1923, b.1878 Japan, a.45, single, 17 years in California and U.S. Comment: Tadaichi-san has one of only two intact private grave markers in Chanate. Probably a contract agricultural worker, Mr. TERAO's tombstone would likely have been provided by his contractor. The characters engraved in the stone mean, "Grave of Terao Tadaichi, deceased, age about 45, from Hiroshima prefecture." The date of death is engraved on the top of the stone in Roman characters. CADI, DC, PV

THIBAULT, Joseph, January 1, 1939 [**103**] b.1860, a.78, a resident of the county farm, aka "THIBAUGH, Joseph." BOI, CADI, CAT

THOMAS, Baby Girl, December 19, 1909, "*Unnamed child female of Mary Thomas,*" b.12-19-1909, a.1 hour, father unknown [but <u>not</u> Willard THOMAS], mother Mary CHIO (b.CA), inquest 1-24-1910 [by Coroner Blackburn], death due to "knife wound in throat, feloniously inflicted by Willard Thomas," buried 12-28-1910 in the county farm cemetery, filed 12-28-1910. Comment: The death certificate reads [the baby's body was] "found Jan. 22-09 3-Blks below Cal. Cannery in creek bed." This is an error since the murder was in December, 1909 with the body being found in January, 1910. The Sonoma County records have this infant indexed under the date of filing of the death certificate rather than the date of death. The burial was delayed because the infant's body, preserved in a jar of alcohol, was used as evidence in three murder trials. ARCH, CADI, CEN, CRT, DC, MIC, NEW

<u>Newspaper records</u>
"Murdered And Flung Into Santa Rosa Creek," *The Press Democrat*, 1-25-1910.
"Confront Man and Woman With Their Confessions," *The Press Democrat*, 1-26-1910.
"Believe Mrs. Thomas Was Implicated in the Murder," *The Press Democrat*, 2-01-1910.
"Man and Woman Are Both Charged With Murder," *The Press Democrat*, 2-04-1910.
"Side By Side on Charge of Murder," *The Press Democrat*, 2-15-1910.
"Murdered Child's Body Brought Into the Court," *The Press Democrat*, 4-20-1910.
"Thomas Collapses and Court Has to Adjourn," *The Press Democrat*, 4-21-1910.
"Life Imprisonment the Fate of Willard Thomas," *The Press Democrat*, 4-22-1910.
"May [*sic*] Thomas Will be Tried Tuesday," *The Press Democrat*, 4-23-1910.
"Had Hoped for an Examination Soon," *The Press Democrat*, 4-23-1910.
"Sentence Passed; Prison for Life," *The Press Democrat*, 4-26-1910.
"Body of Child is Again Produced in Evidence," *The Press Democrat*, 4-27-1910.
"'Arch Conspirator' Says Prosecutor of Woman," *The Press Democrat*, 4-28-1910.
"Thomas Jury Locked Up for Night in Courthouse," *The Press Democrat*, 4-29-1910.
"Eight For Acquittal; Four For Conviction," *The Press Democrat*, 4-30-1910.
"The Second Trial Will Begin Today," *The Press Democrat*, 6-15-1910.
"Jury Secured for May Thomas' Second Trial," *The Press Democrat*, 6-16-1910.
"Life and Death Meet in Contrast in Murder Case," *The Press Democrat*, 6-17-1910.
"Jury Acquits May Thomas of the Charge of Murder," *The Press Democrat*, 6-18-1910.

THOMAS, Eli, June 16, 1910, a.77. Comment: DC has 6-16-1909. This person was not found in the 1900 or 1910 Census. CADI, DC

THOMAS, H. W., December 31, 1904, b.MO, a.50, male, "buried by the county." DEA, REG

THOMAS, Henry, September 1, 1885, left $2.50 to the county. Comment: The 1880 Census has many possibilities but the name is too common to determine accurately which one he might be. PHY

THOMPSON, Alex, October 5, 1908, b.Santa Rosa, California, a.52, single, parents b.Ireland, saloon keeper, died in the county hospital, #5362; 1900 Census

(Santa Rosa) T623-114-348, a.44, b.Canada. Comment: The discrepancy of birth places is unexplained. CADI, CEN, DC, MIC

THOMPSON, Frank, November 11, 1928 [**727**] b.1858, a.70. Comment: This person was not found in the 1920 Census of Sonoma County. CADI, CAT

THOMPSON, James, September 17, 1907, a.72. CADI, DC

THOMPSON, Robert, February 26, 1934 [**231**] b.1866, a.67. Comment: CAT has marker [**213**] in error. CADI, CAT, DC

THOMPSON, Samuel P., July 5, 1923, b.1854 Indiana, age "about 69," widower, farmer, father John THOMPSON, 20 years in California, 10 months at the place of death, died at Camp Meeker, buried 7-07-1923 in the county farm cemetery; possible 1920 Census (Imperial County) T625-99-12, "THOMPSON, Samuel P.," a.66, b.IN-NC-IN, widower, laborer on cotton ranch. CADI, DC, MIC

THORBERG, Axel, January 28, 1934 [396] b.6-11-1868 Sweden, a.66, a resident of Santa Rosa, single, laborer, in U.S. since 1889, in California since 1915, father Matto THORNBERG, mother Annie STOKE. CADI, CAT, MIC

TILLATSON, Marlene, January 16, 1934 [**402**] b.5-19-1933 CA, Indian, a.6 months, father Byron TILLOTSON (b.1-02-1908 CA, d.7-06-1988 Sonoma County, a resident of Healdsburg), mother Delphina or Delphine MANUEL. Comment: Another child of Byron and Delphina, Gladys TILLOTSON died 5-14-1930 in Sonoma County at the age of 1 year 4 months 5 days. Gladys is buried in the Sebastopol Cemetery. No Healdsburg obituary for Marlene. CADI, CAT, CC, DC, MIC

TILLOTSON, Ida [?], December 20, 1933 [**403**] b.1883. Comment: This person, buried next to the infant Marlene, may be a relative, but no record can be found in Sonoma County other than the listing in the *Catalogue of Grave Markers*. A Napa County death was recorded on 12-20-1933 for an Ida TILLOTSON, age 50. She could have been a Sonoma County tuberculosis patient, sent to the Silverado Sanitarium in Calistoga. No Healdsburg obituary was found. The 1920 Census has an Ida TILLOTSON, a.4, b.CA-CA-Norway, daughter of Arthur and Amy TILLOTSON, a resident of Russian River Twp. Ida would have been about 17 years old in 1933. CADI, CAT

TO, Lum, May 10, 1903, a.71, Chinese, a resident of Sebastopol, buried in the county cemetery. DEA, REG

TOBIN, John J., June 18, 1905, b.1838 Ireland, a.67, single, occupation "boot-fitter" [shoe maker], hospital #1942; 1900 Census (Sonoma County Farm and Hospital) T623-114-257B, b.August 1843 Ireland, a.56, widowed, emigrated 1862, 38 years in USA, naturalized citizen, pensioner. CADI, CEN, DC, MIC

TOMBOTAS, Thomas, November 25, 1928 [**728**] b.1828 Sebastopol, Indian, wife Brella (?), died in Santa Rosa, aka "TOMBOTHS, Thomas." Comment: This person was not found in the 1920 California Census. CADI, CAT, DC

TON, Wong, January 5, 1908, b.China, age "about 40," male, single, occupation cook, 20 years in California, 2 months at 408 2nd Street, Santa Rosa, where he committed "suicide by hanging," informant "_____y Sing, DuPont Street, SF," buried 1-06-1908 in the "Sonoma Co. Farm Cem." Comment: The lower left-hand corner of the original death record was cut off; consequently, the first name of the informant is missing. Wong TON cannot be found in 1900 Census or in CADI under TON, TONG, WON, or WONG. CADI, DC, MIC, NEW

Newspaper records
"Chinaman Ends Life By Hanging," *The Press Democrat*, 1-07-1908.

TONG, Harry, December 28, 1918, a.64. CADI, DC

* TOOMBS, Sarah, October 4, 1915, a.3 months. Comment: The death record shows 'Place of Burial or Removal' as "Sonoma Co. Farm," crossed out and "Rural Cem." written in. The information from the burial permit, which was the initial source for this person, is thus negated. It is not known whether the deceased was actually buried in the county cemetery and then moved, or if the burial was in Rural, with the paperwork catching up later. BP, CADI, MIC, RUR

TOOMIRE, Joseph, June 19, 1928, a.76. CADI, DC

TORREZ, Mizel, December 11, 1932 [**418**] b.1870, a.62. Comment: Mizel TORREZ died in Napa County and so cannot be found in the Sonoma County death records. He was probably a tuberculosis patient, one of many sent to the Silverado Sanitarium in Calistoga. CADI, CAT, CEN, MIC

TOURNEUR, Baby Boy, April 28, 1922, stillborn at the county hospital, father Cammillia TOURNIER (b.Italy), mother Annie BAILEY? (b.Hungary), buried in the county farm cemetery. Comment: Not in Fetal (stillborn) CADI except "TOURNOUR, ZZ, San Francisco, 6-04-1922." The family name may be misspelled. DC, MIC

TOWLE, Joseph William, January 17, 1915, a.41. Comment: The Burial Permit has "TOWLE, Charles Wm." (Not in the 1910 Census of Sonoma County.) BP, CADI, CEN, DC

TOWNSEND, George N., November 17, 1936 [**201**] b.1856, a.80. CADI, CAT, DC

TOY, Ah, April 29, 1906, b.China, a.63, female, married, housekeeper, a resident of Sebastopol, 40 years in California, died in Sebastopol, "buried in the County Cemetery." CADI, MIC

TOY, San, September 6, 1917, b.China, age "about 42," female, married, occupation "House Wife," spouse "Van TOY," a former resident of San Francisco, 25 years in California, 1 month 15 days at the place of death, died at the "Joe GRACE Hop Yard, 7 miles northwest of Santa Rosa," buried 9-07-1917 at the county farm. CADI, DC, REG

TRADE, Casper W., August 13, 1935 [**241**] b.1900, a.34, spouse H. TRADE; 1920 Census (135 Naples St., San Francisco) T625-136-15, a.21, b.CA-CA-CA, wife Hedwig a.19, son Charles a.1/12, occupation "mill man in lumber company," living with parents, Charles and Grace TRADE. CADI, CAT, CEN

TRIPI, Tony, April 5, 1937 [**280**] b.1858, a.78. CADI, CAT, DC

TROMBLEE, Joseph, March 29, 1935 [**385**] b.1855, a.89, spouse "A. TROMBLEE," aka "TROMBLEF, Joseph." Comment: Note the ten year difference in age between CAT (1855-1935 = 80) and CADI (89). CADI, CAT, DC

TURNER, George, July 23, 1914, a.34. CADI, DC

TUSCHER, Frederick (Fred), December 22, 1930 [**666**] b.1847, a.81; 1930 Census (Sonoma County Farm and Hospital) T626-222-223A, a.82, b.Switzerland, single, native language French, emigrated 1871, alien, patient. CADI, CAT, CEN, DC

TWIFORD, Thomas L., June 25, 1914, a.69; 1910 Census (Sonoma County Farm and Hospital) T624-109-29A, a.67, widowed, b.U.S.-U.S.-Germany. CADI, CEN, DC

UPTON, Marion, July 19, 1941, b.9-06-1861, a.79, a resident of Mendocino County, aka "UPTON, Wm. Marion." Comment: BOI indicates the expenses of burial were paid by Mendocino County. BOI, CADI, DC

VALENCIA, Alex, December 11, 1928 [**730**] b.1850, a.78; 1920 Census (Glen Ellen) T625-150-105, "VALENCIA, Alec, a.65, b.CA-U.S.-U.S., single, laborer on the farm of Julius WAGNER. CADI, CAT, CEN

VAN PELT, Roy, October 30, 1916, b.10-29-1916, a.24 hours (premature), son of Roy VAN PELT (b.CA), and Laura COLEMAN (b.CA), died in the county hospital, buried 11-03-1916 in the Sonoma County Farm Cemetery. BP, CADI, DC, REG

VANDELOUR, Mathew, January 13, 1913, b.Ireland, a.54, single, occupation "Mucer" or "Muser" [?], parents b.Ireland, two weeks at the county hospital and died there, #6633, buried 1-14-1912 in the county farm cemetery, aka "VAUDELOUR, Mathew." Comment: As written in the death record, the name could be either VANDELOUR or VAUDELOUR (CADI has "VANDELOUR"). Neither name could be found in Census records. CADI, CEN, DC, MIC

VANDERGAW, Cornelias, November 7, 1912, a.80; 1910 Census (Sausalito, Marin County) T624-88-227, "VANDERGAW, Cornelius," a.79, b.NY-NY-NY, 'keeper' of a boarding house, wife Matilda, a.45, b.Germany (his second marriage, her first, married 24 years). CADI, CEN, DC

VANDERWATER, William, June 1, 1929 [**698**] b.7-14-1862 San Francisco, a.66, divorced, laborer, father John VANDERWATER (b.PA), mother Jessie JACKSON (b.LA), aka "VANDERMATER, William." CADI, CAT, MIC

VARONI, Mario, July 30, 1941, b.3-26-1886, a.55, a resident of the county hospital, father VARONI. BOI, CADI, DC

VAUGHARS, Thomas, August 12, 1917, b.11-01-1849 OH, a.66, single, laborer, father John VAUGHARS (b.Cork, Ireland), mother's name unknown (b.Ireland), 52 years in California, died in the county hospital, buried 8-15-1917 in the Sonoma County Farm Cemetery; 1910 Census (Mill Street, Analy Township) T624-109-2, "Thomas VAUGHAN," a.59, b.OH-Ireland-Ireland, marital status illegible, living alone, laborer (odd jobs). CADI, CEN, DC, REG

VERMETTE, Joseph, April 30, 1938 [**153**] b.1870, a.67, single, occupation "horse trainer," a resident of the "Fair Grounds," aka "VERMETTI, Joseph." BOI, CADI, CAT, DC, MIC, NEW

Newspaper records
"Joseph Vermette Passes," *The Press Democrat*, 5-04-1938.

VICE, Martin, October 7, 1934 [**392**] b.1861, a.73, aka "VISE, Martin." CADI, CAT

VIRZARSCONI, Angelo, June 2, 1936 [**260**] b.1-22-1866 Italy, a.70, male, single, b.1-22-1866 Italy, a.70-4-10, laborer, father Antonio VIRZARSCONI, mother Mary (both b.Switzerland), 50 years in Sonoma County, in California, and in the USA, a resident of the county hospital, buried 6-06-1936 in the county cemetery, aka "VIRAZARSCONI or VERZASCONI, Angelo." DC, CADI, MIC, NEW

Comment: This person is not listed in the *Catalogue of Grave Markers* (CAT), which also does not include marker [**260**]. However, he uniquely fits the marker sequence and date in Sonoma County death records, which also say he was buried in the county cemetery. Although the obituary says Virzarsconi lived in Petaluma for 50 years, he does not appear in the U.S. Census records.

Newspaper records
"Aged Petaluman Dies At S. Rosa," *Petaluma Argus-Courier*, 6-04-1936.
"Petaluman Dies At Hospital Here," *The Press Democrat*, 6-04-1936.

VISCA, Antone, December 7, 1941, b.2-23-1866, a.75, a resident of Hewitt Street in Santa Rosa, father VISCA, mother CONTI, hospital #5078. BOI, CADI, DC

VOLPI, Baby Boy, June 1, 1919, stillborn, father Joseph VOLPI (b.Italy), mother Susie FARRIRI (b.Switzerland), resident at 1060 College Avenue, Santa Rosa, buried 6-02-1919 in the county farm cemetery. CADI, DC, REG

VOSS, Frank, August 25, 1938 [**168**] b.8-18-1874 Benton, Butler County, KS, a.64 years 7 days, divorced (wife was Dolly VOSS), retired farmer, father Fred VOSS (b.MI), mother Lydia LYONS (b.KS), a resident of Sonoma, 13 years in California, died at the county hospital, buried 8-29-1938 in the "County Farm Cem.," informant Vorginia [*sic*] VOSS. BOI, CADI, CAT, CEN, DC, MIC

Census records
1880   (Kansas, Butler, Benton) T9-375-74, "VOSS, Frank," a.5, white, male, b.KS. Frank was living with his parents, his sister Ellen, and his mother's brother George Lyons.
1900   (Oklahoma, Woods, Waynoka) T623-1344-135, "VOSS, Frank," a.26, male, white, b.August 1874 KS-MI-IL, farm laborer, wife Bertha (b.January 1879 KS-OH-MO), married 2 years, no children.
1930   (Broadway, Sonoma Town) T626-222-237, "VOSS, Frank," a.52, b.KS-Germany-KS, rents home, doesn't have a radio, married at age 41, proprietor of a garage, wife Dolly (a.37, b.CO-PA-NY), married at age 31, son Charles (a.9, b.SD), daughter Dorothy (a.6, b.OR), daughter Virginia (a.4-5/12, b.CA).

WADE, James H., October 22, 1932 [**527**] b.10-04-1860 OH, a.72, died at the county hospital, buried on 10-24-1932. CADI, CAT, DC

WAGNER, David, January 2, 1937 [**268**] b.1846, a.90; 1930 Census (Sonoma County Farm and Hospital) T626-222-223B, a.84, b.PA-PA-PA, single, inmate. CADI, CAT, CEN, DC, NEW

Newspaper records
"David Wagner, 91, Rancher Here, Dies," *The Press Democrat*, 1-03-1937.

---

* WAGNER or WAGONER, Harry see LATON, Harry (1916).

WAH, Tom, October 30, 1908, a.52. CADI, DC

WAHLGREN, Oscar, November 14, 1931 [**530**] died in Valley Ford, age "about 53," occupation "wanderer," marital status and parents unknown, informant Sheriff's Department, buried 11-18-1931 in the "Co. Farm Cemetery." CADI, CAT, CEN, DC, MIC

Comment: This man's name may have been mistaken for or confused with "Oscar WALDRON," who is listed in CAT but otherwise does not seem to exist. Other than the listing in CAT, "Oscar WALDRON" does not appear in any Sonoma County vital record.

Census records
1920   (Butte Township, Sutter County) T625-152-160, "WALDGRIN, Oscar," a.43, b.Sweden, laborer, emigrated 1901, alien.
1930   (Elkhorn, San Joaquin County) T626-210-205, "WAHLGREN, Oscar," a.52, b.Sweden, single, farm laborer, emigrated 1903, alien.

* WALDRON, Oscar, 1936 [**530**] b.1878. Comment: Not in CADI, not in CA 1920 Census. Possible CAT error, confused with WAHLGREN? No WALDRON deaths 1930-39 in either Sonoma or Napa counties. CADI has only one WALDRON death in 1936, James in Los Angeles. CADI, CAT, CEN

WALKER, David, January 30, 1941, b.1-31-1874 San Francisco, a.66 years 11 months 29 days, divorced, ex-spouse Jeanette WALKER, father David WALKER (b.Nova Scotia), mother Mary KLAHN (b.unknown), a resident of the California Hotel on 4th Street in Santa Rosa, employed in the produce business, 2 years in the community, 2 days in the county hospital and died there, buried 2-05-1941 in the county cemetery. BOI, CADI, DC, MIC

WALKER, Frank, November 2, 1924, b.12-16-1846 Germany, a.77 years 11 months 6 days, single, laborer, father Walter WALKER, mother Theresa HIESLER (both b.Germany), 40 years in the U.S., 21 years 6 months 2 days in California, 4 years 3 months 15 days at the place of death, died in the county hospital, buried in the "county plot." Comment: Not found in the 1910 or 1920 Census in California. CADI, DC, MIC

WALTERS, Fred, January 29, 1938 [**138**] b.1859, a.78, a resident of the county farm. Comment: No Petaluma obit. BOI, CADI, CAT, NEW

Newspaper records
"Petaluman Dies," *The Press Democrat*, 1-30-1938.

* WARDS see WOUK (1933).

WARE, Jaza, May 24, 1933 [**577**] b.1853, a.79; 1930 Census (Sonoma County Farm and Hospital) T626-222-223B, "WARE, Joza," a.76, b.KY-KY-KY, single, inmate. CADI, CAT, CEN

WATSON, Cyrus, February 8, 1881 (41 Deaths 146) b.MI, a.54. Comment: The 1881-82 Sonoma County Financial Report noted a credit of $9.00 from the "Estate of C. Watson, deceased." Watson, like all persons requesting shelter at the county almshouse, was required to turn over all assets to the county upon admission. These assets, usually small amounts of cash, could be drawn upon by the inmate for personal expenses or withdrawn if the inmate was discharged. Should the inmate die, the county was the legal "heir" and kept any funds in the inmate's account. Evidence of such funds being retained by the county is therefore proof the person was an inmate of the county almshouse and died there or at the county hospital. Although this is not proof the person was buried in the county cemetery, it is likely to be true. Mr. Watson must have been a relative newcomer to the county farm or hospital since he is not there in the 1880 Census. DEA, FIN, REG

WEAVER, James, July 13, 1914, a.89. CADI, DC

WEBBER, Charles, November 15, 1925, a.84. CADI, DC

* WEBBS see EBBS (1934).

WEBER, Henry, February 19, 1940, b.5-7-1865, a.74. CADI, DC

WEDNER, Frank, September 22, 1899 (42 Deaths 147) "found dead in bed at the Moffat Log. [Lodging] House, Third Street, Santa Rosa, buried in the county farm cemetery," aka "WIDNER, Frank." DEA, NEW, REG

Newspaper records
"Did This Man Die By His Own Hand?" *The Republican*, 9-23-1899.
"Found Dead In Bed," *The Press Democrat*, 9-23-1899.
"Remains Of Dead Man Are Identified," *The Republican*, 9-23-1899.
"He Is Idnetified," [*sic*] *The Press Democrat*, 9-27-1899.

WEIL, Henry, June 21, 1887, b.1863 IA, a resident of Santa Rosa, left $0.90 to the county; possible 1880 Census (Franklin, Lee County, Iowa) T9-349-105, a.18, b.IA-Bavaria-Bavaria, working on the farm of his father, John WEIL, and his step-mother, Anna (Henry's mother, Lizzie, died before the 1880 Census). CEN, DEA, PHY

WEINGARTNER, Jacob, January 10, 1892, b.France, a.70, died in the county hospital #810, interred in the county farm cemetery. DEA, REG

WEIR, Joseph, March 8, 1924, b.2-11-1854 NY, a.69, single, 20 years in California, died in the county hospital. <u>CADI, DC, REG</u>

WELCH, Arthur A., December 28, 1924, a.72. <u>CADI, DC</u>

WELCH, Homer E., January 27, 1917, b.3-01-1882 NY, a.34 years 10 months 22 days, single, bartender, father William WELCH, mother Ella O. CONA (both b.NY), 28 years in California, died in the county hospital, #7850, buried 1-27-1917 in the Sonoma County Farm Cemetery. <u>BP, CADI, 1914 GR, REG</u>

WELLER, George, September 3, 1913, a.71. <u>CADI, DC</u>

WELLS, Samuel D., November 24, 1920, b.1841 Portland, ME, a.79, single, laborer, father Samuel WELLS, mother unknown (both b.ME), 54 years in California, 9 months at the place of death, died at the county hospital, buried in the county farm cemetery; possible 1920 Census (Sonoma County Farm and Hospital) T625-151-203, "WELLS, Sumner," a.80, b.ME-ME-ME, single. <u>CADI, CEN, DC, MIC</u>

WELSEY, Baby Boy, September 15, 1892, son of Margaret WELSEY. <u>PHY</u>

WELSH, Eugene, September 30, 1942, b.5-29-1861 Pennsylvania, a.81, father WELSH, mother BOWMAN. <u>CADI, DC</u>

WENDT, Robert, February 20, 1913, a.50. <u>CADI, DC</u>

WEST, Gerald, July 21, 1940, b.2-13-1939 Visalia, Tulare County, residence address "Hill Ranch, Forestville" [BOI], a.1 year 5 months 8 days, father William M. WEST, mother Mattie THOMPSON (both b.OK), died in the county hospital (meningitis), buried 7-22-1940 in the "County Burial Grounds, S. R.," informant William WEST, Hill Ranch, Sebastopol. <u>BOI, CADI, DC, MIC</u>

WEST, Helen, October 11, 1938 [**183**] b.1902, a.36, spouse "H. WEST;" 1930 Census (Glen Ellen Township) T626-222-4B, "WEST, Helen," b.CA-CA-CA, a.30, wife of Hammond WEST, 4 children. <u>CADI, CAT, CEN, DC, NEW</u>

Comment: Mrs. West died as a result of the same automobile accident that killed Frank SWED (q.v.), who was also buried at Chanate, next to Mrs. West in [**182**]. It is unusual for a person with a local family to be buried in a pauper's grave. Perhaps the Great Depression had left them without any resources. The 1930 Census shows them to be poultry farmers in the Sonoma area, renting their home in a neighborhood of owners, and not owning a radio. Mrs. West died at the county hospital and the family might not have had the funds to bring her back for burial. Additionally, the newspapers reported Mrs. West was 'estranged' from her husband, who may not have cared where she was buried.

<u>Newspaper records</u>
"Two Die, Two Near Death Here as Car Crashes Into Truck," *The Press Democrat*, 10-04-1938.
"Woman Still Unconscious From Crash," *The Press Democrat*, 10-05-1938.
"New Identity for Woman Victim of Fatal Car Crash," *The Press Democrat*, 10-06-1938.
"Haub Blamed For Causing Fatal Crash," *The Press Democrat*, 10-14-1938.

WEST, Joseph, May 18, 1938 [**128**] b.1865, a.72, a resident of the county farm since 1934. <u>BOI, CADI, CAT, DC</u>

WESTAL, Louis, August 3, 1899, b.Norway, a.50, died at the county hospital, buried in the county cemetery. <u>DEA, REG</u>

WHALEN, Michael, January 14, 1918, b.1-12-1842 Ireland, a.76 years 2 days, widowed, lumber mill worker, a resident of Occidental, father Michael WHALEN, mother unknown (both b.Ireland), 5 years 6 months 1 day at the place of death, 35 years 2 months 10 days in California, died in the county hospital, #6490, buried 1-19-1918 in the county farm cemetery; 1910 Census (Sonoma County Farm and Hospital) T624-109-29B, "WHALEN, Mitchell," a.68, b.Ireland, widowed. <u>CADI, CEN, DC, 1914 GR, REG</u>

WHALEY, Thomas Edwin, March 11, 1931 [**365**] b.3-09-1931 in Sonoma County, a.2 days (premature), father Addler WHALEY (b.AZ), mother Elizabeth (b.KY), buried 3-14-1931 in the county farm cemetery. <u>CADI, CAT, DC, MIC</u>

WHARTON, Henry, May 11, 1907, b.England, a.83, widower, bookkeeper, 25 years in California, 1 year 2 months in the county hospital, buried in the county farm cemetery. <u>CADI, DC, MIC</u>

WHITE, Wilmer, September 10, 1936 [**215**] b.10-03-1870 Ohio, a.65, laborer, father James WHITE, mother Elizabeth SCOURCE (both b.VA), 17 years in California, 10 days at the place of death, died at the county hospital, buried 9-16-1936 in the Sonoma County Cemetery. <u>CADI, CAT, DC, MIC</u>

WHITNEY, W. C., September 1, 1885, left $15.25 to the county. <u>PHY</u>

WHITTAKER, Frank, August 18, 1935 [**242**] b.1853, a.82. <u>CADI, CAT, CEN, DC</u>

Census records
| 1920 | (Sonoma County Farm and Hospital) T625-151-12B, "WHITTACKER, Frank," a.66, widowed, b.MA-England-England. |
| 1930 | (Sonoma County Farm and Hospital) T626-111-223A, "WHITAKER, Frank," a.76, single, b.MA-MA-MA, patient. |

WHITTER, Van Buen, November 3, 1917, b.12-25-1837 IL, a.79 years 10 months 9 days, retired saloon keeper, father Sam WHITTER, mother Dent KENNE (both b.Germany), 2 years at the place of death, 57 years 5 months 2 days in California, died in the county hospital, #7496, buried 11-06-1917 in the county farm cemetery. <u>CADI, DC, REG</u>

---

* WIGHTMAN, Virginia, August 28, 1902, b.CA, a.32 [contradicts age 30 from Census], married (the daughter of Mrs. E. R. BROWN of Santa Rosa), husband George WIGHTMAN, a resident of Sebastopol, "interred county cemetery;" 1900 Census (Sebastopol) T623-114-12, "WIGHTMAN, Vergie" (wife of George W.) a.28, b.May 1872 CA-NY-NY, married 6 years, 4 children. <u>CEN, DEA, MIC, NEW, OLE, REG</u>

Comment: Mrs. Wightman's "constructed" (pre-1905) Sonoma County death certificate states she was under the care of Dr. J. G. Pierce (of Analy Township, hence Sebastopol), died in Sonoma County, and was buried in the county cemetery. However, three newspaper obituaries and a handwritten entry in the O'Leary mortuary records contradict. They say Mrs. Wightman died in Watsonville and was brought back to Sonoma County for burial in Sebastopol.

In this author's opinion, the strongest evidence is the O'Leary record and a notice in *The Press Democrat*:

Records of the E. F. O'Leary Mortuary [OLE]
August 30th 1902
George Wighteman [sic]
To the burial of his wife Virginia C. Wighteman, aged 32 years.
Born in Calif. Died at Watsonville, Cal. Aug 28.
Married, Housekeeper, Female. Race: white.
Cause of Death: peritonitis. Attending physiscain [sic] Saxton Pope.
To use of Hearse and Services: $15.00.
Interred in I.O.O.F. Cemetery.

Newspaper record
George Wightman arrived last night from Watsonville with the remains of his late wife. The interment will take place in Sebastopol. [*The Press Democrat*, 8-30-1902.]

It is clear from the information entered by O'Leary that he was copying from a death certificate, which had to have come from Santa Cruz County, where Mrs. Wightman died. Although the 1900 U.S. Census finds her attending physician in San Francisco, by 1910 the Texas-born Dr. Pope was in private practice at Watsonville, Santa Cruz County. Information in Santa Cruz County (not seen by this author) should show Dr. Pope moved south from San Francisco before August 1902, to treat Mrs. Wightman before her death.

The evidence strongly suggests the Wightman family was not economically distressed. Mrs. Wightman was treated by a private physician in Watsonville; when she died, her body was brought back to Sonoma County for burial by her husband. Such things cost money, the possession of which pretty much eliminates the chance of a burial at taxpayer expense. Therefore, this author concludes the Sonoma County death certificate is in error: Mrs. Wightman died in Santa Cruz County and was buried in the Sebastopol Odd Fellows Cemetery, now Sebastopol Memorial Lawn. Unfortunately, her grave in that cemetery is unmarked.

Additional newspaper records
"Mrs. Wightman Passed To Rest At Watsonville," *Santa Rosa Republican*, 8-28-1902.
"Death of Mrs. Wightman," *The Press Democrat*, 8-29-1902.

WIHELO, Hans, March 17, 1938 [**146**] a.50, a resident of Petaluma, died as a result of an auto accident in Cotati, aka "WIBELO or WILHELO, Hans." Comment: The driver of the car, Sidney J. Elphick (1894-1960), was the son of Ohio-born James F. Elphick of Penngrove. This family was unrelated, or at best distantly related, to the English family of Analy Township for whom Elphick Road, south of Sebastopol, was named. <u>CADI, CAT, CEN, DC, NEW</u>

<u>Newspaper records</u>
"1 Dead, 1 Dying As Auto Hits Pedestrians," *The Press Democrat*, 3-17-1938.
"Hans Wihela, 43, Unidentified Companion, Killed In Auto Accident At Cotati," *Petaluma Argus-Courier*, 3-17-1938.
"Second Victim Hit By Car On Highway Dies," *The Press Democrat*, 3-18-1938.
"Crash Victims' Funeral," *The Press Democrat*, 3-23-1938.

WILBURN, Sophia L., April 4, 1937 [**283**] b.1888, a.49, died in Napa County (probably a tuberculosis patient). Comment: Sonoma County indigents, sent out of county for medical treatment, usually did not get a Sonoma County death record when they died in the host county. They were, however, always brought back to Sonoma County for burial. <u>CADI, CAT</u>

WILFERT, Henry A., September 17, 1939, a.62. <u>CADI, DC</u>

WILKES, George A. <u>or</u> W., January 12, 1899 (42 Deaths 147) b.KY, a.78, "indigent," buried at the county farm; 1880 Census (Santa Rosa Township) T9-84-95, "WILKES, George W.," a.60, b.KY-VA-KY, farmer, married. Comment: There are two entries in the death register for this person. <u>DEA, REG</u>

WILLIAMS, Alexander, December 11, 1937 [**132**] b.1865, a.72, a resident of the county farm, hospital #4325. <u>BOI, CADI, CAT, DC, NEW</u>

<u>Newspaper records</u>
"Graveside Rites," *The Press Democrat*, 12-14-1937.

WILLIAMS, Baby Boy, December 6, 1933 [**576**] b.1933, son of Mr. and Mrs. S. E. WILLIAMS. <u>CADI, CAT, DC</u>

WILLIAMS, John, April 14, 1932 [**414**] b.1845 NY, age "about 87," a resident of Molino (Sonoma County, northwest of Sebastopol), father Samuel WILLIAMS, mother Mary WAGNER (both b.NY), 60 years in California, 4 years 4 months 15 days at the place of death, died at the county hospital, buried 4-14-1932 in the county farm cemetery; 1930 Census (Sonoma County Farm and Hospital) T625-222-223A, a.85, b.NY-NY-NY, single, patient. <u>CADI, CAT, CEN, DC, MIC</u>

WILLIAMS, John, April 26, 1932 [**565**] b.1855 MO, a.77, widowed, laborer, father Joseph WILLIAMS (b.MO), died at home in the South Park district of Santa Rosa, 50 years in California, 2 years at the place of death, informant Joseph WAITE of Merced, Merced County, buried 4-26-1932 in the county farm cemetery; 1930 Census (Sonoma County Farm and Hospital) T625-222-223A, a.75, b.MO-OH-KY, divorced, patient. <u>CADI, CAT, CEN, DC, MIC</u>

WILLIAMS, Louie, Mrs., June 14, 1905, b.1863 England, a.42, married, housewife. <u>CADI, DC, MIC</u>

WILLIAMSON, A., January 12, 1899, b.Scotland, a.76, "indigent," buried at the county farm. <u>DEA, REG</u>

WILLIAMSON, W. T. L.?, February 2, 1886, left #13.00 to the county. Comment: The 1880 Census (California) does not list this person. <u>CEN, PHY</u>

WILLIS, Bailey, August 7, 1913, a.91. <u>CADI, DC</u>

WILLMAN, Lenni, July 24, 1937 [**296**] b.1892 Finland, a.44, spouse F. WILLMAN; 1920 Census (San Francisco) T625-133-40, Frank and Lennie Willman and son Martin. Comment: Frank Willman ran a gas station just west of Santa Rosa. The younger son, Herbert WILLMAN, still lives in Sonoma County, one of few known living relatives of a person buried in Chanate. <u>CADI, CAT, CEN, DC, FAM, NEW</u> (The wedding photo of Mr. and Mrs. Willman was provided by the family)

Newspaper records
"Mrs. Willman Passes," *The Press Democrat*, 7-25-1937.
"Mrs. Willman Funeral," *The Press Democrat*, 7-28-1937.

A plaque for Lenni Willman's grave was purchased with a family contribution.

WILSON, Adam, October 26, 1911, a.81. <u>CADI, CEN, DC</u>

Census records
1900 (Sonoma County Farm and Hospital) T623-114-257B, a.69, born December 1830 NC-NC-NC, single, pensioner.
1910 (Sonoma County Farm and Hospital) T624-109-29A, a.79, single, b.U.S.-U.S.-U.S.

WILSON, Anthony, March 8, 1927, b.11-01-1832 Sweden, a.96, single, 60 years in California, 9 years in the county hospital. Comment: This record was missed in the 1988 compilation of DC. <u>CADI, DC, MIC</u>

WILSON, Baby Boy, February 8, 1934 [**579**] stillborn, father Levi A. WILSON, mother Essie ROBERTS (b.AR). <u>CADI, CAT, DC, MIC</u>

WILSON, Fred, January 28, 1937 [**270**] b.1862, a.74. <u>CADI, CAT, DC, NEW</u>

Newspaper records
[No title] *The Press Democrat*, 1-31-1937.
"Fred Wilson At Rest In Santa Rosa," *Petaluma Argus-Courier*, 2-01-1937.

WILSON, Joseph, January 20, 1930, a.76. <u>CADI, DC</u>

WILSON, Thomas H., March 3, 1922, b.10-09-1849 OH, a.73 years 4 months 22 days, single, farm laborer, father WILSON, b.England, mother unknown, b.England, died in the county hospital, buried 3-08-1922 in the "Co. Farm Cem." CADI, DC, MIC

WILSON, Walter Guy, November 26, 1937 [**316**] b.1877, a.60, a resident of Stewarts Point. Wilson was survived by his widow, Mrs. Ann Wilson, and seven sons and daughters, Betty Ann, Daisy Dean, and Dolly May Wilson, Mrs. Rosemary Sharp, Walter G. Wilson Jr., Henry Wilson and John Wilson. Comment: CAT has "Walter C. WILSON" in error.

The photo shows Walter Guy WILSON with his wife and their two eldest children. The last surviving daughter still lives in Santa Rosa. CADI, CAT, DC, FAM, NEW (Photo courtesy of the family)

A plaque for Walter Wilson's grave was purchased with a contribution from the family.

Newspaper records
"Wilson Rites Held," *The Press Democrat*, 11-30-1937.

WING, Lee, February 5, 1923, b.10-25-1855 China, a.67 years 3 months 11 days, male, "Chinaman," single, laborer, father Lee WING, mother unknown (both b.China), 50 years in California, 3 years at the place of death (620 2nd St., Santa Rosa), buried in the county cemetery. Comment: Lee WING is also listed in the Rural Cemetery Book. This is highly unusual, as Chinese were almost always buried in the county cemetery. Although there is insufficient information currently available to determine where he is actually buried, he is included as one of the Chanate burials. CADI, DC, MIC, RUR

WING, Lo Kim, July 11, 1898, b.China, a.18, married, died in Santa Rosa, "wife of Tom Wing." CC, REG

WING, Tong Chow, September 7, 1893, a.23, female, married, wife of Tom Wing, suicide. Comment: Married only one month, Mrs. WING apparently believed her new husband, who had gone to San Francisco on business, had deserted her. COR, DEA, NEW, REG

WITT, Edwin T., October 11, 1911, a.74. CADI, DC

WOLF, Michael, March 1, 1907, a.80. Comment: This person cannot be found in the 1900 Census (California). CADI, CEN, DC

WOLF, Valentine, April 16, 1938 [**150**] b.1860, a.77, resident on 4th Street, Santa Rosa, aka "WALF, Valentine;" 1930 Census (Sonoma County Farm and Hospital) T626-222-223A, "WOLFE, Valentine," a.59, b.Germany, single, emigrated 1878, alien, patient. BOI, CADI, CAT, CEN, DC, NEW

Newspaper records
"Valentine Wolf Dies," *The Press Democrat*, 4-19-1938.

* WONG see OHIE (1921).

WONG, Ba, September 23, 1900, a.47, male, single. DEA, REG

WONG, Chester, December 27, 1929 [**747**] b.12-09-1913 in Vallejo (Solano County), a.16 years 18 days, male, single, Chinese, schoolboy (Santa Rosa High School), father Ham WONG (b.China), mother Wong LEE (b.Los Angeles), 4 years 2 months 10 days at the place of death, died at 209 4th St., Santa Rosa, buried 12-30-1929 in the Sonoma County Farm Cemetery. CADI, CAT, MIC, NEW

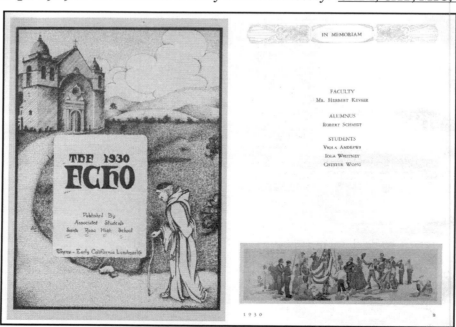

(Santa Rosa High School 1930 yearbook: Sonoma County Library)

Comment: Ham WONG ran a restaurant on 4th Street, which may have been King Fong at 228 4th. Anti-Chinese prejudice had been reduced to where Chester WONG was allowed to go to the public school and even to have his death mentioned in the yearbook but burial was still restricted.

Newspaper records
"Burial Monday for Chinese Boy Student," *The Press Democrat*, 12-29-1929.

WONG, Get, June 14, 1938 [**160**] b.1863 China, a.75, a resident of 2nd Street, retired merchant, 40 years in U.S., died in the county hospital. Comment: WONG was arrested on a narcotics charge. As a life-long opium addict, local officials had planned to send him to a state institution but he died before this could occur. BOI, CADI, CAT, DC, MIC, NEW

Newspaper records
"Death Ends Addiction for Wong, Aged Chair Mender," *The Press Democrat*, 6-15-1938.

WONG, Harry, November 24, 1914, b.10-07-1914 CA, a.1 month 17 days, father Dick Wong, mother Lillie LEE (both b.CA), died at 646 2nd Street, Santa Rosa, buried 11-25-1914 at the County farm. CADI , BP, DC, MIC

WONG, King Laeo, January 3, 1916, age "about 62," b.China, married, father Wong King (b.China), laundryman, 4 years at the place of death, 20 years in California, died on West Grant Street in Healdsburg, buried 1-04-1916 in the Sonoma County Farm Cemetery, aka "LAEO, Wong King." BP, CADI, DC, REG

WONG, Shu, July 9, 1934 [**510**] b.1850, a.84. CADI, CAT

WONG, Sim (Sam), February 17, 1943, b.unknown, age "about 95," a resident of the county farm, buried in the "county cemetery." BOI, CADI, DC

WONG, Tom Wing, February 18, 1918, b.China, a.63, "grocery merchant," a resident of Santa Rosa at 640 2nd St., spouse "Lon WING," 45 years in California, died in the "Santa Rosa [General] Hospital," buried 2-20-1918 at the "County Farm," aka "WING, Wong Ton or Wong Tom." Comment: CADI has both "WING, Wong T." and "WONG, Tom W." with the same state record number. CADI, DC, MIC, NEW

    Although known as "Tom Wing" during his life in Santa Rosa, his name became "Tom Wing Wong" in later years and that is how history knows him. "Tom Wing" was a prosperous Santa Rosa grocery merchant and labor contractor in the late nineteenth and early twentieth centuries. He was known as the "Mayor of Chinatown," which in the early part of the twentieth century was located on Second Street in Santa Rosa.
    Tom Wing was married four times in America and perhaps once before coming to this country (Song Wong's half-brother, Bok Wong, was born in 1889 in China). His first wife, Tong Chow Wing, took her own life in 1893 after only a month of marriage. The second wife, Lo Kim Wing, died of tuberculosis after only 28 days of marriage. For the third marriage, to Toy Lon, he went to San Francisco and had the wedding ceremony performed there according to Chinese customs.

To the fourth wife was born a daughter, Song Wong (1909-1996), who grew up in Santa Rosa, married Charles Bourbeau (1906-1988), and for many years operated the Jam Kee restaurant in Santa Rosa.

Photo: The Song Wong Collection, Sonoma County Museum (Song Wong in her mother's arms).

The family wanted to bury Tom Wing Wong in Santa Rosa but, due to the prejudices of the times, he had to be buried in the county cemetery. A large tombstone was erected over the grave but when Song Wong Bourbeau tried to find the grave years later the cemetery was overgrown and the tombstone was gone. This author's research in and restoration of the cemetery has failed to locate the tombstone or the location of the grave.

Newspaper records
[No title, report of marriage] *The Tribune*, March 1895.
"Possessed Of Beauty Is Tom Wing's Bride," *The Press Democrat*, 1-18-1899.
"Is Superstitious, Tom Wing Afraid Of Another Marriage License, Believes The Licenses Had
       Something To Do With The Death Of His Wives," *The Press Democrat*, 1-25-1899.
"Tom Wing Dies After Several Months Illness," *The Press Democrat*, 2-20-1918.

WONG, Tong, September 30, 1910, b.San Francisco, a.28, male, single, father
       WONG Fong Ging (b.China), mother LOU She (b.China), struck by a freight
       train in Healdsburg, died in Santa Rosa at the Mary Jesse Hospital, aka
       "FONG, Wong." COR, DC, MIC, NEW

Newspaper records
"Dies from His Injuries," *The Press Democrat*, 10-02-1910.
"Inquest Is Held Over Wong Tom," *The Press Democrat*, 10-04-1910.

WONG, Young See, April 18, 1906, b.CA, a.30, male, "yellow," married, merchant, died of injuries sustained in the earthquake at the St. Rose Building, buried in the "County Farm Cem. S. R," aka "WONG, Sue Young" or "John Doe #2." CADI, DC, MIC

WOODLEY, George, August 27, 1921, a.50; 1920 Census (Sonoma County Farm and Hospital) T625-121-12B, a.48 b.MA-U.S.-U.S., married, inmate. No obituary. CADI, CEN, DC

WOODS, James, January 31, 1899, b.Ireland, a.86, "indigent," county farm. DEA, REG

WORTHMANN, Christian, May 2, 1916, a.71, aka "WORTHMAN, Christian." BP, CADI, DC, REG

WOTINK, Robert, July 15, 1937 [**295**] b.1869, a.68, aka "WOTTRIK, Robert." CADI, CAT, DC

WOUK, Louis, December 18, 1933 [**421**] b.1891 Austria, age "about" 42, divorced, in California 20 years, laborer, aka "WONK or WAUK or WARDS, Louis." Comment: "Louis WARDS" is the only CC entry for this date. The handwriting in MIC is difficult to read and could be read "WONK" or "WAUK" as well as "WOUK." CADI, CAT, CC, DC, MIC

WRIGHT, Virginia, August 19, 1937 [**301**] b.1907, a.29, spouse "E. WRIGHT." CADI, CAT, DC

WURST, John, June 23, 1896, b.Germany, a.41, died at the county hospital, #1662, buried at the county farm. DEA, REG

YEE, Chang, February 15, 1937 [**274**] b.1855 China, a.82, a resident of Sebastopol, died at the county hospital. Honorable Chang was survived by two cousins in Oakland. CADI, CAT, DC, NEW

Newspaper records
"Aged Chinese Dies," *The Press Democrat*, 2-16-1937.

YEE, Hy Ly, August 13, 1908, a.57. CADI, CC, DC

YEE, Joe Do, January 14, 1916, b.China, age "about 62," single, laborer, 40 years in California, died in the county hospital, buried 1-15-1916 in the Sonoma County Farm Cemetery. BP, CADI, DC, REG

YEN, Ah, March 14, 1903, b.China, a.50, single, died in Sebastopol, buried in the county cemetery. DEA, REG

YET, Ah, November 21, 1897, a.26, single, opium overdose, buried in the county cemetery, aka "YER, Ah." COR, DEA, OLE

YET, Ah, September 8, 1901, aka "YER, Ah" a.55, died in Sebastopol, buried in the county cemetery. DEA, NEW, REG

Newspaper records
"Celestial's Last Ride," *Santa Rosa Republican*, 9-10-1902.

YEY, Chim, April 18, 1909, a.50, aka "YEY, Lehim" (transcription error, misreading of "Chim"). CADI, CC, DC

YIP, Ah, October 4, 1927, b.China, a.80 or 85, male, retired, a resident of the county hospital, inquest 1-28-1928, buried 1-28-1928 in the county farm cemetery. Comment: YIP drowned in October 1927 but was not found until the following year. The death record has the death in "October 1927" with no date specified; how CADI got October 4 is unknown. CADI, DC, MIC

YON, Dy, January 23, 1894, a.41, female, married, buried in the county farm cemetery, aka "YOU, Dy." CC, DEA

YOUK, Ah, November 16, 1936 [**202**] b.1861, a.75, aka "YOUK, A.H." CADI, CAT, DC

YOUK, Wong Hong, September 26, 1914, a.70, aka "YONK, Wong Hong." CADI, DC

YOUNG, Yep, February 5, 1917, b.1845 China, a.74, single, parents b.China, 50 years in California, died in the county hospital, buried 2-06-1917 in the Sonoma County Farm Cemetery. Comment: Age and dates do not compute. BP, CADI, REG

YOW, Tom, January 29, 1916, age "about 78," single, occupation "chair-maker," died in the county hospital, #7559, buried 2-01-1916 in the Sonoma County Farm Cemetery. BP, CADI, DC, REG

YOW, Wong Quang, April 7, 1920 (60 Deaths 241) b.China, age "about 70," male, married, laundry worker, "body removed to county farm," aka "YOU, Wong Duong." CADI, DC, REG

ZAMPATTI, Louis, November 29, 1940, b.6-24-1879, a.61, resident on G Street in Petaluma, father ZAMPATTI, mother BOLGER. BOI, CADI, DC

ZINNER, Joseph, May 11, 1938 [**155**] b.1875, a.63, died in the county hospital. BOI, CADI, CAT, DC

ZOCHARA, Michael, September 18, 1930 [**739**] b.1853, a.77, aka "ZOCHAKA, Michael." CADI, CAT, DC

ZOPFY, Fred, January 13, 1899, b.Switzerland, a.68, "Indigent, county farm," aka "ZAPFY, Fred." DEA, MIC, REG

ZURBUCHEN, Ulrick, June 8, 1929, b.6-07-1862 Switzerland, divorced, laborer, a resident of Sebastopol, hospital #2383 and died there, parents Peter ZURBUCHEN and Elizabeth RESSER (both b.Switzerland). CADI, DC, MIC

ZUST, John, February 22, 1935, a.44, spouse "C. ZUST." CADI, DC

ZZ UNKNOWN (Chinaman) June 14, 1900, b.China, age unknown, died at the county hospital, buried in the county farm cemetery. CC, DEA, REG

ZZ UNKNOWN (Chinese) April 19, 1930. DC

ZZ UNKNOWN (Chinese male) February 2, 1907 (5 Deaths 23). DC, REG

ZZ UNKNOWN (Jennie DOE) August 12, 1907, a.30. Comment: CADI has her as "ZZ Unknown, Jennie." CADI, DC

ZZ UNKNOWN (John DOE) September 28, 1906, a.48. Comment: CADI has "ZZ Unknown, ZZ." CADI, DC

ZZ UNKNOWN (John DOE) September 1, 1923, b.1863, a.60. Comment: CADI has "ZZ Unknown, ZZ." CADI, DC

ZZ UNKNOWN (John DOE) October 24, 1923, a.38, Mexican. Comment: CADI has "ZZ Unknown, ZZ." CADI, DC

ZZ UNKNOWN (John DOE) March 4, 1936. Comment: Not in CADI. CADI, DC

ZZ UNKNOWN (Male), February 1, 1902 (42 Deaths 142) found in the Laguna de Santa Rosa near Mark West Creek, buried in the county farm cemetery. REG

ZZ UNKNOWN (Male) February 28, 1905, a.65, male, "buried by the county." REG

ZZ UNKNOWN (Male) "presumably 1908," body found at Pine Flat, inquest held 2-17-1911 by Coroner Blackburn, death due to "pistol shot in head," presumed to be suicide, buried 3-03-1911 in the county farm cemetery. DC, MIC

ZZ UNKNOWN (Male) July 24, 1910. DC

ZZ UNKNOWN (Male) March 1, 1911. DC

ZZ UNKNOWN (Male) September 26, 1915, male, white, age "about 60," laborer, coroner's case, body found "in Santa Rosa Township, about 200 yards south of Sebastopol Avenue near N. W. P. R. R. tracks," buried 9-27-1915 in the Sonoma county farm cemetery. BP, DC, REG

ZZ UNKNOWN (Male) August 30, 1917, age "about 70," died in Windsor, buried 9-07-1917 at the Sonoma county farm. DC, REG

ZZ UNKNOWN (Male) July 28, 1921, age "about 60," suicide by hanging, near the Armstrong FAUGHT ranch, 8 miles north of Santa Rosa. The deceased was about five feet eight inches in height and 140 pounds in weight. He had in his possession a "well-used" New Testament. Comment: The death record lists the man's place of burial as Moke's Cemetery. This has to be an error as Moke's Cemetery (originally adjacent to, now part of Santa Rosa Rural Cemetery) was for the well-to-do. See this author's argument under RENALDS, Benjamin George, for details. MIC, NEW

Newspaper records
"Unknown Man Suicide, Will Be Buried in Pauper Grave," *The Press Democrat*, 7-29-1921.

ZZ UNKNOWN (Male) September 13, 1926. DC

ZZ UNKNOWN (Male) December 23, 1936, white, no other personal information; found near the Northwestern Pacific Railroad crossing of Fifth street; buried 1-06-1937. DC, MIC

ZZ UNKNOWN (Male) "found" August 25, 1940 "on Chanate Road," all else in death record "unknown," buried 8-28-1940 in the "Co. Cemetery." Comment: Not in DC, apparently missed by the 1988 volunteer. CADI lists this person as "ZZ Unknown." CADI, MIC

ZZ UNKNOWN (Scotty) January 21, 1931 [543] Comment: Sadly, the only "unknown" with a known grave location; his tombstone would read only "SCOTTY/1931." CAT, DC

ZZ UNKNOWN ("Stone") January 27, 1937. The "aged" man was found dead in a "hobo jungle" near Roberts Avenue in Santa Rosa. DC, NEW

Newspaper records
"Find Man Dead In S. Rosa 'Jungle'," *Petaluma Argus-Courier*, 1-28-1937.
 "Itinerant Found Dead in 'Jungles'," *The Press Democrat*, 1-28-1937.

ZZ UNKNOWN ("Tramp") 1889, mentioned on page 8 of the County Physician's 1889 annual report. PHY

ZZ UNKNOWN ("Transient") July 6, 1936. DC, NEW

Newspaper records
"Tourist Drops Dead At Depot," *The Press Democrat*, 7-07-1936.

ZZ UNKNOWN, April 7, 1907. DC
ZZ UNKNOWN, May 8, 1908. DC
ZZ UNKNOWN, July 9, 1908. DC
ZZ UNKNOWN, September 30, 1908. DC
ZZ UNKNOWN, November 27, 1937. DC

Notes

- A few errors were found in the original records, especially in the 1988 list made from death records and in the "*Catalogue of Grave Markers*." The "*Catalogue*" has numerous spelling differences from county death records. A few persons who are actually buried elsewhere are listed along with their correct place of burial. Other errors are noted with a comment.

- Grave marker numbers are in [brackets]. Numbers in [**bold**] mean the actual numbered concrete marker was located during the research phase of the project. In most cases, the approximate location of the numbered grave is known even if the marker was not located. The location of un-numbered graves is known only generally, based on the date of death.

- Spelling in quoted items is exactly as in the original. The Latin abbreviation *sic* (thus) is used to denote a word appearing strange or incorrect has been quoted verbatim. In particular, newspaper usage in the past often did not capitalize 'street' and similar words when they followed a name, e.g., "Mendocino avenue."

- All photos are by the author except as noted.

- Single U.S. Census records are included in the initial paragraph while multiple records are placed separately with a header "Census records." The absence of a Census record does not mean one does not exist but rather was not found (or searched for) by the author.

- Entries with multiple paragraphs are enclosed in a box.

- Source abbreviations are always underlined and placed at the end of the first paragraph of any entry.

- Entries marked with an asterisk (*) are not included in the total number of known burials; they are duplicates, errors or misspelled names. The author's intent is to include all names listed in any source as Chanate burials and note those that are erroneous. This includes persons no longer buried at Chanate.

- Significant misspellings of last names are handled by inserting a cross reference ("* DARBY see BARBY") since the various sources list both spellings.

- Family (last) names are capitalized in the first paragraph of any entry. Gender is usually obvious from the first name. In cases where it is not, the terms [male] or [female] are inserted. For unnamed infants, "Baby Boy" and "Baby Girl" are used.

- Census records are from Sonoma County, California unless otherwise indicated.

- U.S. Postal Service abbreviations are used for USA states. Names of other nations are spelled out in full. "Unk" means the state is unknown or was not identified.

- The term "mother [last name]" is from CADI; it is the maiden name of the person's mother. Other identification of parents is from the death certificate.

- Census records of 1880 and later identify the place of birth of the subject as well as the subject's parents. This information is abbreviated here to save space by using the two-letter USPS abbreviation for the state and by hyphenating the birthplaces into a short string. For example, "CA-NY-NJ" means the Census subject was born in California, his father was born in New York, and his mother was born in New Jersey. Names of other countries are spelled out in full.

Terminology

Indigent A person dependent partially or entirely on public support. It includes inmates of the county farm (almshouse), patients at the county hospital, and those "outside indigents" living at home but receiving a monthly cash "welfare" payment from the county.

Inmate A full-time resident of the county almshouse, located on the grounds of the county farm. (Persons incarcerated in the county jail were called "prisoners.") Generally, a person without means of support ("indigent") requiring shelter, food, and minimum medical care. Today, we might use "resident" or the politically correct term "client."

Patient A person, usually indigent, being treated for disease or accident in the county hospital; also, a county almshouse inmate receiving full-time medical care.

Pauper A person unable to provide for his or her own care owing to financial circumstances. The term had legal implications in that a true "pauper" was deemed worthy of care at public expense. Such persons were sometimes called the "worthy poor."

Prisoner A person under legal detention in the county jail. A person under suspicion of crime, unable to meet bail, or a person serving a sentence for a petty crime. Persons convicted of a serious crime in Sonoma County served their sentences in the state prison (usually Folsom or San Quentin).

Abbreviations

#	Patient number (assigned by the county hospital)
a.	Age
aka	Also known as
b.	Born
Co./co.	County
d.	Died
d/o	Daughter of
dy.	Days
GR	Great Register of Voters
m.	Married (years)
p.	Page (of Census, newspaper, etc.)
PD	*The Press Democrat*
res.	Resident of or resides at
SD	*The Sonoma Democrat*
s/o	Son of
Son.	Sonoma
Twp.	Township
wd.	Widowed

Death Records

Some of the most important information in this book comes from California death certificates. The form changed over the years; more information may be found in later records and less in earlier ones. In ideal circumstances, a conscientious clerk and a knowledgeable family member or close friend work together to generate an accurate death record. In the real world, this does not always happen. Often, the information comes from the hospital records, which interviewed the deceased upon admission. Sometimes the deceased is a stranger and unresponsive when admitted. Thus, some records have many "unknown" answers.

Interpretation of the questions asked by the death certificate also plays a part. For example, how long a person had lived in the USA, in California, and in the local area was asked although it is not always clear what was meant by "local." Was this the deceased's length of stay in the county or in the city or in the hospital? Readers of this book thus must be cautious to not jump to the wrong conclusions based upon this information.

Right or wrong, the information in the death certificate is official so it is the information used as a primary source, where available, in this book. Further, the California Death Index (CADI) was created from the state's compilation of these records. If significant contradictory information was brought to the author's attention, a note was placed in the entry for that person. Death records were not checked for all persons in the book if there was sufficient information available elsewhere.

The California Death Index (CADI) contains the following information:

1905-1939
Last name
First name
Middle initial
Initial letter of spouse's first name
Unit of age (years, months, days, hours)
Age
County of death
Date of death
Year of registration of death
State death index number

1940–
Last name
First name
Middle name
Birth date
Mother's maiden name
Father's last name
Sex
Birth place
Death place
Residence
Date of death
Social security number
Age

Sources of Information

Periodicals

Argus and Courier, Argus-Courier, Daily Courier, Journal and Argus; Petaluma,
California

Daily Republican and *Santa Rosa Republican*; Santa Rosa, California

Healdsburg Tribune; Healdsburg, California

Press Democrat, The; Santa Rosa, California

Sacramento Bee; Sacramento, California

San Francisco Chronicle; San Francisco, California

Sebastopol Times; Sebastopol, California

Sonoma County Tribune, aka *The Tribune*; Healdsburg, California

Sonoma Democrat, The; Santa Rosa, California (became *The Press Democrat* in
1897)

Sonoma Index-Tribune; Sonoma, California

Sotyome Scimitar; Healdsburg, California

Tribune, The; see *Sonoma County Tribune*

Books

Dillon, Richard H. *The Hatchet Men, The Story of the Tong Wars in San Francisco's
Chinatown*. New York: Coward-McCann, Inc., 1962. Dillon says the 1906
earthquake was the beginning of the end of the tong wars. Chinatown was
destroyed and, in rebuilding it, most surviving Chinese decided to become
Americans, that is, settlers. Although a few of the old battles occurred after 1906,
the killing of Hom Hong in 1917 must be seen as a rare event. Dillon writes "these
were the last spams [*sic*] of dying organisms."

Finley, Carmen. *The Finleys of Early Sonoma County, California*. Bowie, Md:
Heritage Books, 1997. Carmen gives the story of the killing of Hom Hong from
the Finley family's point of view.

Hanson, Patricia Ann Hitchcock. *My Hitchcocks : William to Arthur Henry*. Carson,
Washington: P.A.H. Hanson, c2002. Copies exist in the California State Library
(Sacramento), the Held Poage Research Library (Ukiah, California), and the LDS
Family History Library (Salt Lake City). The Family History Library has the book
in both print (index class 929.273 H636) and film (1573544, Item 8) formats.

LeBaron, Gaye, Dee Blackman, Joann Mitchell, Harvey Hansen. *Santa Rosa, A
Nineteenth Century Town*. Santa Rosa? Calif.: Historia, Ltd., c1985.

Nichols, Jeremy Dwight. *Cemeteries of Sonoma County, California, A History and
Guide*. Bowie, Md: Heritage Books, 2002.

Thomas H. Thompson & Company. *Historical Atlas Map of Sonoma County,
California*. Oakland: Thos. H. Thompson & Co., 1877. Reprinted 2003 by the
Sonoma County Historical Society.

Internet sites
Ancestry http://www.ancestry.com/
Belleek Pottery http://www.belleek.ie/Index.aspx
Free Dictionary, The http://www.thefreedictionary.com/
Heritage Quest http://www.heritagequestonline.com
International Genealogical Index http://www.familysearch.org/
National Postal Museum http://www.postalmuseum.si.edu/starroute/sr_02.html
Political Graveyard, The http://politicalgraveyard.com/
Rootsweb http://vitals.rootsweb.ancestry.com/ca/death/search.cgi
State of California, Department of Consumer Affairs, Cemetery and Funeral Bureau
      http://www.cfb.ca.gov/lawsregs/h_scode.shtml
Vitalsearch http://www.vitalsearch-ca.com/

U.S. Census records

Census dates for the Sonoma County Farm and Hospital are as follows.

Census Year	Census Schedule Date	Census Actual Date
1870	June 1, 1870	July 2, 1870
1880 (farm)	June 1, 1880	June 16, 1880
1880 (hospital)	June 1, 1880	June 30, 1880
1890 (Census records lost)		
1900	June 1, 1900	June 18, 1900
1910	April 15, 1910	November 28, 1910

> Note: For 1910, the Census enumerator wrote on the Census record, "Copied in Office from monthly reports."

1920	January 1, 1920	January 12, 1920
1930	April 1, 1930	April 16, 1930
1940 (not yet released)		

In the 1870 Census, the county farm did not yet exist so all indigents housed by the county were at the county hospital on Humboldt Street in Green's Addition to Santa Rosa. The "patients" were listed under their current or former occupation ("laborer" was the most common) and some may have been there only because they were poor and had no other shelter. In 1880, "inmates" at the farm were all listed as "paupers" while the "patients" of the hospital, still on Humboldt Street, were listed under their actual occupation; additionally, their medical condition was noted. In 1900, they were mixed, but identified as "patient" or "pensioner." In 1910 and 1920, all residents were "inmates," but in 1930 the enumerator again separated the residents into hospital "patients" and poor farm "inmates."

<u>Sources shown by abbreviations in the text</u>

ARCH California State Archives, 1020 "O" St., Sacramento, CA 95814.

BOI *Burials of Indigents, 1937-1966*, provenance unknown, probably compiled by employees of the County of Sonoma, a typescript document created over the years 1937 through 1966 and being apparently a list of expenses associated with public (indigent) burials. The original document has been lost but a microfilm copy exists in the Family History Library, Salt Lake City, Utah (microfilm number 924903 Item 2). The FHL lists the author as the Sonoma County Coroner but the current employees have no knowledge of the document. A print copy has been placed in the Sonoma County Library, Local History and Genealogy Annex, 3rd Street at E, Santa Rosa.

BP "Burial Permits 1914-1917" (unpublished) extracted by members of the Sonoma County Genealogical Society from discarded Sonoma County records. Typed manuscript in the files of the society.

CADI *California Death Index*, by the State of California, Department of Public Health, Bureau of Vital Statistics and Data Processing. Available on microfilm at libraries and on the Internet from *Vitalsearch* (1905-1939) or *Rootsweb* (1940-1995). The California State Library in Sacramento has a complete copy in print; the legibility of this copy is superior to either the microfilm or Internet copies.

CAT *Catalogue of Grave Markers*, provenance unknown, probably by employees of the County of Sonoma, a typescript list of 453 burials created about 1939 when the original wooden grave markers at the Sonoma County Cemetery were removed and replaced with concrete "soup can" markers. This list, covering primarily the 1930s, gives names, dates, and grave marker numbers. It was found at Community Hospital (now Sutter Medical Center) in 1987. Copies exist in the Sonoma County Library and the original is in the Sonoma County Recorder's Office.

CC Sonoma County Clerk, current keeper of vital records in Sonoma County.

CEN U.S. Census population schedule. Sonoma County and California is assumed unless otherwise indicated. The year of the Census is given. Location references, if included, may be either a page number or in a code such as "T623-88-39" which is the "Series-Roll-Page" terminology used by *Heritage Quest* (http://www.heritagequestonline.com).

CHSQ *California Historical Society Quarterly*, California Historical Society (San Francisco: California Historical Society, 1922-present).

COR *Sonoma County Coroner's Inquests 1852-1898*, part of CD #1841: *Sonoma County [CA] Records*, Volume 1, Sonoma County Genealogical Society (Bowie, Md: Heritage Books, 2001).

CRT Sonoma County Court Records office, Room 118-J, Sonoma County Hall of Justice, Santa Rosa, California.

CS "Census Substitute." *Reconstructed 1890 Census*, a part of Compact Disk 1841: *Sonoma County [CA] Records*, Volume 1, Sonoma County Genealogical Society (Bowie, Md: Heritage Books, 2001).

DEA *Sonoma County, California Death Records 1873-1905*, second edition, part of CD #1841: *Sonoma County [CA] Records*, Volume 1, Sonoma County Genealogical Society (Bowie, Md: Heritage Books, 2001).

DC   List of some Sonoma County death certificates (1905-1964) as researched by an unknown volunteer in 1988. The volunteer noted the name, date of death, and book/page number for all records in which the deceased was buried in the "county cemetery" or words to that effect. A few errors and omissions have been found but the work was 99% accurate. Not included are records in which the place of burial was given only as "Santa Rosa," since that could mean any one of four cemeteries (Calvary, County, Odd Fellows, Rural). The original handwritten copy (a stenographer's notebook) is on file in the Sonoma County Recorder's Office. Photocopies are available in the Sonoma County Library, Local History and Genealogy Annex, 3rd Street at E, Santa Rosa, California.

DIR   Sonoma County directories, various publishers, kept at the Sonoma County Library, Local History and Genealogy Annex, 3rd Street at E, Santa Rosa.

DM   Depot Park Museum, operated by the Sonoma Valley Historical Society, 270 1st St. West, Sonoma, California. Telephone (707) 938-1762.

FAM   Information received from a family member.

FIN   *Financial Report of Sonoma County*, biennial report, fiscal years 1881-82 and 1882-82. From the files of the Healdsburg Museum, 221 Matheson Street, Healdsburg, CA 95448. Telephone 707-431-3325. Open Wednesday-Sunday, 11:00 am - 4:00 pm. http://www.healdsburgmuseum.org/

GR   *Great Register of Voters*, Sonoma County, various years, a good source of information for between-Census years, adult (age 21+) citizen males only until 1912. Available on microfilm in the Sonoma County Library, Local History and Genealogy Annex, 3rd Street at E, Santa Rosa.

IGI   International Genealogical Index. http://www.familysearch.org/

IND   *Indigent Records in Sonoma County California 1878 to 1926*, Sonoma County Genealogical Society (Bowie, Md.: Heritage Books, 2006).

MIC   Microfilm copies of original death certificates, in the Sonoma County Recorder's office. These records are not available to the public due to laws respecting privacy. As a county volunteer, the author was allowed access to the records in order to create this burial list, which the county is required by state law to maintain.

MIL   Military Records (draft registration, service records, pension records, etc.), from various sources.

MIN   *Minutes of the Sonoma County Board of Supervisors.* (1857-present) Reports before 1906 are in the county administration offices (575 Administration Drive, Santa Rosa, California). After 1906, the reports are in the county archives. Contact the staff of the Local History and Genealogy Annex, Sonoma County Library, Third and E, Santa Rosa.

NEW   Newspaper story, obituary, or death notice.

NPRC   National Personnel Records Center, St. Louis, Missouri.

OLE   O'Leary (Sebastopol) Mortuary Records, available on microfilm in the Sonoma County Library, Local History and Genealogy Annex, 3rd Street at E, Santa Rosa. The originals are in possession of the Pleasant Hills Memorial Park (successors to O'Leary), [south of] Sebastopol, California.

PHY   Reports of the Sonoma County Physician, on file in the county archives. These are monthly reports by the Sonoma County Physician, detailing the activities at the county farm and hospital. The reports are primarily statistical, listing numbers of persons admitted, released, died, etc. Occasionally, names of decedents are mentioned, especially if the deceased left money in his/her account. Contact the staff of the Local History and Genealogy Annex, Sonoma County Library, Third and E, Santa Rosa.

POL Police records, various jurisdictions in Sonoma County.

PRO Probate records (microfilm), Sonoma County Hall of Justice, Room 110-J, 600 Administration Drive, Santa Rosa. Comment: As of 2009, this source is open to the public Monday-Wednesday-Friday from 8:00 A.M. to 12:00 Noon.

PV Personal Visit by the author.

REG *Sonoma County Register of Deaths* (original hardbound ledgers) on file in the county archives. A notation such as "40 Deaths 26" means "Death Register, Volume 40, Page 26." These records are not available to the public due to laws respecting privacy.

RUR *Burials in the Santa Rosa Rural Cemetery 1853-1997* (CD-ROM version) by the Sonoma County Genealogical Society, published by Heritage Books of Bowie, Md.

SAN Sanborn fire maps, various years. Original bound volumes and microfilm for the City of Santa Rosa, in the collection of the Sonoma County Library, Local History and Genealogy Annex, 3rd Street at E, Santa Rosa.

Acknowledgements

The author gratefully acknowledges the assistance of the following persons.

John Dennison, metal detector operator and finder of "soup can" grave markers.

Doris Dickinson and **Carmen Finley** for proofreading and for advice on formatting this book.

Holly Hoods of the Healdsburg Museum and Historical Society, who helped me with information on people from that city.

Sonoma County Librarian **Tony Hoskins**, for assistance with the Sonoma County Archives.

Sonoma County General Services Manager **Dave Kronberg** (retired), who so easily could have forbade me to work in the old county cemetery but did not, and additionally asked "what can we do with volunteers and donations" when it was clear the county could not restore the cemetery without help.

Sonoma County Chief Deputy Recorder **Stephen Lehmann**, for access to and assistance with county records.

Lois Nimmo, for typing the 1988 "Steno Book" list of Chanate burials.

Ray Owen, my fellow volunteer and researcher, for his constant advice and for finding the Reverend Halahan Killigrew DUNBAR.

Katherine Johnson Rinehart, who advised me on questions involving persons from Petaluma.

Diane Smith, who researched several people with connections to the City of Sonoma.

Third District Sonoma County Supervisor **Tim Smith** and his assistant, **Allison Sanford** (both retired), both of whom encouraged me in my research and in my work to restore the Chanate Historic Cemetery.

About the Author

Lead, follow, or get out of the way.

Jeremy Dwight Nichols graduated from Macalester College in St. Paul, Minnesota, receiving a B.A. degree with a major concentration in physics. His working career was spent in Silicon Valley, as an engineer at several major electronics firms. At one of these he met Laura Cline, who became his wife in 1976. He retired in 1997 and moved to Sonoma County, where he lives in a rural setting with his wife and two cats, *Calvin* and *Hobbes*.

Potter's Field is his second book. He previously wrote *Cemeteries of Sonoma County, California, A History and Guide* (Bowie, Md: Heritage Press, 2002). The latter book was the winner of the first Peterson Prize in 2003. The Peterson Prize is awarded annually by the Sonoma County Historical Records Commission for writing about Sonoma County history based upon research in the public records.

Index
(Names Mentioned in the Text)

Farley	Johnson, Cassie	Langford	Patterson, Frank
Farriri	Volpi, Baby Boy	Larson	Carlson, Frank M.
Felker	Flage, Frederick	Lazzari	Grisetti, Frank
Fetters	Morrison, Delta May	Lee	Wong, Chester
Fidlar	Barry, Ray	Lee	Wong, Harry
Finley	Hong, Hom	Leper	Quarry, Jack Pete
Fitzgerald	Meyer, Baby Boy	Lou	Wong, Tong
Fleming	Green, Nelson F.	Lucas	Ryan, Frank
Fleming	Quay, Edward	Lundstrom	Erikson, Eric
Flock	Newell, Hershel V.	Luper	Hall, Alta
Ford	Haley, John	Lyons	Ehlich, Henry
Frau	Stahl, John	Lyons	Voss, Frank
Freitas	Barone	Mamal	Dominguez, Lilly E.
Gardner	Garcia, Mary	Mangels	Schlobohm, Guse
Garihan	Keys, Frank B.	Manuel	Tillatson, Marlene
Gauden	Guillermir, Marcel	Marie	Maurelli, Lawrence
Gausch	Nell, John	Mass	Ehlers, Henry
Genetti	Petri, Norisco	Mathews	Johnson, Baby Boy
Gibson	Myers, Charles Benjamin	Maxwell	Fothergill, John
Goudati	Leupelloni, Frank	McCauley	Blagg, Donald
Grace	Toy, San	McCauley	Romona, Manuel
Green	Morton, William Sidney	McConnik	Murry, Michael
Greenfield	Carpenter, William	McDowell	Earley, Raymond Carl
Greif	Koenig, Ernest	McDowell	Gingrich, William
Grirole	Gregori, Camille	McDarlan	Richards, Eliza
Hadden	Morrison, Delta May	McGuire	Ray, Edward
Hammon	Harris, Wylie	Mecordia	Colli, Frank M.
Harris	Lillard, Newton Abraham	Medina	Cassio, Leonora Rose
Haub	Swed, Frank	Meins	Arbuckle, Robert
Hayes	Chase, Wilmot	Melinski	Kroll, Frank
Heaton	Baldwin, John	Melsling	Marky, George
Hoover	Gibson, Samuel J.	Meyer	Porter, William
Hopkins	Keith, Richard Edward	Miller	Asmussen, Andrew
Hopper	Hitchcock, Jasper Newton	Miller	Koster, Frank J.
Horton	Boakes, Jacob N.	Mills	Renalds, Benjamin George
Howard	Browne, Frederick S.	Mitchell	Smith, Derian Warren
Huff	James, Elmer	Moore	Lewis, Fred
Humphries	O'dell, Simpson George	Moore	Nicholson, Grover
Hunter	Robinson, William	Moyer	Calini, Joseph
Hurley	Sullivan, Patrick	Murray	Reynolds, Roy
Hutchinson	Miller, Garnet	Mykie	Davis, Joe
Jackson	Vanderwater, William	Naklectal	Huber, John
Jenkins	Dunbar, Halahan	Narra	Peracca, Rudolph
Johnson	Nelson, Louis	Noble	Evans, Baby Girl
Juls	Dias, Antonio	Noil	Rice, David P.
Kenne	Whitter, Van Buen	Norman	Beal, Charles
Kieth	Harmison, Douglas D.	Olsen	Henderson, Christ
Kirkpatrick	Spurr, Leonora (Nora)	Olsen	Knudsen, Healma
Klahn	Walker, David	Olsen	Peterson, John
Klobus	Niedrusghane, Harry	Oren	Sather, Peter
Lafitte	Beall, Daisy L.	Orther	Eck, John

Otten	Rugen, John	Steen/Steer	Garner, Lemuel
Ozona	Renalds, Benjamin George	Stoke	Thornberg, Axel
Padesta	Bacci, Santi	Stoker	Lingo, Margaret E.
Padilla	Navarro, Charles	Stoops	Hamer, Sylvester T.
Palacio	Rodriquez, Isabel Palacio	Stuart	Moloof, Baby Girl
Palmary	Mirone, Andrew	Swindell	Amedeo, Lewis
Panina	Moloof, Baby Girl	Taylor	Bradt, George Washington
Pereiva	Ocacio, Carmilio	Thernberg	Keith, Louis
Pete	Dominguez, Lilly E.	Thihl	Kurch, Otto
Peterson	Johnson, Bert	Thomas	Quarry, Jack Pete
Phillips	Pinola, Minnie	Thompson	West, Gerald
Pierce	Martin, Mr.	Tinen	Bruines, Martin
Pihl	Kallman, Andrew	Trippo	Cardova, Floyd James
Pike	Bradley, Wayne	Trumbella	Spinetti, Henry
Piroka	Broka, Larry	Tucker	Sweatman, Solomon
Polidori	Giusti, Guiseppe	Vack	Alpen, Peter
Pope	Wightman, Virginia	Vagery	Perring, Leo
Pulida	Navarro, Marcos	Valejo	Ortiz, Ustocia
Rader	Ruland, Joseph	Vali	Gelpi, Luigi
Rafferty	Mulvehill, Jerry	Villa	Flores, Jesus
Ramsay	Isdell, William	Waggins	Stone, Baby Boy
Rays	Rodriguez, Manuel	Wagner	Cline, Frank
Regler	Patack, Bert	Wagner	Valencia, Alex
Resser	Zurbuchen	Wagner	Williams, John
Richards	Ford, Guilford	Waite	Williams, John
Roberts	Wilson, Baby Boy	Walker	Field, Baby Girl
Robinson	Gibson, Samuel J.	Walker	Nell, John
Roland	Brown, Alice	Wallace	Drimmer, David
Rossi	Benedetto, Frank	Waller	Conkel, Roy
Roundtree	Brooks, Frank	Walton	Relyea, Bert Garfield
Ruro	Cavedon, Virgil	Watson	Merritt, Edward
St. Clair	McDaniels, Oliver	Watts	Lemmon, Helen
Sanders	Carroll, Baby Girl	Wester	Olsen, Julia
Santa	Carubbi, John	White	Powers, Maurice Vincent
Sashay	Hayden, Andrew	Wilcox	Gray, Baby Boy
Schley	Kittz, Adam	Wilson	George, Baby Girl
Scource	White, Wilmer	Wilson	Ivans, John E.
Sherman	Hawley, Delia Annie	Wilson	Laird, Samuel Wilson
Sloan	McNeil, Andren	Wilson	Saabeclea, Augustine
Slocomb	Lawrance, Thomas	Wohlford	Jones, Clarence
Small	Johnson, Richard Welch	Wong	Ohie, Wong
Smith	Baker, John A.	Worden	Hawley, Delia Annie
Smith	Gillam, John	Wyana	Lorentino, Larry
Sportsman	Hilligas, Mary Lee	Yee	Ohie, Wong

Made in the USA
Charleston, SC
02 September 2012